SHOTGUNS & CARTRIDGES
FOR GAME AND CLAYS

Barrel boring by the traditional, but still unsurpassed, spillboring process

The boring bit is a straight square-section bar with one cutting edge, which is packed against the side of the bore by a wooden spill. Strips of paper, visible on the bench, are inserted between the spill and the boring bit according to the cut required

Shotguns & Cartridges for Game and Clays

GOUGH THOMAS

(G. T. Garwood, M.Sc., C.Eng., F.I.C.E., F.I.E.E.,
Gun Editor, the *Shooting Times*)

*New and enlarged edition
with line illustrations by the author*

ADAM & CHARLES BLACK
LONDON

First published 1963 by Electrical Press Ltd,
Maidenhead, Berks

Revised and enlarged edition
published 1970, reprinted 1972
Third edition published 1975,
reprinted 1977, 1981
by A & C Black (Publishers) Ltd,
35 Bedford Row, London WC1R 4JH

© 1975 G T Garwood

ISBN 0-7136-1583-4

To Mildred, my Wife

Printed in Great Britain by
Butler & Tanner Ltd,
Frome and London

CONTENTS

CHAPTER   PAGE

      Preface to the Second Edition   11

      Preface to the Third Edition   13

      Introduction   14

  1. Historical Background   17

  2. Modern Guns   24

  3. Choice of a Gun (Type)   43

  4. Choice of a Gun (Performance)   51

  5. Patterns   60

  6. Choke   71

  7. Cartridges   83

  8. Home-Loading and Reloading   100

  9. Clay Pigeon Guns   113

10. Magnum Guns   118

11. Self-Opening Guns   123

12. Special Guns   129

13. The Shotgun Barrel   131

14. The Shotgun Action   141

15. Boxlock or Sidelock?   148

16. Weight and Recoil   152

17. Balance   158

18. Problems of Vision   165

19. Stocks and Fitting   171

20. Pointability   180

21. Sighting the Shotgun   184

22. Problems of Accuracy   187

23. Shot and Shot size   196

24. Shooting Ailments   204

25. Care and Maintenance   208
26. Muzzle-loaders   213
27. In the Field   219
28. Miscellanea   228
    Appendix 1 The Proving of Guns   240
    Appendix 2 Metric Equivalents   243
    Appendix 3 Firearms and the Law   245
    Bibliography   249
    Index   250

ILLUSTRATIONS

Barrel boring   *Frontispiece*

PAGE

1. Early Tudor matchlock   17
2. Rifled matchlock   18
3. Early flintlock   19
4. Perfected flintlock by Purdey   20
5. Percussion muzzle-loader by S. & C. Smith   20
6. Lefaucheux-type pinfire by Joseph Lang   21
7. Sliding barrel pinfire by Harvey of Exeter   21
8. The hammer gun at the peak of its development   25
9. A typical Anson & Deeley gun   25
10. Anson & Deeley action   26
11. Machined body of boxlock gun   27
12. A typical London pattern sidelock gun   28
13. A conventional sidelock   28
14. The French Darne sliding breech gun   29
15. The trigger plate mechanism of a Perazzi gun   30
16. The Purdey-Woodward over-and-under   30
17. The Webley-Greener Martini action GP gun   31
18. The Southgate ejector   32
19. The Deeley ejector   32
20. The Baker ejector   32
21. Winchester inertia-type single trigger mechanism   34
22. Release trigger   34
23. A typical American pump-gun   36
24. The FN Browning long-recoil automatic   36
25. Working principle of a long-recoil automatic   37
26. The FN Browning short-recoil automatic   36

7

27. Working principle of a short-recoil automatic 38
28. The Benelli fixed barrel recoil-operated automatic 40
29. Working principle of the Benelli fixed barrel recoil-operated automatic 38
30. A popular American gas-operated repeater 40
31. An American bolt action repeater 40
32. An inexpensive Spanish gun 41
33. An AYA 25-inch-barrelled boxlock 41
34. Effective ranges 56
35. 80-yard pattern, fully choked repeater 61
36. A shot charge in flight 63
37. A typical modern plastic wad 63
38. 40-yard pattern, improved cylinder 66
39. 40-yard pattern, full choke 66
40. 20-yard pattern, improved cylinder 67
41. 20-yard pattern, full choke 67
42. 15-yard pattern, rifled barrel 68
43. Types of choke 74
44. Spread of small and large bores 75
45. Full choke and improved cylinder spread compared 76
46. Aiming target for demonstrating spread 78
47. The Cutts compensator 79
48. The Winchester 'Winchoke' 80
49. A collet-type adjustable choke 80
50. Nominal muzzle constriction for choke in various gauges 81
51. A modern Eley cartridge 86
52. The Winchester compression-formed cartridge 86
53. Cold welding of shot pellets 88
54. Balled shot and cold welded pellets 89
55. An automatic loading machine 91
56. Testing Eley cartridges in a pendulum gun 92
57. X-rayed cartridges 93
58. Effect of progressive powders 94
59. Full choke with a $1\frac{1}{16}$ oz. and $1\frac{1}{4}$ oz. shot compared 95
60. High-velocity and normal cartridges compared 96
61. The Wanda cartridge 98
62. The Redding Model 16 loading machine 102
63. The Lyman loading machine 102
64. The Lyman 'Ohaus' beam balance 102
65. The FN Browning over-and-under trap gun 116
66. The SKB over-and-under trap gun 116
67. The Churchill 'Hercules' boxlock 123

68. The Smith easy-opening action 124
69. The Purdey self-opening action 124
70. The Holland & Holland self-opening mechanism 125
71. The author's self-opening action 126
72. Methods of assembling shotgun barrels 132
73. Monobloc barrel assembly 133
74. Typical twelve-bore shotgun chamber and cone 135
75. Flexure of shotgun action at instant of firing 142
76. Demonstrating the flexure of the shotgun action 144
77. Basic types of top extensions 146
78. The Greener 'Empire' action 150
79. An American-type recoil reducer 155
80. The principle of a muzzle brake 156
81. Composite gun movements resolved into components 159
82. Measuring balance 161
83. Equivalent distribution of weight 162
84. Displacement of object when seen obliquely through glasses 169
85. The measurements of a gun stock 173
86. Curing low-shooting gun by straightening stock 175
87. Attachment of stock to action by means of a stock-bolt 178
88. Normal Birmingham method of attaching stock to action 179
89. Forces of recoil and reaction 188
90. Effect of mirage in rifle shooting 190
91. Clay target and squared background as seen over cold barrel 191
92. Clay target and squared background as seen over hot barrel 192
93. Convection currents and heat shimmer from O/U barrels 193
94. Notional view of pellets undergoing rapid acceleration in gun barrel 197
95. Comparative performance of No. 3 and No. 5 shot on duck 200
96. Stacking of shot (theoretical) 201
97. Stacking of shot (practical) 202
98. The perfected form of the flintlock 215
99. Twenty-bore flintlock with powder and shot chargers 217
100. Curve showing the author's characteristic aiming errors 226
101. Semi-diagrammatic view of a well-designed safety sear 229
102. Twelve-bore rifled slug 230
103. The Singlepoint SP 270 sight 231

104. Barrel burst by plug of mud or snow at muzzle 233
105. O/U action showing marked obliquity of strikers 235
106. A modern breech-loading punt gun 237
107. Screw breech for a punt gun 237
108. Cartridge for a punt gun 238
     Current nitro-proof marks 241
     Current foreign nitro-proof marks 242

TABLES

PAGE

1. Minimum patterns 53
2. Percentage patterns for all borings at all ranges 54
3. Striking energy for individual pellets 54
4. Pellets in game charges 58
5. Definition of choke 72
6. Diameter of spread 74
7. Black powder loads 104
8. Recommended loads (80 powder, paper tube) 108
9. Recommended loads (80 powder, plastic tube) 109
10. Recommended loads (60 powder, paper tube) 110
11. Recommended loads (60 powder, plastic tube) 111
12. Balance data—best guns 163
13. Balance data—other guns 163
14. Punt gun sizes and loads 238

PREFACE TO THE SECOND EDITION

The first edition of this book was criticised as being too short. It was, indeed, written under severe limitation as to space. In the present edition that limitation has been substantially relaxed and I have taken advantage of the opportunity to add much new material, including three completely new chapters, and to bring the book thoroughly up to date.

In its present form it will, I hope, provide the practical but enquiring sportsman with all he needs for an adequate understanding of modern shotguns and their ammunition. At the same time, several of the matters now briefly dealt with, more especially as concerning the choice, testing and appraisal of guns, are elaborated in my *Gough Thomas's Gun Book*. The two books, indeed, are largely complementary—a fact that will, I hope, excuse the several references to the latter herein.

I gratefully acknowledge the help and guidance I have received in the choice of matter for the present edition from the extensive correspondence I have conducted over the past decade with readers of the *Shooting Times* which I have had the privilege of serving in the capacity of Gun Editor.

In conclusion, I have to thank the proprietors for permission to make use of matter originally published in that journal; Imperial Metal Industries Limited for permission to reproduce Tables 2, 3, 4 and 6 from their admirable publication *The Shooter's Year Book* (57th edn.), as well as for other data and co-operation generously afforded by Mr. J. W. Huskins on their behalf. I also have to thank the following firms and others who kindly supplied illustrations, namely, Imperial Metal Industries Ltd., Messrs. James Purdey & Sons Ltd., Westley Richards & Co. Ltd., Webley & Scott Ltd., Gallyon & Sons Ltd., Anglo Spanish Imports, Etablissements Darne, L. LePersonne & Co. Ltd., Millard

11

Bros., O. F. Mossberg & Sons, The Remington Arms Co., Thomas Bland & Sons, BSA Guns Ltd., Leslie Hewitt Ltd., Holland & Holland Ltd., the Lyman Gun Sight Corporation, Olin (Winchester-Western Division), Polychoke Co., Singlepoint (GB) Ltd., The Worshipful Company of Gunmakers and the Proof Master and Guardians of the Birmingham Proof House. My cordial thanks are also due to Joan Clifford for generously undertaking the duties of amanuensis and critic.

PREFACE TO THE THIRD EDITION

Since the second edition of this book there have been some notable changes in the British shooting scene. In particular clay pigeon shooting has continued to grow in popularity, with increasing specialisation in relation to game shooting. I have therefore taken advantage of the publishers' readiness to double the size of the book to go more fully into several aspects of guns and ammunition in which trap and skeet shooters are especially interested. At the same time I have endeavoured to provide the enquiring game shooter with more information conducing to a better understanding of his weapon in relation to himself, leading, I hope, to better performance in the field. Lastly, I have tried to provide more for those enthusiasts who revel in guns for their own sake.

I gratefully acknowledge the valuable information and comments I have received from I. M. Crudgington, C. D. Cradock and Roger Barlow, who also supplied several illustrations for this edition.

Once again I have to express my appreciation of the indulgence I have enjoyed at the hands of the proprietors, editors and readers of the *Shooting Times*, and the generous and indispensable help I have had from Joan Clifford in preparing this edition for publication.

INTRODUCTION

I always feel that it is a pity for a shooting man to be too keen on guns—
it seems to be subordinating a major to a minor interest. There is so
much more in shooting than the mere weapons of the chase. In many
ways it takes a man back, body and spirit, to the places where he
belongs, and gives him back so many of the things of which modern
commercial civilisation has deprived him. Air, freedom and exercise;
wild nature; the good companionship of dogs and men; and the etern-
ally thrilling pursuit of a wild quarry destined for wholesome food, are
surely its main sources of delight.

And yet there is a very special relation between a man and his gun—
an atavistic relation with its roots deep in pre-history, when the primitive man's personal weapon, so often his only effective defence and food-
provider, was nearly as precious to him as one of his own limbs. Small
wonder that instinct should invest the modern man's gun with some
faint aura of this quality, enhanced, as it may well be, by his recognising
it as an old friend, the indispensable companion of some of his best
days and the agent of some of his best-remembered successes.

And so, within their love of shooting, many men find room to love
a gun. I count myself as being of their company; and it is for such as
these that I have written this book, knowing, as my work for the *Shooting
Times* has taught me, the sort of things on which they and their sons
most often seek further knowledge and guidance. I have not written
for the specialist, amateur or professional, in any branch of gun-know-
ledge or practice. Rather, I write as an ordinary shooter, whose qualifi-
cations are a lifelong interest in guns and shooting, a long experience,
and a professional training which throws light on some aspects of the
subject.

In planning my coverage, I have adopted, as being more appropriate to the times, a less insular approach than that of most previous British writers in this field. Indeed, there has never been a time when such an approach was justified in a general work. As stated in the preface to this edition, I have also had fuller regard for the increasingly specialised needs of competitive trap and skeet shooters.

CHAPTER ONE

HISTORICAL BACKGROUND

To understand how modern guns came about, and to form certain judgments about them, it is necessary to consider something of their history.

In this country, the use of firearms for taking feathered and ground game may be conveniently dated from the end of the Wars of the Roses in 1485, during which the smooth-bore matchlock (fig. 1) was perfected. This was a gun in which the charge was ignited by a smouldering cord or 'match' worked by a simple trigger mechanism.

The troubled times had no doubt acquainted many humble folk with the use of this crude but exciting new weapon, and had shown them that it could be more fruitfully employed in augmenting food supplies than in killing men. A number of factors were thus brought into combination which were destined to bring about great social changes. On

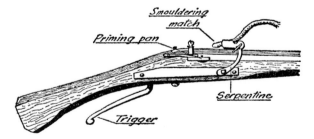

Fig. 1. Early Tudor matchlock. This exciting new weapon—or so it must have appeared to a peasant of the period—notably improved the standard of his winter living by enabling him to take toll of the great numbers of wildfowl that flocked the undrained meres of fifteenth-century England—not to mention, less lawfully, the herds of wild deer that roamed royal chase and lordly domain

17

the one hand, there was the gun itself, an effective arm against sitting targets; and on the other there were seemingly inexhaustible stocks of game, wildfowl and other edible birds against which it could be successfully employed. When to these were added the endemic winter food shortages that existed among the poorer classes, and the fact that, over the greater part of the country, fowling was lawful and free to any man who could possess himself of the means to practise it, the great upsurge that took place in shooting can be seen to have been inevitable. Attempts to check it by legislation, inspired by legitimate fears for our national supremacy in the use of the longbow, and no doubt with some thought for the fillip which the gun had given to deer-poaching—not to mention robbery with violence—were totally unavailing. In the absence of effective enforcement, nothing could deter the rustic population from using this new means for stocking their scanty larders. Besides, we may be sure that the shooting peasantry of early Tudor days thoroughly enjoyed their pot-hunting; for although the matchlock was incapable of wing shooting, it offered all the thrills of stalking. And so, as Shakespeare indicates, its popularity spread upwards to the new, well-fed, mercantile classes of the Elizabethan era.

Fig. 2.   Rifled matchlock—probably the property of a member of a Continental shooting guild (*c.* 1600)

But the nobility and privileged classes remained almost wholly outside this movement: for their sporting, they continued to rely on horse, hound and hawk, whereby the nascent gun trade of this country languished for lack of aristocratic and wealthy patronage.

Not so on the Continent, where the upper classes appear to have been less conservative. There the matchlock was freely used, both as an adjunct to the conventional chase and as a hunting weapon in its own right. From its early days it had been rifled, and had thereby gained greatly in power and precision, so that it could be used effectively against deer and wild boar up to about 200 yards. The beautifully made and ornamented specimens to be seen in our museums provide abundant evidence of its eager adoption by the Continental aristocracy, whose patronage and encouragement soon established flourishing *ateliers* for the manufacture of high-class sporting arms in most of the centres that remain famous to this day—St. Etienne, Liège, and Brescia among others.

A new impetus was given to the sport of shooting and to the Continental arms industry by the development of the wheel-lock in Nuremburg around 1520. This invention, with what must have seemed to be its well-nigh miraculous quality of giving instant fire, enabled a gun for the first time to be loaded and kept in a state of constant readiness and instantly discharged by the touch of a trigger. It was a weapon of considerable complexity, the art of making which, though highly cultivated abroad, hardly spread across the Channel. The relatively few specimens seen in this country were invariably importations, procured by wealthy enthusiasts, among whom that royal gun-lover, Henry VIII, stands pre-eminent.

Shooting becomes fashionable

The origin of the next great invention—the 'pecking-hen' flintlock—is obscure, but by 1625 a typically English form had been developed. It was, however, slow in action, and did little or nothing to extend the stalking tactics or social background of shooting. But with the return of Charles II from his exile in France in 1660, there was a big change, for he brought with him in his entourage many who had learnt the

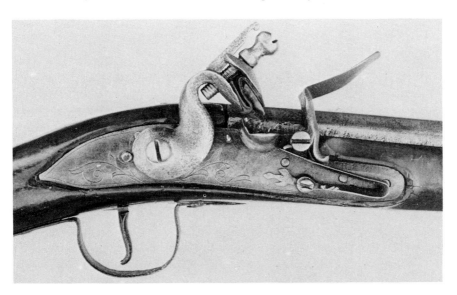

Fig. 3.   Early flintlock incorporating French improvements (*c.*1690)

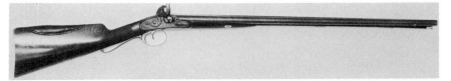

Fig. 4.   Perfected flintlock by Purdey (*c*.1820)

new French sport of shooting birds on the wing, which French improvements in the flintlock had rendered possible. The sport quickly became fashionable, and stimulated our home gun trade into meeting the demand for the new, improved fowling pieces. From that time onward, shooting became what it has been ever since—one of our great national sports, the love of which is rooted in all classes.

By the end of another century, say by 1760, the best English gunmakers had more or less caught up the long start of their Continental rivals; and in the next half century, they succeeded in overtaking them. They did this, be it noted, not by any Heaven-ordained superiority, but by the sheer excellence of their guns—their shooting powers, their faultless workmanship and their severe elegance, in which, latterly, the pervasive influence of Beau Brummel on the taste of the period can be distinctly traced.

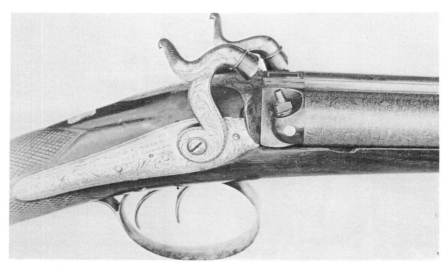

Fig. 5.   Percussion muzzle-loader by S. & C. Smith (*c*.1850)

Fig. 6. Lefaucheux-type pinfire by Joseph Lang (1863). (Note absence of extractor and mechanical ineptitude of breech-locking arrangement)

Fig. 7. Sliding barrel pinfire by Harvey of Exeter (*c.*1860)

A sporting revolution

The overthrow of the perfected flintlock by the percussion muzzle-loader, to which we may attach the date of 1825, though a technical revolution, is of little significance to the present theme. It was the introduction of the pinfire breechloader by the Paris gunmaker, Lefaucheux, towards the middle of the century, that revolutionised, not only guns, but the whole sport and practice of shooting. The English gunmakers, still the world-leaders, threw themselves into the task of perfecting the new weapon with furious energy. Urged on by a large and wealthy clientele, who demanded weapons equal to the exacting requirements of driven game shooting and the making of enormous bags, and at the same time of the highest elegance, safety and lasting quality, they evolved our modern hammerless ejector. It was a weapon forged in a white heat of competitive ingenuity and cunning craftsmanship for which it would be hard to find a parallel. Small wonder that, after three-quarters of a century, it should have changed so little.

The American contribution

We pass now to America, where, throughout the nineteenth century, the imported English gun held pride of place. But by historical imperative the USA was destined to become the birthplace of the repeater. The Civil War had left an arms industry with a large surplus capacity for the production of arms, including repeating rifles, by modern methods. Around the fringe of the settled areas were immense stocks of game and wildfowl which were slaughtered without limit by market-gunners. There was therefore a large potential demand from a protected home market for a cheap repeating shotgun, as well as the means for satisfying it. In the circumstances, the ultimate production of such weapons was inevitable; and when they duly emerged towards the end of the century, they were favourably received by a people eager for whatever was new and ingenious and American. And so repeaters took root and flourished on American soil. But these highly mechanical weapons cannot be regarded simply as part of the continuing evolution of the sporting gun: they were a development *sui generis*—an offshoot of a war industry, the mark of which they bear to this day. Europe, with commendable discrimination, remained faithful to the conventional double-barrelled gun. Though repeaters have been on sale here for fully half a century, for a long time they made no material progress, and apparently it did not occur to Burrard even to mention them when he wrote his monumental work on the shotgun over forty years ago. But in recent years, the repeater has attracted many adherents among the younger shooters, and those who entered the sport through clay pigeon shooting.

The modern picture

The present position of the sporting gun in this country is possibly fairly reflected in two personal observations—that in some fifty years' experience covering every type of shooting practised in and around the British

Isles, I have never yet seen anything but conventional side-by-side guns in use in regular shooting parties of which I have been a member. For clay pigeon shooting, however, the over-and-under is now the standard weapon. The side-by-side has virtually disappeared from competitive events, and in recent years the various repeaters have much declined in favour.

CHAPTER TWO

MODERN GUNS

As a preliminary to considering the choice of a gun in the next chapter, we must survey the guns available to the modern shooter in this country. They are single and double guns of 4, 8, 10, 12, 16, 20, 28 and ·410 bore, with the 12-bore greatly preponderating. The 4- and 8-bores are rare and obsolescent, production of the ammunition having now ceased. It is a matter for conjecture how long it will be before the 10-bore follows them. For the rest, these guns fall into two broad divisions to which I have had difficulty in assigning fair and proper descriptions.

The first division includes all guns made by the traditional methods of the gun trade—a trade, incidentally, which is not in its origins a branch of engineering, but is traceably descended from that of the mediaeval armourer. These guns are made to designs evolved in the field and based on fitness for purpose rather than on the exigencies of economical manufacture. The cheaper sort are made by fundamentally the same methods, but of less expensive materials and to simpler designs, and are put together by less highly-skilled and highly-paid craftsmen in far less time. Less time is also spent on general finish and on adjusting and regulating the mechanism, and perhaps no time at all on testing or regulating the shooting.

The other broad division comprises all guns made by modern machine-shop methods. They are made to designs evolved on the drawing board rather than in the field, with a view chiefly to mass production by machinery. The best of them, regarded as engineering products, are beautifully made, and are good value for money.

One is tempted to label these two broad divisions as handmade or gunmakers' guns, and machine-made or engineers' guns. But that would be misleading, for the maker of the traditional type of weapon, even in its most costly form, uses machine-shop methods so far as possible to get down to the outside tolerances of action and barrels, and

Fig. 8. The hammer gun at the peak of its development, with rebounding locks, small, neat hammers entirely below the line of sight when cocked, top-lever, snap-action, Purdey double bolt, Greener cross-bolt and Purdey side-clips

Fig. 9. A typical Birmingham-made Anson & Deeley gun (see also fig. 10). This simple and durable kind of weapon, costing about £10 before World War I, and sold in very large numbers, chiefly sustained the high reputation of English guns in the remoter parts of the world

very rightly so; whilst the manufacturer of the allegedly machine-made kind is no doubt unable to avoid putting in a considerable amount of hand-work in finishing, assembly and adjustment, to an extent dependent on the type and quality of the weapon. So, to avoid unfair and misleading implications, I will take advantage of the fact that the newer kinds of guns are almost invariably repeaters to label my broad division conventional guns and repeaters respectively.

Conventional guns

These are predominantly the double-barrelled, drop-down guns, which can be either side-by-side or over-and-under. The single-barrelled kind must also be included. Other candidates for inclusion are the French sliding-breech type pioneered by Darne and possibly the combination gun-rifle favoured in Germany and Central Europe, and most commonly seen in the form of a drilling—a three-barrelled weapon comprising a double shotgun with a rifle barrel beneath. The Darne is entitled to rank under this heading because it is a gunmaker's gun with a history as long as that of the conventional hammerless ejector—also because of its availability on the British market and its suitability for British sport. But because it hardly conforms to this last particular, I have excluded the *drilling*.

The outstanding features of the guns I have grouped in this main division are as follows.

DOUBLE-BARRELLED, SIDE-BY-SIDE.   Five subdivisions of this category must be considered.

(*a*) *Hammer—non-ejector*. A strong and simple design. Old, high quality specimens can be very beautiful but, as found, are usually proved for black powder only, and unless and until re-proved, are unsuitable for use with modern smokeless ammunition. Prone to inadvertent discharge, irrespective of quality, by faulty manipulation;

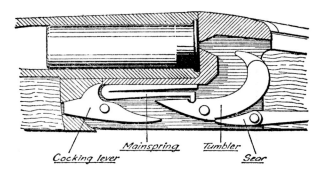

Fig. 10.   Anson & Deeley Action. Introduced in 1875 by Westley Richards, this triumphant simplification is still the most widely used of all conventional gun actions. As shown, it is in the cocked position ready for firing. Pulling the trigger depresses the nose of the sear clear of the notch or 'bent' in the tumbler, which is thereupon impelled by the mainspring to strike the cartridge. When the gun is opened after firing, the cocking lever, carried around by the fore-end, restores the tumbler to the position shown. See also illustration on page 25

Fig. 11. Machine-shop methods are used so far as possible to get down to the outside tolerances of actions and barrels. (Webley & Scott fully-machined action body for A. & D. boxlock gun)

though many eminent sportsmen, including King George V, continued to prefer this type long after hammerless guns had come into general use. They are slower in action than hammerless guns, unless made, as a few were, with ejectors. (Self-cocking hammer guns with ejectors are currently being manufactured in Italy by Armi Famars of Gardone Val Trompia and possibly by other makers.)

(*b*) *Hammerless boxlock (ejector or non-ejector).* Usually, if English, made on the Anson & Deeley system—the simplest, most robust, best understood and most readily repaired and adjusted of all sporting guns. Except only for the hammerless sidelock, the least accident-prone. Made in all qualities, and easily the most thoroughly proved sporting gun in the world. The simple lockwork is accommodated in slots machined out of a solid action body. Some Continental boxlocks, loosely described as 'Anson & Deeley' are variants, and need individual appraisal. Balance and handling qualities, fair to very good. Normal weight of a $2\frac{1}{2}$-inch, 12-bore with 28-inch barrels—6 lb. 6 oz. to 6 lb. 8 oz.

(*c*) *Hammerless sidelock (usually ejector).* The locks are mounted on detachable plates let into the side of the action and stock. They usually incorporate intercepting safety sears as a safeguard against the lock jarring off, as by a fall. A more elegant weapon than the boxlock—somewhat less simple and a good deal more costly, but usually better balanced and with superior trigger pulls. Everlasting in the best grades if well treated, but cheap versions need critical buying. Some of them are not true sidelocks, but boxlocks with

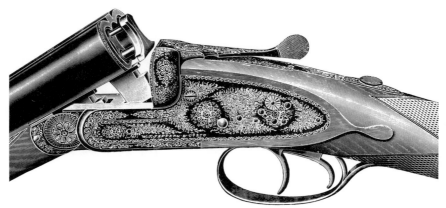

Fig. 12.   A typical London pattern sidelock gun incorporating locks as shown in fig. 13 and a Southgate ejector as shown in fig. 18

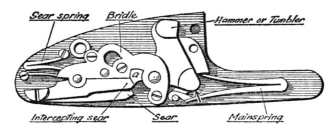

Fig. 13.   A conventional sidelock. Here shown in the fired position. When the gun is opened, a see-saw lever (not shown) pivoted in the knuckle of the action and carried around by the fore-end, lifts the hammer or tumbler where shown by the arrow and restores it to the cocked position. Pulling the trigger depresses the nose of the sear and also that of the intercepting sear, thus allowing the hammer to fall; but if the sear alone is disengaged, as by a jar, the intercepting block *a*, which is part of the tumbler, is arrested by the nose of the intercepting sear, thus preventing the fall of the hammer

dummy side-plates, etc. Others are true sidelocks but much simplified variants, without intercepting sears. Corresponding weight— 6 lb. 4 oz. to 6 lb. 6 oz. (See also below under EJECTORS, SINGLE TRIGGERS and SELF-OPENING ACTIONS.)

(*d*) *Sliding breech (Darne).*   Barrels are fixed in relation to stock; the gun is loaded by sliding back the standing breech. Strong, light, simple and highly elegant in the better grades. Light recoil. Balance

Fig. 14. The French Darne sliding breech gun—strong, light, simple and highly elegant in the better grades. Here shown (a) closed, and (b) open. In the latter position the fired cartridge has been selectively withdrawn with the breech and when clear of the chamber falls to the ground

and liveliness outstanding because of the rearward disposition of weight. Hand-detachable locks and ejectors in all models. Gun takes down into two parts only. Corresponding weight—6 lb. 2½ oz.

(e) *Trigger plate actions.* In these, the whole of the percussion mechanism is mounted on the trigger plate and is detachable therewith. Only British representative is the Dickson 'round action', normally a side-by-side. An outstanding Continental representative is the Italian Perazzi side-by-side or over-and-under), in which the mechanism can be dismounted merely by an extended movement of the safety catch. Ideal for cleaning and maintenance, and for protection against theft. Favours the attainment of good balance and handling quality.

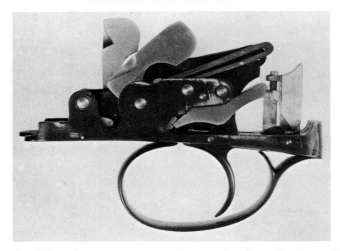

Fig. 15.   The trigger plate percussion mechanism of a Perazzi gun

OVER-AND-UNDER (O/U).   Outstandingly the favoured weapon of trap and skeet shooters and latterly available in many moderately-priced models by Continental, American and Japanese makers. A few costly and beautiful specimens are made by English firms, usually in sidelock form. Mechanism is less direct than in side-by-side, and loading is less easy. Weight is normally greater for equal duty.

SINGLE-BARRELLED, DROP-DOWN.   Available in top quality for serious trap-shooting, but usually seen in cheap machine-made form. With cylinder boring and fitted with sights, becomes a valuable weapon for close-country deer shooting, using the rifled slug (see Chapter 28). Variable choke a useful addition (see Chapter 6). Mentionable here, as a variant is the W. & C. Scott, Martini-action 'GP' gun—outstanding for strength and rearward disposition of weight, making for superior liveliness and balance. Preceding remarks on rifled slugs particularly apply.

Fig. 16.   The Purdey-Woodward over-and-under, probably the most elegant of all guns of this type

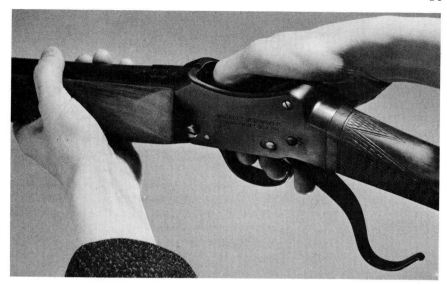

Fig. 17. The W. & C. Scott Martini action GP gun, a notably strong, durable and well-balanced weapon of its grade

PARADOX BALL AND SHOT GUN. This gun, usually a 12-bore side-by-side of normal appearance, except for its having sights, is in a category of its own. It is distinguished by having a short length of rifling at the muzzle end only of the barrels, and is capable of firing either a heavy (735 or 750 grain) bullet with the accuracy of an Express rifle, or a charge of small shot to a good cylinder pattern. The Paradox was particularly suitable for jungle shooting, and was effective against any soft-skinned dangerous game. It is now obsolete, as the special ammunition is no longer manufactured, but surviving specimens can make good use of the rifled slug (see fig. 102).

EJECTORS. When the double gun was being perfected in the 1890s, numerous ejectors were designed for throwing out the spent cartridge or cartridges. Notable examples are the Holland & Holland, more usually described as the Southgate, the Deeley and the Baker. The first has most deservedly and conspicuously survived. It comprises only two parts, as shown in fig. 18 and is housed in the fore-end of the gun.

The mechanism is in duplicate—one set for each barrel—and is therefore fully selective: it operates only if the gun has been fired; and if one barrel only has been discharged then it ejects only the appropriate case.

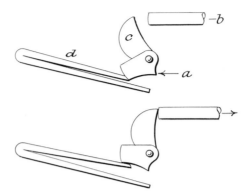

Fig. 18.   The Southgate ejector, the simplest and by far the most popular of all ejectors, works on the over-centre principle, like the blade of a penknife. It comprises only two parts, the cam or 'kicker' *c* and the vee-spring *d*. The top view shows it cocked and ready for action. When the gun is opened after firing, the end of the cocking lever, which projects from the knuckle of the action, engages the appropriate kicker at *a* and forces it around its pivot until the over-centre position is reached, whereupon the spring flicks it over (bottom) so that it strikes the end of the extractor rod *b* and ejects the appropriate cartridge. The re-closing of the gun forces the kicker back to the position shown in the top view

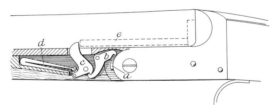

Fig. 19.   The Deeley ejector

The Deeley ejector, especially favoured by Westley Richards, is also housed in the fore-end. It comprises what is essentially a lock of the form shown in fig. 13, in which the hammer or tumbler becomes the kicker acting on the extractor rod, the sear being triggered by the forward movement of the mainspring of the fired lock, acting through a 'slipper' or detent (see fig. 19).

The Baker ejector, again housed in the fore-end, is shown semi-diagrammatically in fig. 20. The kicker *a* is formed at the end of the rod *b*, and is actuated by the coil spring shown. These parts are contained

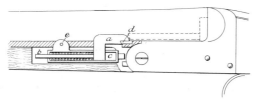

Fig. 20. The Baker ejector

in a box c pivoted at e. In the ready or unfired position shown, the kicker is restrained from movement by a notch or bent engaging with a stop d in the fore-end iron.

When the gun is opened after firing, a slipper or detent, as in the former example, raises the hinged box and disengages the kicker from the stop d, whereupon it is impelled forward by the spring, thus striking the extractor rod and ejecting the appropriate cartridge case.

The Baker ejector was especially favoured for big-game rifles because it continues to function even if the spring is broken.

All these ejectors are normally re-cocked by the action of the standing breech on the extractors when closing the gun.

The ejectors of the more popular over-and-unders do not involve any new principles. The FN Browning, for example, has a fore-end ejector, comprising a kicker actuated by a coil spring and controlled by a sear, which, when the gun is opened after firing, is tripped by a rod projecting from the fore-end and under the control of the hammer.

The Japanese Miroku employs a similar arrangement, but uses a vee spring instead of a coil.

As hitherto made, ejectors are always operative provided that the gun has been fired. But owing to the reloading potential of the now common plastic cartridges and to the indestructible litter they make if scattered on the ground, I have urged that ejectors should be made 'optional', so that they can be switched out of action if the speed in reloading of which they admit is not called for by the sport in hand.

I am pleased to see that this suggestion has been taken up by some foreign gunmakers, and have myself published particulars* of a convenient way of converting the popular Spanish AYA guns from ordinary to optional ejection.

SINGLE TRIGGERS. These are generally favoured by clay pigeon shooters because they enable the second barrel of an over-and-under to be fired without shifting the grip, and thus contribute to the accuracy

* 'Case Salvage Made Easy', by Gough Thomas—*Shooting Times*—June 21, 1969

Fig. 21. Winchester inertia-type single trigger mechanism. The sear lifter (A) is hinged on the trigger blade and is thrown backwards by the recoil from the firing of the first barrel, as shown, at which stage the involuntary pull takes place harmlessly. The lifter is then returned to the forward position, when it engages the second sear

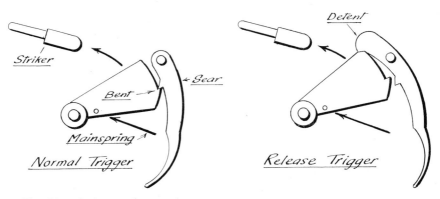

Fig. 22. Release trigger (diagrammatic only). Pulling the normal trigger (left) releases the hammer, which is then impelled by the mainspring to hit the striker and fire the gun. Pulling the release trigger (right) disengages sear from bent, but brings into action a detent which holds the hammer back until the trigger is released

with which the second shot can be placed. On game guns, however, I regard them as a great mistake unless the shooter is satisfied that their many disadvantages are more than compensated by the accuracy with which he can place his second shot. They seem to add nothing to speed, for I find that the finger can usually beat the eye, and their drawbacks are formidable. Whether selective or otherwise, they deprive the double gun of its great advantage of instant availability of open or choke boring; they add appreciably to the cost and complexity of a gun; they habituate the user to a minority system; and they are prone to get out of adjustment or to fail unless periodically cleaned and overhauled by a gunsmith who really understands them. I shall never forget the lesson of two fellow-members of a grouse-shooting party in one of the remotest parts of the Highlands, whose single triggers failed them at the height of the season. The undoubted popularity of the single trigger in America, where it is widely regarded as a *sine qua non* on a good double gun, irrespective of the class of sport for which it is required, is due, I believe, to gadget-appeal, though it acquires merit as an aid to shooting in colder regions, when fingers are numb or when gloves are worn.

An interesting variant of the single trigger principle is the double selective trigger. A double gun thus equipped has two triggers of ordinary form. The front one, pulled twice, fires first the bottom barrel of an O/U and then the top. The back one fires first the top barrel and then the bottom. Pulling the front and back triggers in normal sequence fires the two barrels correspondingly. This ingenious arrangement would appear to give rise to confusion unless the shooter adopts one particular usage and sticks to it.

RELEASE TRIGGERS. These triggers, practically unknown in this country, have a limited and possibly increasing following abroad. The trigger is pulled immediately *preparatory* to firing, and the shot is fired by letting the trigger go. Release triggers are claimed to be a cure for flinching (both physical and psychological forms) and are discussed further in Chapter 9 (Clay Pigeon Guns).

SELF-OPENING ACTIONS. Although personal preference is the deciding factor, no double gun intended for game shooting is really up-to-date in my opinion unless it has a self-opening action. This not only adds to the pleasure of using the gun, but it materially increases personal fire-power. I have repeatedly noticed in driven partridge shooting that with a self-opener I am able to reload more quickly than my next-in-line, if he is without that advantage. The most famous action of this sort is the Purdey, which is a true self-opener in the sense that irrespective of whether the gun has been fired or not, it opens by itself when the top lever is pushed over. As explained in Chapter 11, this is not

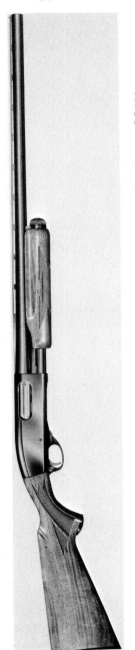

Fig. 23. A typical American pump gun. The model shown is the popular Remington M870

Fig. 24. The FN Browning long-recoil automatic. The first self-loading shotgun working on the long-recoil principle, and still one of the favourites. See also fig. 25

Fig. 26. The FN Browning short-recoil (2-shot) automatic, introduced in direct competition with the conventional double-barrelled gun. See also fig. 27

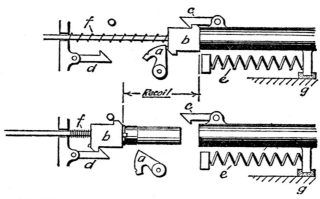

Fig. 25. Working principle of a long-recoil automatic. Upper diagram shows conditions at instant of firing—hammer *a* has just struck firing pin. Barrel and breechblock *b*, locked together, then recoil to extent indicated, recocking hammer in the process. (Part of energy of recoil is absorbed by friction brake *g*.) Breechblock lock *c* is then tripped and breechblock caught by latch *d*, as in lower diagram. Recoil spring *e* then returns barrel to original position, leaving empty case attached to breechblock by extractor hook, from which case is flicked sideways through ejection port by a projection on an extension (not shown) of the returning barrel. The returning barrel also trips the latch *d*, whereupon the action spring *f* restores breechblock to its original position, feeding a fresh cartridge into the chamber in the process. (Actual constructional details do not correspond to indications of the diagram.) See also illustration on page 36

the case with some guns, which are self-openers only when they have not been fired.

Repeaters
These are operated manually, by recoil or by gas pressure, and subdivide as follows.

(*a*) *Manually-operated repeaters.* The slide-action, trombone, or pump-gun, as it is variously called, and the bolt-action only need be considered under this head.

In the pump-gun the spent case is ejected and the gun recocked by pulling back the sliding fore-end. Pushing back the fore-end reloads and closes the breech ready for firing. Usually designed for five shots. This is the standard American shotgun and is a proved type. Because of the forward disposition of weight, balance is bad. (For the weights of repeaters, see the note on page 39).

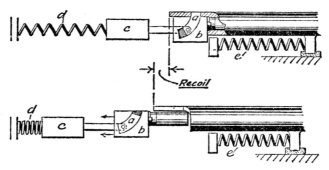

Fig. 27. Working principle of short-recoil automatic. Upper diagram shows conditions at instant of firing, whereupon barrel and breechblock *b*, locked together by sector-shaped bolt *a*, recoil for short distance as shown. Barrel is then stopped; but the impulse thus given to inertia weight *c* causes it to continue travelling to the rear, which it does by pulling the bolt *a* out of engagement with the barrel and compressing the action spring *d* (see lower diagram). The breechblock also withdraws the spent case, which is finally flicked sideways out of the ejection port. Recoil spring *e* meanwhile returns barrel to original position. Action spring *d* then returns breechblock and locks it in position, feeding a fresh cartridge into the chamber in the process. Hammer (not shown) is cocked by breechblock as in fig. 25. (Note that Winchester M50 automatic works on identical mechanical principle, except that barrel remains fixed and a floating, sleeve-like chamber only recoils.)

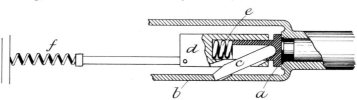

Fig. 29. Working principle of the Benelli fixed barrel recoil-operated repeater. Diagram shows mechanism at the instant of firing. The cartridge is held in the breech by the obturator head *a*, which is locked in the receiver *b* by the diagonal bolt *c*. The recoil of the gun causes the obturator head to deliver a blow to the heavy floating breechblock *d* via the strong spring *e*. The breechblock is thereby impelled backwards against the action of the return spring *f*, lifting the bolt *c* out of engagement in the process and extracting the fired case, which is finally flicked sideways out of the ejection port. The spring *f* then returns the breechblock and obturator head to their original positions, picking up a fresh cartridge from the under-barrel magazine and chambering it. The hammer, not shown, is cocked by the recoiling breechblock, as in fig. 25

The bolt-action is the poor relation of the repeater family, but for line, balance and handling quality is probably the best of all. Unfortunately, it has a low rate of fire.

(b) *Recoil-operated automatics.* These are now of three basic types—the original long-recoil kind exemplified by the FN Browning 5-shot, in which the barrel recoils some 3 inches into the action on firing; the short-recoil FN Browning 2-shot, in which the recoil of the barrel is reduced to about $\frac{3}{4}$ inch; and the fixed barrel kind recently introduced by Benelli. The floating-chambered Winchester M50, in which the barrel remains fixed and the sleeve-like chamber only recoils, is a variant of the 2-shot Browning. All standard models are badly balanced and slow handling because of the way in which the weight is dispersed from the point of balance. Some may be had in lighter versions with aluminium alloy receivers. The FN Browning 2-shot and the Armalite go further and rectify forward heaviness by the use of an aluminium alloy barrel. This is an optional feature in the Browning.

(c) *Gas-operated automatics.* In these, a portion of the propellent gas is diverted into a cylinder in the fore-end containing a piston which works a breech mechanism similar to that of a pump-gun. In form, weight and balance, these guns resemble the recoil-operated automatics.

Weight of repeaters

Repeaters being mass-produced, they must be taken as they come, which invariably means with $2\frac{3}{4}$- or 3-inch chambers and of appropriate weight, even though they will be used with British standard $2\frac{1}{2}$-inch cartridges.

It is difficult to generalise on the weight of these weapons, because many of them are available in so-called 'lightweight' models with aluminium alloy receivers, etc. The following examples, however, are believed to be representative.

The standard Winchester M1200 pump-gun ($12 \times 2\frac{3}{4}$ in. $\times$ 30 in.) weighs about 7 lb., as compared with $6\frac{3}{4}$ lb. for the 'Featherweight' version. The 3-inch magnum weighs $8\frac{3}{4}$ lb.

The standard FN Browning long-recoil, 5-shot automatic ($12 \times 2\frac{3}{4}$ in. $\times$ 30 in.) weighs about 8 lb., as compared with $7\frac{1}{2}$ lb. for the lightweight model and 7 lb. for the super-lightweight.

The standard FN Browning 2-shot ($12 \times 2\frac{3}{4}$ in. $\times$ 27 in.) weighs about $7\frac{3}{4}$ lb. as compared with about 7 lb. for the lightweight model and 6 lb. for the model with light alloy barrel. The Benelli ($12 \times 2\frac{3}{4} \times 27$ in.) is available in normal game gun weight.

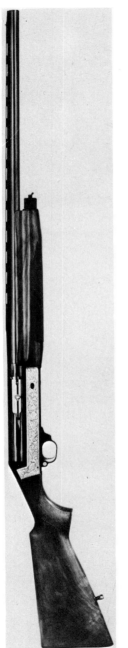

Fig. 28. The Benelli fixed barrel recoil-operated automatic. See also fig. 29

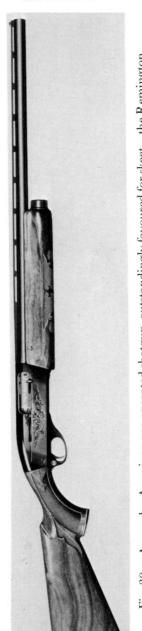

Fig. 30. A popular American gas-operated shotgun, outstandingly favoured for skeet—the Remington 1100. The gas cylinder which operates the breech mechanism is housed in the fore-end

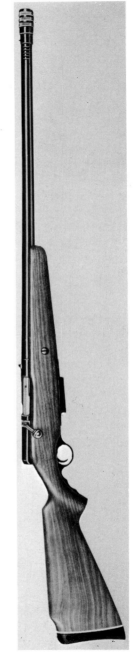

Fig. 31. An American bolt action repeater. This Mossberg gun is fitted with a collet-type variable choke. Guns of this kind are usually among the most inexpensive of shotguns, but possess the merits inseparable from the basic design.

Fig. 32. An inexpensive Spanish gun (AYA No. 1). Faithfully modelled on best quality English guns, it captures much of their beauty and elegance

Fig. 33. An AYA 25-inch-barrelled boxlock—a well-built and serviceable weapon of attractive appearance

Gas-operated automatics seem to come out at about the same weight as the pumps.

This necessarily imperfect catalogue of the leading features of the different kinds of guns available on the British market admits of a broad summary.

Summary
Conventional guns, if good specimens, are distinguished by their lightness, elegance, balance and fast-handling qualities; also, unless they are decidedly inferior, by their ease of manipulation, reliability, durability and, outstandingly, their safety. This last quality comes from its being instantly manifest whether or not they are loaded, and from the tempting ease with which they may be unloaded on every occasion when it is desirable to take this precaution in the field. It is even easier to make them safe—and obviously safe to all around—by merely dropping the barrels; and the ease with which the bores may be inspected when shooting in mud or snow is a contributory factor.

The repeaters are generally characterised by inelegance and bad balance, and by a semblance to military weapons which many find objectionable in a sporting arm. Manipulation is less easy, and safety in use much less assured, since *all* the features mentioned above as contributing to the safety of conventional guns are missing. The automatics are prone to malfunctioning from a variety of causes, and, quality for quality, their life expectancy is lower than that of other guns. Their recoil should be less than that of fixed breech guns, but it can be considerably more severe if they are incorrectly adjusted. This point is examined further in Chapter 16.

Owing to large-scale production and a highly competitive market, most repeaters are surprisingly cheap, and the better kinds offer conspicuously good value for money, despite the harshly critical attitude towards them of so many European and some American writers.

The pros and cons of conventional guns and repeaters are elaborated in Chapter 3.

CHAPTER THREE

CHOICE OF A GUN (TYPE)

The logical approach to the choice of a shotgun is to consider the kind of game chiefly in view and the greatest range at which it will normally have to be taken for its effective pursuit. With this information, plus due regard for the skill of the shooter, which will determine how much choke he can use to advantage, the required pattern at the limiting range can be worked out and the necessary charge calculated. From this to the selection of a gun suitable for firing the charge so determined is but a step.

But it is this step with which the present chapter is solely concerned: questions of performance are dealt with later in Chapter 4. This departure from strict logical order is justified by the various ways in which the average man or boy approaches the acquisition of a gun.

If he requires a gun for general rough shooting in this country and has a shooting background, the question will probably be decided for him, either by the general force of family example, or by the kind of gun his father is prepared to make over to him, or if he is lucky, to buy him on a special occasion. In these circumstances the gun will almost certainly be a conventional double. But if he is a newcomer to the sport, and particularly if he is chiefly interested in clay pigeon shooting, he may be seriously exercised in his mind as to whether he should buy a conventional gun, an over-and-under or a repeater. Even if he leans towards the conventional weapon, he may share the indecision of the established sportsman requiring a new gun as to whether the money he has available can best be spent on an English gun, a Continental one to a more elaborate specification, or an equivalent, but second-hand, one of English make.

Conventional gun or repeater?

I will deal with the first question first. It is one that causes heated controversy, which is a pity, because much of it arises out of ill-conceived attempts to dictate what is properly determinable by the tastes and fancies of others. I would offer it as an acceptable principle that *so far as a man shoots for pleasure, and shoots alone, the best gun for him is the one that serves his pleasure best, whether it be a repeater, a conventional gun, an over-and-under or a muzzle-loader.* It is only so far as he shoots with others, or by their favour, that he owes any consideration to their views, and it may be, their prejudices. Prejudice undoubtedly exists. The young shooter or other newcomer to the sport must recognise that it is still strong against repeaters in regular game shooting circles in this country. It arises from a feeling that such weapons are unethical or dangerous or both. What is worse, they are sometimes regarded as the mark of a greedy or unsporting shot. The fact that the prejudice may be without foundation is beside the point. What is much to the point is that a man who is in the way of receiving shooting invitations would miss many if he were known as a repeater man.

But the solitary wildfowler or rough shooter, or the clay pigeon enthusiast, need be deterred by none of these considerations—he can safely regulate his choice by the simple principle I have put forward. If he does not know, or cannot make up his mind, which kind of gun would best conform to that principle, I would recommend him to consider the various criteria by which a gun can be fairly judged and to make his decision accordingly.

The criteria in question are weight, recoil, balance and handling quality; ease of manipulation and safety; quietness of operation; ease of take-down and reassembly; ease of cleaning and general maintenance; portability and transportability. On a slightly different plane come reliability, durability and repairability. Different again are firepower and adaptability; and yet again, beauty. I must comment on all these points.

Weight and recoil. These must be considered together. For a conventional gun or a manually-operated repeater intended for game, the minimum weight necessary to keep recoil within limits acceptable to the average man is usually taken as 96 times the weight of the shot charge—say 6 lb. for 1 oz. of shot, 6 lb. 6 oz. for $1\frac{1}{16}$ oz. and 6 lb. 12 oz. for $1\frac{1}{8}$ oz. Anything in excess of this is unnecessary in a game gun because conventional guns can readily be built down to these figures. But most other types cannot, or are not available in such weights. They should be marked down accordingly. Extra weight may not tell in a gun-maker's shop, but it will at the end of a long day, however young you may be. It is a characteristic of young men to tend to over-gun themselves; but they invariably learn to regard it as a great mistake, as I myself did. Indeed, if a shooter has to walk long distances for a few shots he may do well to submit to rather more recoil in order to enjoy the advantages of a lighter gun.

In the case of automatics, the 96 : 1 relationship may be affected by other considerations, which are dealt with in Chapter 16. For clay pigeon shooting, heavier guns are desirable—say, $7\frac{1}{2}$ to $8\frac{1}{4}$ lb. for 12-bores firing $1\frac{1}{8}$ oz. of shot. Anything much lighter will expose the shooter to loss of performance through undue recoil.

Balance and handling quality. This most desirable attribute of a gun is hard to overrate. A well balanced gun seems to join eagerly in the game, whereas a badly balanced one hangs inertly on the hands in a spirit of complete non-co-operation. The subject of balance is so important that I have devoted the whole of Chapter 17 to it. Here I will merely say that the better conventional doubles, the Darne, the Greener GP, the bolt-action repeater and the FN Browning 2-shot *with the aluminium alloy barrel* are the best balanced and fastest-handling guns I have tested, though there are tactile aspects of balance, referred to in the chapter on the subject, from which some of these guns appear in a less favourable light.

Ease of manipulation and safety. These two also are bound up together. A gun should be easy to open and close. It should be equally easy to load *and unload*; and it should be particularly easy to check that it is indeed unloaded. From both the safety and convenience aspects, easy unloading is essential. When shooting over cultivated land, with its gates and ditches, it is necessary to unload very frequently—how frequently I never realised until the day when an unconventional weapon caused me considerable inconvenience in this respect. Unfortunately, it is not enough to make your gun safe by merely operating the safety device provided by the manufacturers. Your friends know nothing of the efficacy of such devices: *they want ocular evidence that your gun has been emptied*, or that it has been made demonstrably safe, as by the dropping of the barrels of a conventional gun. If the kind of gun you are using does not enable you to afford them that satisfaction, you may find yourself being avoided. Prejudice apart, this is one of the good reasons for the unpopularity of repeaters in the shooting field.

Ease of loading is much facilitated in conventional guns by a good 'gape': the breech ends of the barrels should stand well up above the standing breech. If the gun has only a poor gape, there may be difficulty in regulating the ejectors.

For what they are worth, safety catches should be accessible without changing the grip on the weapon, and their state should be instantly visible and capable of being checked by touch alone. See also Chapter 27.

Finally, it should be easy to check, even in bad light, that the barrels are free from obstruction—particularly mud and snow. All the repeaters and the Darne are at a disadvantage here.

Quietness of operation. To avoid putting game on the *qui vive*, it is always desirable and frequently necessary to load or unload silently. This is easy with a conventional gun, but most repeaters are noisy in all their operations.

Ease of take-down and reassembly. This is important from the safety as well as from the convenience point of view. If a gun does not come to pieces with the ease of the conventional type, there is a temptation to keep it together—in a motor car, for example; and one day, there may be a cartridge left in it.

Ease of cleaning and general maintenance. The barrels of a gun should be instantly and conveniently demountable, or otherwise made accessible, for cleaning and inspection. Ideally, this should also apply to the breech-locking, percussion and ejector systems, which should be separable from the woodwork for drying out by warmth, or for immersion in cleaning or lubricating baths. The Darne and the bolt-action repeater alone fully conform to this ideal, but are closely followed by trigger-plate actions such as the Perazzi and by the sidelock. The box-lock and the remaining repeaters are less easy of access to their internal parts.

It must always be remembered that guns get very wet at times and that, if many cartridges are fired, impacted water is likely to become sprayed into every part of the weapon. Small coil springs can quickly rust through if water is allowed to remain in their working cavities; and there are no less than fifteen coil springs, large and small, tucked away in one of the most popular of the automatics.

Portability. A gun is not always in the hands. It has to be carried for long walks in the crook of the arm or triggers-upwards over the shoulder. A gun which cannot be carried thus in comfort is not a good shooting companion. Bottom-loading repeaters, in which the underpart of the receiver is reduced to two narrow rails, need critical regard from this point of view. So does the over-and-under, with its narrow action. When its breech is closed (but not otherwise), the Darne, with its rearward weight and broad wooden bar, is the most comfortable of all guns to carry, with the ordinary doubles running it very close.

Transportability. A gun should pack away in a small case for easy transport by motor car.

Reliability, durability and repairability. The reliability and durability of the conventional gun are a byword. Cases within my knowledge that come immediately to mind are a BSA that went straight back into service after being recovered from the muddy bottom of an African river; an old Gallyon pinfire which was *ploughed up* on the glebe of a sporting parson friend of mine, and which he used for some years after merely having it cleaned and re-proved; and a Boss sidelock, now retired, which survived the firing of over 1½ million rounds in the testing department of the Kynoch works. There may be comparable cases of repeaters, but I have never heard of them. The pump gun is known to be a durable weapon, but not so the self-loaders, which have a comparatively short trouble-free life. The latter are also prone to malfunctioning from a number of causes, including swollen, malformed or unsuitable cartridges and sand or mud in the mechanism, to which the open, cage-like receivers of some types are particularly accessible.

It should not be overlooked that a broken spring or the like, which may put one barrel of a double gun out of action, is unlikely to affect the other, so that the weapon is not wholly incapacitated by such an accident.

The ease and speed with which a weapon can be repaired is an important consideration. The great bulk of the repairs required to conventional guns are broken springs and dented barrels, with which any practical gunsmith in this country can cope. Whether he would be so competent to deal with the repair and adjustment of repeaters is open to some doubt, and the prospective purchaser of one of these guns would do well to check this point with his local gunsmith.

Any unusual materials or modes of construction in a gun should be critically regarded from the repairability point of view, and the availability of spare parts should always be checked, especially in the case of imported guns.

Fire-power and adaptability. I believe it is generally admitted by those who have taken the trouble to make the experiment that the *sustained* fire-power of a conventional hammerless ejector is greater than that of a 5-shot self-loader—in other words, that over a period one can get off more shots with the former than with the latter. It is argued for the repeater that where birds are coming in bunches at short intervals the user of a 5-shot repeater is nevertheless at an advantage; but it is not explained how the bunches are persuaded to time their arrival so as to avoid the occasions when he has only one or two cartridges in his magazine, or the relatively long periods required to replenish it.

The adaptability of the repeater, with its single barrel, can be extended by the fitting of a variable choke. Not so the double. But then the latter, if a two-triggered weapon, offers an *instant* choice of choke or open boring, as well as a similar choice of shot sizes, or even shot and ball. This last can be a valuable feature abroad, where dangerous big game may turn up unexpectedly in a drive.

Beauty. I make no apology for adding beauty to my list of desiderata. A gun is, so to speak, an intimately manual implement which has to be used with speed and precision. It should thus possess in the highest possible degree the quality of conforming instantly to its user's intentions, without distracting him in any way from the object of his pursuit. This requires that it should not only be light and well balanced, and smooth and elegant, but that its form and proportions should be altogether in harmony with the muscular reactions and tactile sense of the shooter. If it possesses all these qualities, the gun will have functional beauty—a kind of beauty that may be observed in many things that have become perfectly adapted over the centuries to human use and handling. What we are concerned with here is no mere whimsy, but the last refinement of efficiency. It is a kind of beauty that may be seen to perfection in a fine English game gun, and is in no way dependent on applied adornment. Even cheap conventional guns, if well designed, can claim it in goodly measure. An example is the Spanish gun shown in fig. 32. But the broken lines of the repeaters shown, and in particular the gravid appearance of the self-loaders are, in my opinion, aesthetically painful and constitute a serious defect.

So much, therefore, for the factors to be considered by the uncommitted shooter in choosing a gun for general rough shooting in this country. If I were asked for a recommendation, I could only say that, on the counts I have listed, the side-by-side double seems to me to be by far the superior weapon.

A harsh evolution

This is hardly surprising, for few mechanical inventions can ever have been subjected to such a harsh process of evolution. It was, as I have already indicated, developed empirically over many decades by a highly inventive and highly competitive trade to meet the needs of a world market, including, at one extreme, a large social class of wealthy and critical customers, who, regardless of cost, demanded the highest degree of functional efficiency combined with outward elegance; and at the other, a multitude of humbler gunners, ranging from the rabbiting rustic of the home country to the hunters, traders and prospectors of the new dependencies beyond the seas. Both these classes subjected their guns to gruelling conditions of service: the first by the large number of cartridges they fired—five to ten thousand in a season was not uncommon—and the second by exposing them to every hazard that rough treatment and neglect could possibly entail. Yet the double gun not only survived these extremes of usage, but proved itself to have a liberal margin of endurance and dependability, so that even when worn, neglected, out of proof, and shaking in all its joints, it could still continue to withstand the shocks and stresses of discharge.

So far as the type of weapon is concerned, therefore, the game shooter, the wildfowler or pigeon shot, who chooses a conventional gun can hardly go wrong. The serious clay pigeon shooter will choose the over-and-under version, but the others are likely to be better suited with the side-by-side. In its most highly developed form, which, in my opinion, is the London pattern sidelock with rebounding locks and self-opening action, it will cost as much as a superior motor car, though it will last a lifetime and cost next to nothing to maintain. For a mere fraction of the price, however, it is possible to buy an honest and seemly foreign boxlock which (especially if its regulation and adjustment have been checked by a competent gunsmith) is capable of eminently satisfactory service.

As for the more general question of English versus foreign guns, it is widely recognised that some wage rates abroad are so far below ours as to give the makers an important economic advantage. This, however, is partly offset by import duty, and by the existence of makers of bad, cheap guns who are out to exploit the demand that has been created in this country by their more reputable compatriots. The buyer's protection is to confine his choice to guns offered and recommended by an established retailer, preferably a member of the Gun Trade Association, who thereby covers them by his own implied warranty as to fitness for purpose. Such warranty, I am advised, is fully valid in law.

Second-hand guns present a more difficult problem. Good second-hand guns are becoming increasingly scarce and dear. 'Gun coping' is much on the increase, and the path of the inexpert buyer is beset by pitfalls. For example, guns can be tightened by unsound or even dishonest methods whereby they shoot loose again after a few shots. They may be lapped to remove pitting until they are out of proof; or lapped to the verge of proof without quite successfully removing all of the pitting. An unscrupulous vendor might then assert that the pitting is a trifling blemish which could easily be removed at any time. So it might seem until the barrel is gauged, when it would be apparent that any further lapping would involve re-proof, with all its attendant risks and expense. Unless, therefore, a prospective purchaser is particularly astute and well informed, he should avoid transactions with unknown private individuals, or at least insist on having any gun offered by such a one scrupulously vetted by a first-class practical gunsmith. He should refuse even to look at a 'bargain' offered at a low price for a quick sale by a stranger who is reluctant to afford him the opportunity of thus having the gun checked; and for the rest, he should confine his choice to guaranteed weapons offered by such a retailer as I have described.

For my own part, I would rather buy a second-hand gun straight off the field, with all its blemishes and signs of wear, than after it had been done-up by someone I did not know and trust implicitly.

Buyers should remember that it is still lawful to sell guns which have never been nitro-proved, and which, irrespective of their condition, must therefore be regarded as unsuitable and potentially unsafe for use with modern smokeless ammunition. Only a gunsmith is likely to be able to say whether a gun has been duly nitro-proved *and is still in proof*.

CHAPTER FOUR

CHOICE OF A GUN (PERFORMANCE)

We now come to those questions of power and range which logically come first in the choice of a gun, but which I deferred in the last chapter for the reasons indicated. Although most men requiring a gun for general rough shooting in this country can safely short-circuit these questions and go straight for an ordinary 12-bore, there are others who cannot do so—not, that is to say, if they want to get the best satisfaction from their sport. They are chiefly those who pursue their game under exceptionally difficult conditions, arising out of the kind of territory they shoot over, or the nature and habits of the game concerned, or even out of some physical limitation or disability of their own. They may well require something different from the standard 12-bore game gun firing a standard charge, such as would best suit the general rough shooter. There is also to be considered the man who inherits or acquires a non-standard gun, and needs some knowledge of its potentialities.

So we come down to the fundamental requirements of a gun for a particular class of sport, which are independent of any question of the type of mechanism it possesses for opening and closing the breech, etc. These requirements can only be determined by the kind of game mainly in view and the maximum range at which it must normally be taken for its effective pursuit. This poses straightaway the question of how to specify the range of a gun. That is easy, one might say: the range of a gun is simply its maximum killing range.

But that would never do, because birds may occasionally be killed by individual pellets finding a vital spot at distances far in excess of the gun's normal reach. Regularly used at such distances, it would produce a dismal record of misses, relieved—if that is the right word— by a few instances of birds being hit, but not killed, and going off merely pricked, or maybe wounded, with one or two pellets in non-vital parts.

In the process, the shooter would endure endless frustration, and would experience, we may hope, many qualms of conscience.

Clearly then, both on ethical and practical grounds it is necessary to abandon any conception of the maximum killing range of a gun, and to substitute that of the maximum effective range, which, unlike the former, can at least be defined. Thus, *the maximum effective range of a gun in relation to a given kind of game is the greatest range at which it is reasonably certain that a clean kill will be made by a truly aimed shot*, it being understood that the size of shot used will be within the range of sizes normally employed for that particular purpose.

Even so, it will be noted that the definition lacks precision, because of that word 'reasonably'. But it cannot be omitted, for even with the most accurate shooting, and guns and cartridges giving unexceptionable performance, there will inevitably be marked variations in the number and location of the pellets striking a target of given size at a given distance. *The maximum effective range of a gun and load against a particular kind of game is not, in fact, a specific distance*—it depends partly on what sort of performance the shooter is prepared to accept. If he demands 100 kills from 100 accurately aimed shots, he must be prepared to regard his gun as having a shorter effective range than that commonly assumed. I shall return to this point a little later.

But having defined it, how is the maximum effective range to be determined? As an experimental addict, I have always found the question a baffling one, inasmuch as it cannot be answered out of hand by direct practical trial. If one took a particular gun into a country thick with the appropriate kind of game, and shot it hard for a whole season, it would not be possible to extract the required answer from the record. In the first place, since the effective range merges insensibly into the region of flukes, it would be impossible to say whether distant birds struck dead *ought* to have been struck dead or whether they were merely unlucky. Conversely, it could not be said whether those that escaped did so because of the inadequacy of the weapon or the unskilfulness of the shooter. And then there would remain the overall practical difficulty of saying in each case what exactly was the range from the gun in mid-air. (How do some shooters decide, I wonder, that such and such a bird was killed, say, 'fully 70 yards off?' If it means, as it usually does, that it was 70 *paces* from the shooter's position to the point at which the bird fell, the account is not of much value to the serious enquirer.)

The Burrard method
In the circumstances, it seems that the method followed by Burrard, in his well-known and painstaking attempt to find a general answer

to the question of the effective range of shotguns, is the most feasible one. What Burrard did was to measure the sizes of various birds, or, more strictly, the areas covered by their vulnerable regions, and to regard these as targets which he then proceeded to relate to the known pattern distribution of various guns. Then, having decided from experience how many pellets could be taken as a minimum to ensure a clean kill, he was able to calculate the minimum patterns necessary to achieve this purpose. The greatest distance at which a given gun with a given load would be capable of throwing such a pattern could thus be taken as its maximum effective range. There is no theory involved in the method—it merely puts together two sets of practical measurements. The results had, of necessity, to be hedged in within limits prescribed by the minimum striking energy of the individual pellets. Also a 10 per cent allowance had to be made for stringing. The calculations, as finally worked out by IMI for a standard 2½-inch 12-bore, are summarised in a well-known table published in *The Shooter's Year Book*. They assume that the minimum requirements for a clean kill are:

Small Birds, such as snipe—2 pellets, each having a striking energy of at least 0·5 ft. lb.

Medium Birds, such as grouse—3 pellets, each having a striking energy of at least 0·85 ft. lb.

Large Birds, such as geese—4 pellets, each having a striking energy of at least 1·5 ft. lb.

This table has stood unchanged for many years, and undoubtedly gives a widely accepted picture of the capacity of a standard 12-bore.

TABLE 1.   Minimum Patterns (including allowance for stringing)

Game	Shot Size	Minimum Pattern in a 30-inch circle
Snipe	8	270
Woodcock	7	150
Squirrel	7	180
Partridge	6	130
Grouse	6	130
Pheasant	6	120
Pigeon	6	130
Rabbit	5	120
Teal	6 or 7	150
Duck	4	80
Hare	4	100
Goose	3	70

(*Note:* The above minimum patterns are subject to the preceding remarks on minimum pellet energy—see also Table 3.)

Such reservations as I have come to acquire since the first edition of this book can be dealt with conveniently a little further on.

Proceeding by Burrard's method, it is easy to work out certain minimum patterns as being necessary to ensure that sufficient pellets are likely to strike the kind of bird concerned to bring about a clean kill. They come out as in Table 1, which, for consistency's sake, I have back-calculated from *The Shooter's Year Book* table and rounded off.

If, to this information, we now add particulars of the percentage patterns at all ranges thrown by guns of different boring, we shall find ourselves in a position to give at least a *prima facie* answer to a considerable variety of questions on shotgun range and performance. The required further particulars are those set out in Table 2 below.

TABLE 2.   Percentage Patterns for all Borings at all Ranges

Boring of Gun	Range in yards						
	30	35	40	45	50	55	60
True Cyl.	60	49	40	33	27	22	18
Imp. Cyl.	72	60	50	41	33	27	22
¼ Choke	77	65	55	46	38	30	25
½ Choke	83	71	60	50	41	33	27
¾ Choke	91	77	65	55	46	37	30
Full Choke	100	84	70	59	49	40	32

In order that individual pellet energies may be checked where necessary against the minimum figures already quoted, I give them for all ranges and sizes in Table 3 below.

TABLE 3.   Striking Energy in foot-pounds for Individual Pellets fired at Observed Velocity of 1,070 feet per second

Size of Shot	Range in yards						
	30	35	40	45	50	55	60
3	4·48	3·92	3·43	2·99	2·59	2·23	1·94
4	3·54	3·08	2·66	2·30	1·97	1·68	1·42
5	2·60	2·23	1·90	1·61	1·36	1·14	0·93
6	2·03	1·71	1·44	1·20	1·01	0·82	0·67
7	1·52	1·27	1·06	0·86	0·70	0·57	0·45

(N.B. The energies listed are true only of those pellets that have preserved their original form and substance intact. The 'Observed Velocity' is the average velocity over 20 yards.)

We should now be able to say what charge of shot is needed to deal effectively with a given kind of game at a given range; and with that information to decide what kind of gun is required to throw it.

The procedure is simple. A partridge, say, is seen from Table 1 to require a minimum pattern of 130 pellets of No. 6 in a 30-inch circle at whatever may be the maximum effective range. All we have to do then is to find out from Table 2 what is the greatest range at which the gun and load we are using will make such a pattern.

Say we are using an improved cylinder 12-bore firing a standard game cartridge loaded with $1\frac{1}{16}$ oz. of No. 6 shot. From Table 4 (page 58) we see that this will comprise 287 pellets, of which we already know that we need to throw 130 or 45 per cent into the 30-inch circle; and if we turn back to Table 2, we find that an improved cylinder will make such a percentage pattern at something rather more than half way between 40 and 45 yards, or, say, 43 yards.

But on the evidence accumulated since the first edition of this book, I consider that the kills to cartridges ratio implicit in the foregoing example, and any others worked out in the same way, is somewhat too low to satisfy the 'reasonable' expectations of an expert shot who is also a humane sportsman. The Burrard method, as applied, may indeed be criticised as being too dependent on averages, and having insufficient regard for the wide variation from round to round in the number and incidence of the pellets striking a target of given size, even with guns and cartridges giving unexceptionable performance.

Comprehensive performance diagram
With these considerations in mind, I have prepared the diagram shown in fig. 34, which affords immediate and I believe realistic answers to all the questions commonly arising in this context. It shows the maximum effective range of various charges of shot against game and wildfowl, irrespective of the calibre of the guns from which they are fired, provided only that they are fired at standard velocity to make good regular patterns with shot of appropriate size.

(It should never be forgotten in this context that birds are not killed by guns, but only by charges of shot, and then only by those pellets of adequate size, travelling with adequate velocity, which the regularity and density of the pattern, combined with the skill of the shooter, are together capable of bringing to bear.)

The diagram is based on the same principle of relating minimum pattern to target size, but the effective ranges so calculated have been scaled down to what I regard as a more appropriate level. They thus fall into line with the judgment of generations of experienced sportsmen in that they key in with the traditional effective range of the 12-bore with its old standard load of $1\frac{1}{8}$ oz.—namely, 40 yards if bored improved cylinder and 50 yards if full choke.

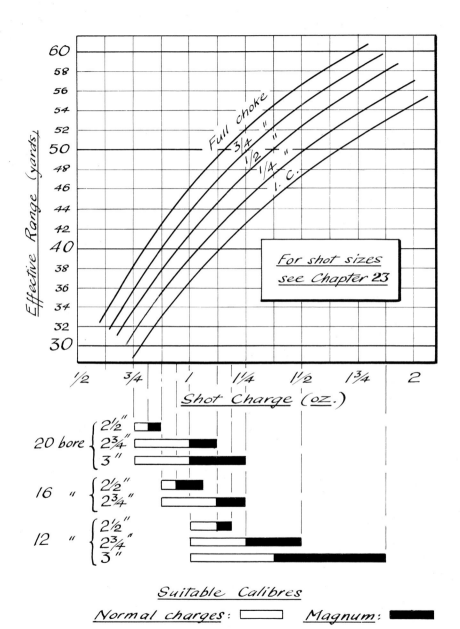

Fig. 34. Effective ranges of various guns and loads

The diagram has five curves, one for each of the common gun bor-ings. So if a shooter wants to know, say, the approximate maximum effective range against pigeon of the 16ga. $2\frac{3}{4}$-inch cartridge, with its one-ounce load, when fired from an improved cylinder, he follows the vertical line from '1 oz.' on the base line of the diagram up to the IC curve, and from that point horizontally to the range scale, where he reads about 36 yards. On reference to the lower part of the diagram, he sees the alternative calibres available for firing this charge, and whether it would constitute a magnum or a normal load. As to choice of calibre, see Chapter 10. It is interesting to note that the diagram gives the maximum effective range of the $1\frac{1}{16}$ oz. 12-bore load as 38 yards for an improved cylinder and not 43 as previously.

Answers are also given to more involved questions. A *Shooting Times* reader wanted a 'good 50-yard duck gun' for flighting, and wondered whether he could suitably adapt a strong, heavy $2\frac{1}{2}$-inch 12-bore, weigh-ing 7 lb. and bored improved cylinder and half-choke. A gunmaker was prepared to rechamber the gun for $2\frac{3}{4}$ in. cartridges and to improve the shooting of the right barrel to quarter-choke.

Referring to the diagram, and starting from 50 yards on the range scale, we find that a quarter-choke would need a charge of $1\frac{1}{2}$ oz. to give the necessary minimum pattern for duck. Reference to the lower part of the diagram shows this to be a magnum load for a $12 \times 2\frac{3}{4}$ in. gun.

The practical limit, having regard to the $3\frac{1}{4}$ tons maximum working pressure for which the gun would normally be re-proved, and the heavy recoil of magnum charges in a gun of this weight, would be the $1\frac{1}{4}$ oz. Alphamax, which can be seen from the diagram to have an effective range of about 45 yards with a quarter-choke and 47 yards with a half-choke.

Minimum pellet energy
Although the minimum pellet energies previously specified are believed to be adequate for medium game birds up to the size, say, of a grouse, they should be stepped up for larger birds, such as cock pheasants, which I consider need 1·5 foot-pounds for reasonable results. Duck (e.g. mallard) also need 1·5. The smaller geese should be allowed 2, and the big Canadas, 3.

The pellet energy available at the ranges indicated by the diagram should always be checked for adequacy in the light of the foregoing by reference to Table 3.

Owing to the rapid deterioration of patterns at extended distances, I have not attempted to legislate for ranges in excess of 60 yards.

TABLE 4.   Pellets in Game Charges

Oz. of Shot	Size of Shot					
	3	4	5	6	7	8
$1\frac{1}{2}$	210	255	330	405	510	675
$1\frac{7}{16}$	201	244	316	388	489	646
$1\frac{3}{8}$	192	234	303	371	468	618
$1\frac{5}{16}$	183	223	289	354	446	590
$1\frac{1}{4}$	175	213	275	338	425	562
$1\frac{3}{16}$	166	202	261	321	404	534
$1\frac{1}{8}$	157	191	248	304	383	506
$1\frac{1}{16}$	149	181	234	287	361	478
1	140	170	220	270	340	450
$\frac{15}{16}$	131	159	206	253	319	422
$\frac{7}{8}$	122	149	193	236	298	394
$\frac{13}{16}$	113	138	179	219	276	366
$\frac{3}{4}$	105	128	165	202	255	338
$\frac{11}{16}$	96	117	151	186	234	310
$\frac{5}{8}$	87	106	138	169	212	282
$\frac{9}{16}$	78	96	124	152	191	254
$\frac{1}{2}$	70	85	110	135	170	225

I am well aware that some shooters, and particularly wildfowlers, will regard the ranges given by the diagram as being inferior to those of their favourite guns and cartridges; and it must be admitted that the large sizes of shot used against duck and geese retain sufficient energy to score kills well outside the effective range if only a lucky pellet hits a vital spot. But deliberate reliance on this kind of happening is not sport and cannot be taken into account in any serious study of the effective power and range of a sporting gun. Wildfowlers should pattern their guns at the range at which they believe them to be effective. They will not fail to note the rapid deterioration in pattern density and quality; and if they are using the maximum charges their guns are capable of shooting, they may well find that the dense part of their full choke patterns is passing well below the point of aim.

Particulars of the number of pellets in game charges, as needed for performance calculations, are given in Table 4.

A necessary warning

The preceding diagram and examples must not be taken for more than they are worth. The maximum effective range of a shotgun being partly dependent on the shooter's interpretation of that word 'reasonably', as explained, the diagram is best regarded as affording a broad picture of the range and power of various guns and loads and especially their *comparative* effectiveness. It shows more accurately, and perhaps more revealingly than anything else, the relatively small gains due to increased or magnum loads. *It will be seen that every extra eighth of an ounce of shot is worth only 3 or 4 yards in terms of range*—a distance too small to be judged in the air, and under the varying conditions of light and background met with in the course of shooting.

There is a further point. Calculations like those on which this diagram and the preceding examples are based depend absolutely for their realism on guns and cartridges that not only give approximately standard performances in terms of velocity and percentage patterns at stated ranges, *but which also give patterns of good uniform quality.* If the patterns are appreciably below standard in quality or pellet-count, as they may be with cartridges that are bad or unsuited to the gun, or with a gun that is badly bored or otherwise defective, then the conclusions are of less practical significance. Patterns frequently fail before velocity, and invariably so with the larger sizes of shot, and no sportsman can afford to be indifferent to the patterns thrown by his gun and cartridges unless he is content to take his game at short range or to depend on fluke shots. I deal with these points more fully later.

But subject to these remarks, the foregoing conclusions would, I think, be endorsed by any experienced shooter; and, so far as they go, they confirm the practical nature of the method employed and its applicability to a wide range of problems involved in the choice of a gun.

Extreme range

Proper consideration for the safety of beaters and others requires a recognition of the maximum or extreme range of a shotgun—not to be confused with the maximum *effective* range.

It may be taken that, when suitably elevated, a normally loaded gun will have an extreme range of about 2·2 yards multiplied by the diameter of the pellets in thousandths of an inch. Thus, the diameter of No. 6 shot is given in *The Shooter's Year Book* as ·102″ or 102 thousandths. The extreme range would therefore be about 2·2 × 102 or 224 yards.

The angle of elevation is not critical, and varies with the size of the pellets, but it may be taken that a gun will realise something closely approaching its extreme range at any elevation between, say, 15 and 30 degrees to the horizontal.

As for the danger of wounding other members of a shooting party, cases are on record of blood being drawn by bird shot at distances of over 150 yards.

CHAPTER FIVE

PATTERNS

In the last chapter I think I made it clear that for consistent and predict-able performance, it is necessary to have patterns reasonably conform-ing to the nominal boring of the gun and also of good, uniform quality. If the actual performance falls conspicuously below this ideal, the shooter is left to a greater or less extent in the dark. Let us consider the practical effect of bad, patchy patterns on the performance of a competent shot, who is taking all his birds within what he has a right to regard as a fair sporting range for the gun and cartridges in question. Some birds will be caught with a dense part of the pattern. These will be struck decisively dead even if well out towards the limiting range, and will impress the shooter as indicating that his gun is good and his cartridges thoroughly effective. But other birds, at all ranges, struck by weak, open parts of the pattern, will either escape or go off pricked or feathered or with a leg down. The baffled shooter will not know who or what to blame, though it is all too likely in the circumstances that he will blame himself, and thereby start a hoodoo which may take weeks to get rid of.

Good patterns are supremely important for clay pigeon shooting, not only because of the small size of the target, but because a single lost bird out of a hundred, which would hardly be remarked by a game shooter, can mean the loss of a competition. The wildfowler shooting flighting duck or geese at maximum ranges is also much dependent on pattern quality. Express and magnum loads and high velocity have a deadlier sound than pattern, but it is the pattern that tells. *This, as I have already indicated, is because, with the shot sizes in common use, the wild-fowler's patterns fail before velocity*—a fact which should never be lost sight of by the long-range shooter.

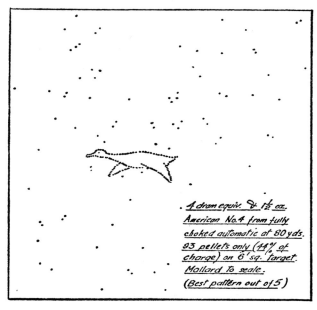

Fig. 35.   80-yard pattern made by 1½ oz. of American No. 4 shot (equivalent to English No. 3) from a fully-choked American automatic

A practical test

Some years ago I examined in the *Shooting Times* the claim of an American author respecting some of his compatriots who were stated to be 'constantly dropping mallard well out towards the 80-yard mark with their trusty 12-gauges'. For this purpose I arranged for a test to be carried out, in the course of which five shots were fired from a new, fully-choked, 2¾-inch 12-bore, bearing the name of a world-famous American maker, from a carefully measured distance of 80 yards. The cartridges were a premium grade, loaded with 1½ oz. of American No. 4 shot, corresponding to English No. 3. I reproduce in fig. 35 the best of the five diagrams. It will be seen that the pattern at this range had utterly failed, and that it must have failed a good way back. More than half the pellets never reached the six-foot target, and those that did had no recognisable pattern-centre. Nevertheless, the individual pellets, though much depleted of their original velocity and energy, had still retained about 1.0 ft. lb., which is the same as the minimum still sometimes accepted. This is, therefore, an extreme case in point; for at the stage when velocity might still have been just adequate, pattern had gone, and with it, any assurance of an effective shot.

Does it matter?

Before considering the factors that affect pattern, it might be well to consider the views of the practical sceptics who deprecate all discussion of patterns as being totally unnecessary, morbidly introspective and bad for shooting. Some may declare that any kind of cartridge does for them, provided it makes a bang, and they may appear to justify themselves by performing admirably in the field. But I have never known these men to seek out bad cartridges. If they take the first that come, they probably get good ones nearly every time. I know that if I went into my village shop and asked for some 12-gauge cartridges—'anything you've got will do'—I should get *Grand Prix* No. 6s. And even if they were something inferior, I might do better with them than another man with the best, if only I were a good enough shot to take my birds consistently with the centre of the pattern rather than the fringe. So I would never allow any breezy evidence of this sort to blow my conclusions out of the window. Birds are not killed by bangs, and I have seen enough of the results of bad cartridges, both at the plate and in the field, to know that good patterns are indispensable for the best results, more especially for the longer reach.

Factors affecting pattern

The factors chiefly influencing patterns are the boring of the gun (not merely the degree of choke, but the whole of the boring, including the cone); the peak pressure of the cartridge; the velocity; the kind of wadding and turnover; the size and quality of the shot and the amount of deformation it suffers on being propelled from the gun. There are good grounds for believing that plated shot gives better patterns than plain, for the reasons explained in Chapter 7 (Cartridges), which amplifies several of these points.

Tightly bored and well choked guns exert the firmest control over pattern; but loosely bored and only slightly choked guns are capable of some of the best game-getting patterns, though they need more careful boring and regulating and greater care in the choice of cartridges. Especially do they need high-quality wadding and moderate velocity loads. High peak pressures and high velocity are usually bad for patterns, whatever the boring of the gun. Large shot generally makes better quality, though, of necessity, thinner patterns than small. But a grave drawback of unduly large shot, such as BB in 12-bore charges for duck shooting, is that it seriously reduces the consistency from round to round

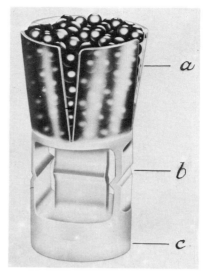

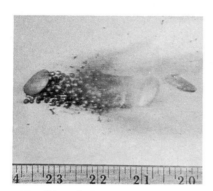

Fig. 36. A shot charge in flight two feet from the muzzle, showing interference of the top wad with the development of the pattern

Fig. 37. A typical modern plastic wad, incorporating *a* a shot protector, *b* a collapsible portion for cushioning the initial rise of pressure of the powder gases, and *c* a cup-washer gas-seal

in the number of pellets striking the target. Its undoubted ability to bring off occasional kills at extraordinary distances has thus to be paid for by an increased risk of wounding when smaller shot would have scored a clean kill.

The nature of the closure or turnover is important, the more so with open-bored guns. The crimp closure improves the percentage pattern which they throw by as much as 5 to 10 per cent, and eliminates the occasional 'blown' or abnormally scattered pattern caused by the over-shot card interfering with the emerging pellets. The improvement is less marked with guns carrying more choke.

The modern plastic wad, incorporating a protective shot cup which enfolds the charge during its passage up the bore, and so reduces the abrasion of the pellets by the barrel wall, tends to improve the quality and density of patterns, more especially from closely bored guns.

It also tends to increase the average energy of the pellets by reducing the number rendered comparatively ineffective through the loss by attrition of their original spherical form—and indeed of much of their substance.

Being a better obturator than most modern fibre wads, the skirted plastic wad reduces, or even eliminates, the dangerous balling of the charge, i.e. the fusing together of clusters of pellets caused by the escape of hot powder gases among them. This is an important subject, which is dealt with fully in Chapter 7 (Cartridges).

Testing for pattern
It was a familiar article of faith with shooters in the muzzle-loading days that every gun had a load with which it shot best. This is equally true of modern breechloaders, which can give widely different results, even with different brands of *good* cartridges. If therefore a shooter, and especially a comparative beginner, has confidence in his cartridges as suiting his gun, I would strongly recommend him to forget all about patterns and velocity and the like and to concentrate on shooting. He has much to lose and little to gain by worrying about these things. But if he strongly suspects his cartridges and cannot reasonably put the suspicion out of his mind, he should test his gun for pattern at the plate, and dispose of the matter one way or the other.

But the test *must* be properly carried out. It is worse than useless firing a single shot at a newspaper draped over a gate and from a distance that has not been accurately measured. Patterns are judged by firing not less than five shots from a previously fired barrel at a sheet of plain paper, or better, a whitewashed iron plate, at least four feet square, at a distance of 40 *measured yards* (not paces) from the shooter's position. The apparent centre of the pattern is selected by eye, and a 30-inch diameter circle described about it. The pattern enclosed in the circle is judged for uniformity, including freedom from undue central concentration. Any balling is particularly noted as being a serious defect. The number of pellets inside the circle is then counted and noted. When this has been repeated for each shot, the average of the pellet-counts is taken and the percentage of the total pellets in the charge worked out. It is advisable to open one or two cartridges in the batch and check the number. Short weight is not unknown.

The nominal percentage patterns corresponding to the various borings are given in Table 2; but I would emphasise that average pellet-counts corresponding precisely to these figures are decidedly not to be expected. If a gun is supposed to be bored improved cylinder, throwing a nominal pattern of 50 per cent, at 40 yards, and it actually gives an average of, say, 48 or 52 per cent of *well-distributed* pellets, with a fair consistency from round to round, the shooter should be well satisfied. The larger sizes of shot always tend to give higher *percentage* patterns than do small.

The testing of shotguns and the appraisal of patterns is gone into more fully in my *Gough Thomas's Gun Book*.

Figs. 38 and 39 show good quality 40-yard patterns made by $1\frac{1}{16}$ oz. of No. 6 shot fired from improved cylinder and full choke barrels respectively. Figs. 40 and 41 show corresponding results at 20 yards, and, incidentally, demonstrate the advantage of open boring for shots taken at the shorter ranges. (See Chapter 6).

Advantage should always be taken of any properly conducted pattern test to ascertain just where each barrel centres its charge in relation to the point of aim. Guns for general rough shooting or driven game should desirably shoot about 6 inches high at 40 yards if the pattern is to be delivered with maximum effectiveness under practical conditions. Failing this, the gun may need re-fitting. (See Chapter 19).

An aspect of patterns neglected in this country arises from the fact that whereas shooting at distances beyond, say, 40 yards needs progressively more choke, shooting at distances below 30 yards often needs more open patterns than those thrown by a true cylinder. When shooting woodcock in covert, for example, many shots may have to be taken at 10 to 20 yards.

Continental sportsmen provide for such situations either by using 'spreader' cartridges—that is, cartridges specially designed to give normal patterns at very short ranges, such as the FN 'Dispersante' with its cubic shot—or by using guns rifled with a slow twist of about one turn in twelve feet.

'Plomb disco', that is, flattened shot, is another means for obtaining abnormal spread. It has the advantage of being controllable, according to the degree of flattening imparted, but excessive flattening may be objectionable. My limited experiments with this kind of shot suggest that it may produce patterns which are of inferior quality for a given overall spread.

Perhaps the most popular spreader cartridges are those in which the shot charge is divided lengthwise into four compartments by means of two interlocking rectangles of cardboard. Rifled shot barrels are not available in this country, and if imported would appear to require a Firearm Certificate.

Misleading patterns. The patterns thrown by a given gun with a given charge of shot will vary with the velocity. If the powder charge is such as to give an unnecessarily high velocity, accompanied by a high muzzle

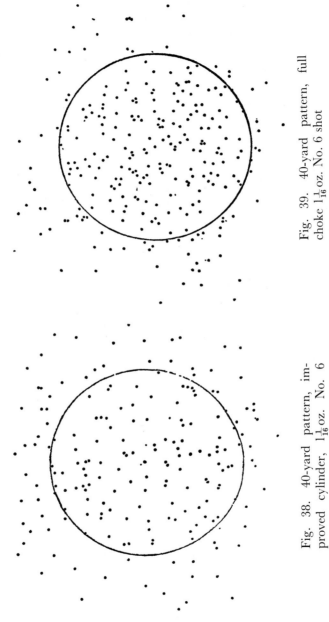

Fig. 39. 40-yard pattern, full choke $1\frac{1}{16}$ oz. No. 6 shot

Fig. 38. 40-yard pattern, improved cylinder, $1\frac{1}{16}$ oz. No. 6 shot

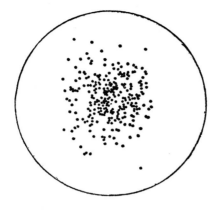

Fig. 41. 20-yard pattern, full choke, $1\frac{1}{16}$ oz. No. 6 shot

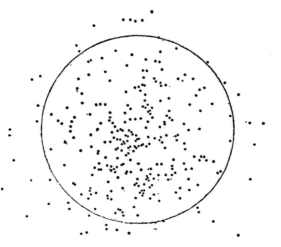

Fig. 40. 20-yard pattern, improved cylinder, $1\frac{1}{16}$ oz. No. 6 shot

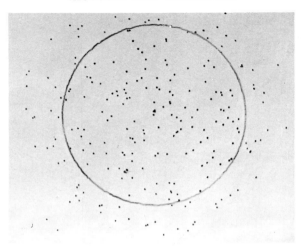

Fig. 42.   15-yard pattern made in 30-inch circle by a Bretton rifled shot-gun barrel with $1\frac{1}{8}$ oz. of No. 6 shot. The pattern has already opened up sufficiently to kill game at this range without undue damage

pressure, the patterns will be wild; yet with the same charge, thrown to a more moderate velocity, the gun may make patterns of unexceptionable quality.

Although the 'pepper pot' pattern—that is to say, one in which the pellets are distributed with geometrical regularity, like the holes in a pepper pot—remains the ideal, the existence of a certain number of obvious voids or vacant patches is not necessarily an indication of inferiority. Indeed, in a strictly normal pattern, the number of voids of a given size is predictable by the laws of chance, and, given the number of pellets in the circle, it can be calculated with uncanny accuracy. Thus, the 40-yard improved cylinder pattern shown in fig. 38 should, by calculation, contain 6 to 7 vacant 5-inch diameter patches. It actually contains 6. It is only when a 30-inch circle contains more than about 300 pellets that the expectation of voids of this size falls to zero.

Accepting their existence, it should be recognised that they do not, as is commonly thought, represent a corresponding number of opportunities of a bird's escaping unhurt. Remembering that the shot charge in flight is elongated into a 'string'—perhaps two or three yards in length at full sporting range—it will be seen that the existence of a void on the pattern plate represents a vacant tunnel running from front to back of the string. But unless a bird were flying strictly in line with it, it would have no assurance of escaping: it would be likely to fly into some of the pellets at the sides of the tunnel.

Again, two identical patterns, as seen on the plate, would not necessarily be of equal merit in the field. One might represent a long shot-string and the other a short one, and their performance on game might be noticeably different.

It should always be recognised that the function of a shotgun is to fill the game-bag, or to break clay targets, and not to make pattern diagrams on a plate. If, therefore, performance in the field is in every way satisfactory, the shooter is well advised to count his blessings and leave well alone. Pattern testing at 40 yards has undermined the confidence which many a gun has fairly earned at its proper work.

Critical appraisal of patterns

In the preceding section, *Testing for pattern*, I have described the common and empirical method of judging patterns 'by eye'. When the eye is that of an experienced man, the method is by no means to be despised—indeed, it is largely adequate. But both the amateur who is not sure of what to expect of his patterns and the expert who needs a more critical method of appraisal will find that set out in *Gough Thomas's Gun Book* likely to meet their needs.

This convenient and reliable method is derived from Oberfell & Thompson,* and I consider it to be the best of the several I have examined. It assesses the merit of the pattern on two observations, namely, (a) the overall uniformity of distribution, as determined by comparing the number of pellets in the inner and outer halves respectively of the pattern circle; and (b) the 'patchiness', as determined by the number of voids or vacant patches of a given size. The numerical values attached to these observations are combined to produce a single figure of merit for the pattern, which affords a reliable indication of its practical, game-getting quality.

In my quoted book, I have given two simple diagrams based on Oberfell & Thompson's conclusions which enable the merit of patterns to be quickly assessed. The first of these diagrams is concerned with the overall uniformity of distribution, as judged by the pellet count in a 20-inch circle as compared with that in a 30-inch at 40 yards. As a 20-inch circle includes about 45 per cent of the area of a 30-inch, it follows that in an ideally distributed pattern the smaller circle would contain about 45·per cent of the pellets, irrespective of the boring of the gun.

---

* *The Mysteries of Shotgun Patterns*, Oberfell & Thompson, Oklahoma State University Press

In fact, with normal patterns, the degree of central concentration is likely to fall within the following limits:

	Percentage of pellets in 20-inch circle
True cylinder	46–51
Improved cylinder	48–54
Half choke	52–57
Full choke	57–62

Merit lies in the extent to which the observed figure approaches the ideal of 45 per cent. It will be seen that the full choke pattern is the worst performer in this regard.

The second diagram shows the merit assignable to the pattern according to the number of non-overlapping 5-inch circles that can be fitted into the vacant patches it reveals, in relation to the total pellets in the 30-inch circle. With normal patterns the number of such patches is shown to be as follows:

No. of pellets in 30-inch circle	*No. of 5-inch vacant patches*
50	13–19
100	8–11
150	4– 7
200	2– 5
250	0– 3
300	0– 2

Merit, of course, lies in the smallness of the number of vacant patches actually observed; and it is stressed that *this figure of patchiness is all that is practically needed to assess the effectiveness of the pattern in the field*, assuming normal velocity and an adequate size of shot. This is so far the case that leading ammunition manufacturers use the patchiness rating as an adequate routine check on pattern quality.

CHAPTER SIX

CHOKE

Choke is the name applied to a constriction at the muzzle end of the bore of a gun barrel whereby a portion of the emerging shot pellets are given an inward impulse, so that they spread less in the course of their flight, and make a smaller diameter pattern circle at a given distance than would otherwise be the case, and one that is therefore more densely garnished with shot.

There are two main kinds of choke as shown in fig. 43(a) and (b). To these must be added the variable choke, described below. In the ordinary choke shown at (a) the bore diameter at the constriction is less than that at any other point. In the 'recess' or 'jug' choke shown at (b) the constriction comes at the end of a local enlargement and is not necessarily of smaller diameter than the rest of the bore. Recess choke has the advantage of being the only kind that can be *added*. It may thus be applied to restore some degree of choke to barrels that have lost what they originally had, through being shortened. It is, however, incapable of being used to introduce more than a slight degree of choke, and is more frequently used by the makers of good-class guns as a regulating device for adjusting patterns, in which case it may be associated with an ordinary choke.

The degree of choke carried by a barrel is expressed in several different ways, namely, (a) by a familiar system of terminology; (b) by the percentage pattern thrown; and (c) by the actual amount of the constriction, measured in thousandths of an inch, or 'points'. If we put these three systems together, we get Table 5 overleaf.

Some modern guns intended for skeet shooting have a kind of negative choke—an exaggerated conical, parallel or trumpet shaped enlargement of the bore at the muzzle, which is claimed to improve the quality of patterns and possibly to increase their spread.

Occasionally, a clay pigeon shooter's outstanding success at some major international competition will be attributed by him or others to some marvellous new system of boring. This is a subject that is in every way likely to involve elements that have nothing to do with practical ballistics; and in view of the fact that every conceivable variation in the boring of shotguns—every possible combination of features—appears to have been tried, one is entitled to treat any such accounts with reserve.*

TABLE 5. Definitions of Choke

(a) *Type of boring*	(b) *Percentage Pattern (in 30-inch circle at 40 yards)*	(c) *Approximate Points of Choke in a 12-bore*
True Cyl.*	40	—
Imp. Cyl.	50	5
¼ Choke	55	10
½ Choke**	60	20
¾ Choke	65	30
Full choke	70	40

(* Also known as 'Skeet' or 'Skeet No. 1')
(** Also known as 'Skeet No. 2')
(See Chapter 9 for Continental Choke markings)

(N.B. The above figures refer to ordinary sizes of game shot. Large shot tends to give higher percentage patterns with a given boring.)

An anomalous system

The system of definition of normal chokes given in Table 5 is riddled with anomalies. For example, to obtain a full-choke pattern, one gunmaker may use 40 points of choke, but another (more probably nowadays) may use only 35. Again, a gun which gives a 70 per cent or full-choke pattern with 35 or 40 points of choke and a certain load or cartridge, may give only a 60 per cent pattern with another load or cartridge. To cut through these anomalies it is necessary to recognise that unless he is contemplating firing some kind of solid projectile, a shooter is not in the slightest degree interested in the amount of the constriction in the muzzle of his gun. I emphasise this because I have known one who felt deceived in respect of an allegedly fully choked

---

* For example, the boring of the gun with which Eugeny Petrov, the Russian Olympic gold medallist, broke 200 skeet targets straight at Phoenix, Arizona, in 1970 was stated to have had a 4-inch parallel enlargement, slightly choked at the muzzle, preceded by an internal ridge. My belief is that the ridge could indeed be valuable in breaking up any 'crypto-balling' (see Chapter 7), whereafter the charge would be re-aligned in the parallel portion and finally brought under such degree of choke as might be found expedient.

But Greener described what is essentially that kind of boring 60 years ago.

gun when he found that the muzzle constriction was less than the 40 points he had expected. The actual constriction, then, is a design feature and is purely the gunmaker's concern. The shooter's concern is not the gun's design but its performance; and so, when discussing or specifying choke, it is best for him to define it by reference to the percentage pattern.

For the reasons already explained, however, the idea of percentage pattern must always be associated with the idea of a particular load or cartridge. If I am specifying the boring of a gun I always say that I want a *well-distributed* pattern of *about* 50 per cent (or whatever it may be) when using, say, the standard *Grand Prix* cartridge loaded with $1\frac{1}{16}$ oz. of a given size of shot and with a crimp closure.

The practical effect of choke from the ballistical point of view may be seen from Table 2, which I repeat here for convenience.

TABLE 2. Percentage Patterns for all Borings at all Ranges

Boring of Gun	Range in yards						
	30	35	40	45	50	55	60
True Cyl.	60	49	40	33	27	22	18
Imp. Cyl.	72	60	50	41	33	27	22
¼ Choke	77	65	55	46	38	30	25
½ Choke	83	71	60	50	41	33	27
¾ Choke	91	77	65	55	46	37	30
Full Choke	100	84	70	59	49	40	32

It will be recalled that in Chapter 4 the maximum effective range of a gun in relation to a given kind of game was defined as the greatest range at which it is reasonably certain that a clean kill will be made by a truly aimed shot; also, that this range was determined by the greatest distance to which the gun would throw the necessary minimum pattern. Referring to the above table, we see that the 40 per cent pattern thrown by a true cylinder at 40 yards is extended to over 45 yards by an improved cylinder; to 50 yards by a half choke and to 55 yards by a full choke. This then is the ballistic effect of choke—to extend the effective range of a gun.

But choke has other and no less practical effects. They arise from the reduced spread of the shot charge, the extent of which is apparent from Table 6.

The figures repay careful study: they show that, at the ranges at which game is most frequently shot—probably between 20 and 30 yards—the diameter of spread, and therefore the margin available for covering the shooter's aiming errors, is much larger for the open borings than it is for the heavy chokes (see also figs. 38–41). But there are two

TABLE 6.   Diameter of Spread (being the diameter in inches covered by the bulk of the charge of a gun at various ranges for all calibres*)

Boring of	Range in yards						
Gun	10	15	20	25	30	35	40
True Cyl.	20	26	32	38	44	51	58
Imp. Cyl.	15	20	26	32	38	44	51
$\frac{1}{4}$ Choke	13	18	23	29	35	41	48
$\frac{1}{2}$ Choke	12	16	21	26	32	38	45
$\frac{3}{4}$ Choke	10	14	18	23	29	35	42
Full Choke	9	12	16	21	27	33	40

(*Special Note: Because of the persistent fallacy that small-bore guns throw a smaller pattern circle than those of larger bore, it is necessary to emphasise that this is not the case. All bores throw approximately the same diameter circle, and the above table is therefore true for all calibres as stated—see fig. 44.)

important points to be borne in mind here. The first relates to over-choke. It is a fact that a gun with an excessive degree of muzzle constriction may give tighter patterns when some of the choke is removed; and it is more generally true, as the preceding table itself indicates, that the concentrating effect of choke on patterns diminishes with the range. This is well brought out by fig. 45, which shows the proportionate diameters of full choke patterns in relation to those thrown by an improved cylinder at various ranges. At the more extended ranges, therefore, the patterns thrown by a heavily choked gun approximate ever more closely to those of one which is open-bored, until, at distances beyond the effective range of either, it would be hard to determine whether the shot charge had come from a choke or a cylinder.

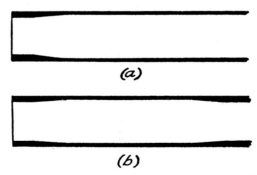

(a)

(b)

Fig. 43.   Types of choke. In normal choke (a), constriction is confined to end of muzzle; in recess-choke (b), constriction comes at end of a local enlargement. Note that a recess-choke can conveniently be applied eccentrically to modify the mean impact of the shot charge.

Tables 5 and 6, critically regarded, furnish a joint explanation of the history of choke in the shooting field which it is instructive to examine.

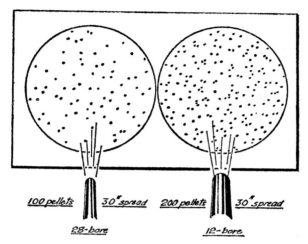

100 pellets   30" spread   200 pellets   30" spread

28-bore   12-bore

Fig. 44.   Small and large bores give the same spread

The verdict of a generation

On the strength of his British Patent No. 1501 of May 29, 1866, William Rochester Pape of Newcastle probably has the best claim to be regarded as the inventor of choke boring, though the practical development of the invention in this country is justly credited to the famous Birmingham gunmaker, W. W. Greener. By 1874, he had so far perfected the art of boring guns in this way as to guarantee patterns of a closeness previously unknown. Indeed, his results attracted so much scepticism as to induce the *Field* to hold a grand trial in 1875, when the choke system thoroughly vindicated all the claims made on its behalf. It proved, in short, that it was capable of substantially extending the range of a gun. As a natural consequence, there was a rush of sportsmen to acquire guns with the new boring which had so decisively proved its superiority—at least, so far as its ability to make close patterns was concerned. But in the succeeding years there was a movement, less precipitate perhaps, but of comparable volume, in the opposite direction. It had in fact been found that the patterns thrown by heavily choked guns were too small in diameter to cover the aiming errors of the average shot, or even of the average good shot, and that the game tally had

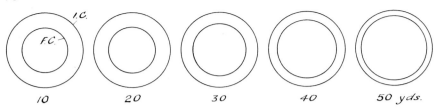

Fig. 45.   Comparative spread of full choke and improved cylinder at various ranges. Note the weakening effect of choke with range and the higher standard of marksmanship it requires at the shorter distances

usually suffered from the abandonment of the open boring. In consequence, the best boring for a game gun for the average man shooting in this country has long been recognised as improved cylinder for the right barrel and half to three-quarters choke for the left.

Nowadays we seem to be witnessing a double movement, both towards and away from choke boring. On the one hand, many newcomers to shooting, and other uncritical shooters, are buying guns that carry too much choke for best results. On the other hand, considerable numbers of the more knowledgeable ones, headed by the skeet shooters, are rediscovering the virtues of open boring. The former class—the new class of patrons of the full choke—adopt this boring for a variety of reasons, chiefly because they consider it more suitable for pigeon shooting and wildfowling, but partly, I have no doubt, because of its psychological appeal and for no better reason than that that happens to be the boring of guns offered to them in the shops.

Considering that a whole generation of shooters, after having eagerly taken to heavily choked guns, turned away from them, chastened and disillusioned, it may well be asked why do so many foreign and American gunmakers still send their guns out with this kind of boring? There are two simple reasons—choke can easily be removed if it is not wanted; and on those occasions when a fully choked gun is held really straight on a distant quarry, the result is likely to give the shooter a good impression of his weapon, and to divert all blame for frequent misses to himself. He is unlikely to lump the gun and himself together as an inefficient combination, and in the absence of any capacity for self-improvement, to blame the gun as the defaulting partner. Yet, all too frequently, that is what he should do.

Another thing he should do is to take a note of the modern, crimp-closed cartridge as a significant development in this context. Not only do open-bored guns show a 5 to 10 per cent improvement in pellet-count when using these cartridges, but they are also free from the old reproach of 'blown' patterns.

The full plastic wad with protective shot cup is also regarded as being responsible for a tightening of patterns, frequently to the shooter's disadvantage. But the ammunition manufacturers, notably Winchester, have convincingly argued that this is not so, and that the only effect of their Mark 5 protective collar (and equally that of the full shot cup) is to 'bring in the fliers'—that is to say, by avoiding pellet-abrasion, to cause many low-energy pellets, which would otherwise fly wildly to the extreme outer fringe of the pattern, to fly truly and make their contribution to the effective part.

For all that, shooters of undeniable experience maintain that, for 'upland shooting', protective shot cups and collars do indeed tighten patterns unduly, and reduce their prospects of success in the field.

I myself am impressed by both these sources of evidence, and can only reconcile them on the consideration that there is no specific distinction between what constitutes a 'flier' and what constitutes a working pellet, and that many a bird in the field falls to pellets which are arguably either. In blunter language, most of us owe some at least of the birds we put into the bag to the outer fringe of our patterns. It must also be borne in mind that at the relatively short distances at which most birds are taken, the pellets in the fringe are likely to have adequate striking energy, and to do their share of execution.

An important maxim

My own experience and observations, and the views expressed to me by many correspondents, leave me in no doubt that unless the conditions of sport imperatively demand a gun of maximum range, the average man is better served by the more open borings. Indeed, I would unhesitatingly say that *the best degree of choke for filling the game bag and avoiding the displeasure of the cook is always the least degree consistent with the requirements of the class of sport concerned.*

This follows from the fact that, provided there is a sufficiently close pattern to ensure a kill at the average range at which birds are being taken, it is better that any surplus pellets available should be devoted to increasing the spread rather than increasing the already adequate density. Thereby hits are scored which might otherwise be misses.

A good idea of the relationship between choke and personal aiming error may be obtained by loading a familiar gun with dummy cartridges or 'snap-caps' and taking snap shots at a target as in fig. 46. The shooter should face the target at the stated distance; then close the eyes and turn away. Then open the eyes and fire at the aiming mark as quickly as possible without fluster, pulling the trigger just as the gun comes into the shoulder and 'calling' the shot—that is, mentally photographing the position of the foresight at the click of the hammer. Shots falling as at *A* would be misses both with an improved cylinder and with a full choke barrel. Shots as at *B* would be misses with the choke but hits with the cylinder; and only those as at *C* would be hits with the full choke. The *B* shots are obviously the significant ones. If you repeat this practice several times on successive days and keep a record of your scores, you will have a fair idea of the possible significance of spread in your particular case.

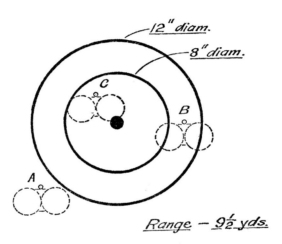

Fig. 46. Aiming target for demonstrating difference between spread of full choke and improved cylinder boring. (Equivalent to 25 yards actual range.)

Choke for trapshooting

I have already referred to the open patterns necessary for skeet, but the best degree of choke for DTL or trapshooting deserves further consideration. Many aspirants at this latter kind of sport seem to take it for granted that the proper boring for a trap gun is obviously full choke in both barrels. This is not an unreasonable conclusion considering the small size of the target, especially when it is seen edgewise, as in this case. But if a shooter has quick reactions, so that he takes his targets at relatively short range, but is not outstandingly accurate in his point-ing, there is good reason to expect that he would do better with some-thing less than full choke in his first barrel and also with smaller shot—say No. 8 instead of No. 7.

Variable chokes

These comparatively modern devices, adaptable to all single-barrelled weapons, take three forms. The first comprises a short extension screwed on to the barrel and incorporating a plain choke as illustrated in fig. 43 (*a*). It is usual for the sportsman to have a set of these extensions, each incorporating a choke of different degree.

The second kind, unlike the first, is truly variable. It is sometimes called a collet choke, after a kind of mechanic's chuck which it resembles, and comprises a constriction divided by longitudinal cuts into a number of fingers, rather like the petals of a closed flower. These fingers are held together at their outer ends by a conical ring which may be screwed in or out, thus squeezing or releasing them and varying the amount of the constriction. The screw ring has a clicking mechanism and is marked on its outside so that the degree of choke may be identified.

Both the foregoing chokes are frequently associated with a muzzle-brake for the reduction of recoil, which takes the form of a short tube with slots or holes for the release of propellent gases at right angles to the axis of the bore. (See Chapter 16 for an explanation of this device.)

The third kind of variable choke is the automatic variety, which con-sists of a collet-type variable choke in which the controlling ring is shifted on firing by a spring-opposed inertia weight. The effect is that the second shot is fired to a closer pattern than the first—truly a strenuous attempt to repeat in a single-barrelled weapon an inherent facility of the double.

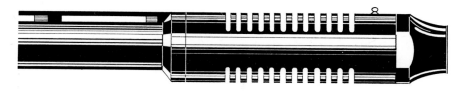

Fig. 47.   The Cutts Compensator with short choke tube attached. For principle of action see fig. 80

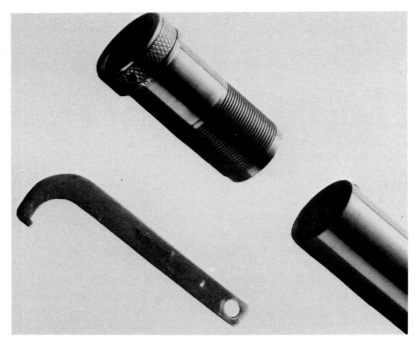

Fig. 48.   The Winchester 'Winchoke'—a choke tube that is concealed inside the muzzle of the gun

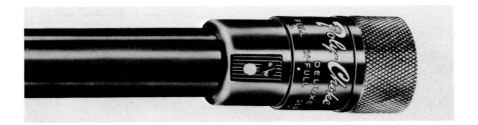

Fig. 49.   A collet-type adjustable choke. These ingenious and attractive devices need expert fitting, and the careful checking of their performance

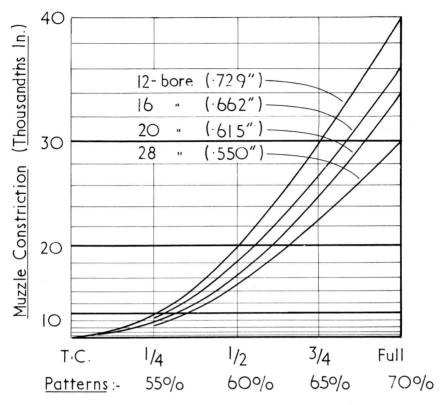

Fig. 50. Nominal muzzle constriction for various degrees of choke in various gauges

Examples of these three kinds of variable choke are (1) the Cutts Compensator; (2) the Poly-choke and (3) the Adjustomatic. This last has an integral muzzle brake.

As a means for adding flexibility to single-barrelled weapons, these devices are attractive, but they all, in varying degrees, involve hanging extra weight on to a gun at the very place from which gunsmiths have laboured for a century and a half to remove it. The automatic chokes are particularly bad in this respect, weighing, as they may, as much as six ounces, and adding possibly 50 per cent to the moment of inertia of a game gun (see Chapter 17) and a corresponding amount, therefore, to the energy demanded from the shooter for its active manipulation.

The collet-type adjustable chokes are especially disappointing. Despite their convenience, they cannot normally be relied on to give consistent patterns of the density conforming to the indications of the setting. The performance of these devices should therefore never be taken for granted. They have the further disadvantage that, especially if they are regularly used at the full choke setting, they are unduly prone to shoot clean off the end of the gun. I cite these disadvantages with reluctance, because, from the mechanical viewpoint, variable chokes have considerable attractions.

At the same time, it should be noted that variable chokes, being larger in diameter than the barrels to which they are fitted, depress the bore axis in relation to the line of aim. They also tend to increase the negative 'flip' of the barrel on firing, so that their overall effect is normally to cause the gun to shoot low. To correct this fault, so damaging to performance, the firms that fit these devices usually give the barrel, or the ventilated portion of the attachment, a slight and scarcely perceptible upward set. The fitting of these chokes and the correction of the shooting is thus a matter for a skilled gunsmith accustomed to the work.

Replaceable choke tubes which screw *inside* the muzzle of the gun are now offered by some makers. They are free from the above-mentioned defects.

CHAPTER SEVEN

CARTRIDGES

Modern British cartridges for game, wildfowl and clay target shooting range from the $2\frac{7}{8}$-inch 10 gauge loaded with $1\frac{7}{16}$ oz. of shot to the 2-inch 0·410 with five-sixteenths. Notable recent newcomers are the two Eley 12-gauge magnums—the $2\frac{3}{4}$-inch loaded with $1\frac{1}{2}$ oz. and the 3-inch loaded with $1\frac{5}{8}$.

The standard Eley $2\frac{1}{2}$-inch, 12-gauge game cartridge is a waterproof cartridge with a crimp-closed, polyethylene case, a non-corrosive cap and a vegetable felt wad, throwing a charge of $1\frac{1}{16}$ oz. of medium shot to an average or 'observed' velocity, measured over the first 20 yards of flight, of about 1,070 feet per second, corresponding to a muzzle velocity of, say, 1,320.

The corresponding Eley cartridges for clay target shooting are similar to the foregoing, but the loads and ballistics, and the hardness and quality of the shot, are modified as necessary to give the best results for the various classes of sport. These cartridges range from the old-established 'Trapshooting' brand, with its paper case and vegetable felt wad—still a prime favourite—to the newer plastic-cased 'Super' grades for trench, trap and skeet, with skirted plastic wads and shot-protectors.

At the time of writing, paper-cased cartridges are still available in several British-made and imported varieties, and are preferred by some shooters who believe that they give more regular ballistics. There is some *prima facie* reason for this belief, based on the greater compressibility of paper as opposed to plastic. This is believed to absorb inevitable variations in the maximum pressure developed from round to round. When one considers the remarkably sensitive relationship that exists between chamber dimensions and pressure, as explained in Chapter 13, the possibility that paper may indeed act in this way

appears to be a lively one. They are also free from some curious contamination phenomena* that have been observed, chiefly in America,
and are not yet fully explained.

The cartridge case. The case has at least three functions—(a) it has
to act as a container, preferably waterproof, for the components of the
charge, including the cap; (b) it has to restrain the emergence of the
shot until the powder is properly ignited; and (c) it has to seal the
breech against the pressure of propellent gases. Of these three functions,
the last is unquestionably the most important. Apart from the screw
plug, no mechanical device ever succeeded in efficiently sealing small-
arms at the breech until the elastic cartridge case was invented. Breechloaders with hand-fitted, inelastic metal cartridges have been known
for centuries. Henry VIII had such a weapon, which may still be seen
at the Tower of London. But the simple idea of a cartridge case which
was sufficiently elastic to expand and fill the chamber as the gas pressure
rose inside it, and thus to seal the junction between chamber and
breech, even in the absence of any accurate fitting of the mechanical
parts, was slow to arrive. It was the elastic, breech-sealing, pin-fire cartridge, invented by Houiller in the 1840s and adopted by Lefaucheux,
which more than anything else ensured the success of the drop-down
breechloader that bears the latter's name—the first modern sporting
gun.

It will be obvious that the use of paper for cartridge cases is an economic compromise. The case should be waterproof, but paper is not.
Nor is it sufficiently elastic under certain conditions. The chief defects
of paper are that when it becomes damp it swells and may cause the
cartridges to jam in the gun, particularly if it is a self-loader; and that
if it becomes abnormally dry and thereby loses elasticity, it is prone
to split. In extreme cases, this may cause 'cut-offs', when the body of
the case becomes completely detached from the head. For this and other
reasons paper cartridges should never be stored in excessively warm
and dry situations, such as airing cupboards, nor should they be left
for long in closed motor cars exposed to the hot sun. They are best
stored under the ordinary, temperate, indoor conditions to be found
in dry houses in this country.

But despite the disadvantages of paper cases, they have served
shooters well for over a century, and with commonsense and by no
means onerous precautions, are as nearly as possible troublefree. It is
not surprising that some ammunition manufacturers and shooters still
pin their faith to them. Perhaps the greater reloading potential of some

---

* See 'Cartridge Chamber Contamination' by Gough Thomas—*Shooting Times*, March 15, 1969

plastic cases is their only important advantage to trap and skeet shooters.

The litter problem.   A marked disadvantage widely attributed to plastic cartridges is the indestructible litter the empty cases make when left on the ground. It has been stated that polyethylene is not in fact indestructible, and that it slowly deteriorates and presumably decays under the influence of ultra-violet light. But if that is so, the process is obviously too slow to be of any consolation to keepers and others who may have to undertake cleaning-up operations around stands or in butts after a heavy shooting day.

There is, however, some hope that future plastic cartridge cases may incorporate an additive, such as that marketed by the Coloroll Company of Nelson, Lancashire, whereby the cases would become 'biodegradable'. Polyethylene cases to which this substance has been added remain fully durable in stock, but once they touch the ground, soil enzymes initiate a process of deterioration whereby the case quickly rots away. It is to be hoped that we may hear more of this.

As stated in Chapter 5 (Patterns), the closure of the case by crimping instead of by using a cardboard top-wad has a beneficial effect on patterns.

Length of case.   Cartridges were hitherto denoted by the length of the unloaded case, which was never greater than the length of the chamber. Since crimp closures became the rule, they have been denoted by the minimum length of the chamber for which they are designed, as stated on the carton. *They must never be used in chambers of any lesser length.*

Incidentally, the 2-inch 12-bore cartridge should never be used in chambers of any greater length. The powder charge has insufficient reserve to allow for the fall in pressure and temperature inevitably resulting from the use of this cartridge in longer chambers, with their greater volume, especially in cold weather.

Powders.   Modern powders are 'double-based' (i.e. nitroglycerine and gelatinised or fibrous nitro-cellulose) compounds. Progress latterly has been chiefly in the direction of improving the consistency of their performance and in their stability with age and under widely varying conditions of storage, which, as an eminent specialist complained to me, may be anything between the equator and the poles, or between the bread-oven and the shed at the bottom of the garden. Notable progress has also been made in improving the controls regulating the rate of burning. For example, Eley now have no less than seven grades of their Nobel-Glasgow powder available, ranging from the fastest-burning sort normally required for driving light charges of shot at high

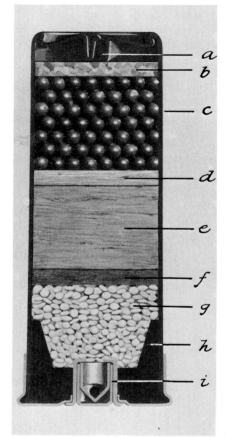

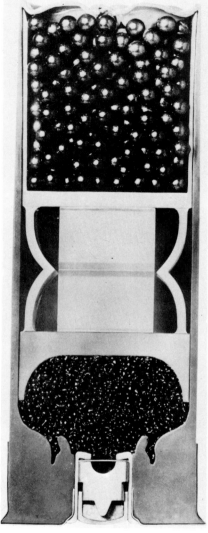

Fig. 51. A modern Eley cartridge, showing *a* crimp closure, *b* frangible waterproof seal, *c* plastic case, *d* under-shot card, *e* vegetable felt 'Kleena' wad, *f* over-powder card, *g* double-based powder, *h* compressed paper base-wad, and *i* cap or primer

Fig. 52. The Winchester compression-formed cartridge. The case of this cartridge is formed from a solid slug of polyethylene plastic and by a process that greatly increases the strength of the material

velocity, to the slowest-burning or progressive kinds required for magnum loads, including that of the 3-inch 0·410. We shall need to return to these graded characteristics of modern powders when considering loads.

The cap. Intimately connected with the powder is the cap or primer. For the best results, it must be adapted to match the powder, the various kinds of which vary in their ignitibility. Dangerous pressures can be developed with normal loads of powder and shot by the use of unsuitable caps, and the possibility is examined more fully in the chapter on home-loading (Chapter 8).

The modern non-corrosive or styphnate cap is a great advance over the highly corrosive caps of the past. Used in conjunction with a suitable powder, it eliminates the bugbear of barrel corrosion, and has largely reduced the business of gun-cleaning to that of merely preventing common atmospheric rusting. Further, unlike earlier caps, its correct functioning is independent of the quality of the striker blow; if it goes off, it goes off properly.

Wadding. The wad has a vital function to perform in the cartridge. It has to seal the bore, and to confine the white-hot, high-pressure, propellent gases to the space behind the shot-charge. Any leakage of gas among the pellets is highly detrimental to patterns and may result in clusters of them becoming fused together, or balling—a dangerous thing, for such a cluster is capable of travelling far beyond ordinary shot and inflicting injury on someone who might be considered well out of range. There is reason to believe that more balling takes place in shotguns than is commonly recognised. That is because when shot is fired into the air the existence of balling is not revealed unless a cluster of pellets happens to strike a bird. Also, balling may take place within the barrel but may be broken up by the choke. I call this crypto-balling. This subject is so important that I deal with it more fully below.

The sealing-power, or obturating-power as it is called, of a wad is dependent on its elasticity and its ability to translate the powerful thrust of the powder gases into a lateral thrust against the sides of the bore. Best quality, greased, white felt is one of the most efficient wadding materials ever known, but it has the drawback of being expensive. Brown felt can be good, but it lacks the uniformity necessary for regular ballistics. A great variety of other material has been tried, notably cork, but cork lowers ballistics and has the peculiar disadvantage of accepting a high degree of longitudinal compression without developing any corresponding lateral thrust. It is, in fact, a poor obturator, as may be seen by putting a felt wad and cork wad side by side in a vice and squeezing them up together. By the time they are compressed to half their original length, the felt wad will have spread out greatly in diameter but the cork wad hardly at all.

Apart from simple materials, many composite wads have been developed. Among those that have survived, cork and felt appear to be the favourite components.

By far the most popular wad in this country in recent years has been the 'Kleena' wad, developed by Eley. This is a vegetable felt originally made of sugar-cane fibre. It is claimed to have the merit of consistency and to prevent the leading of the bores.

The plastic wad, incorporating a protective shot cup, as described in Chapter 5 (Patterns) is now being introduced in certain Eley cartridges, and its use will almost certainly be extended.

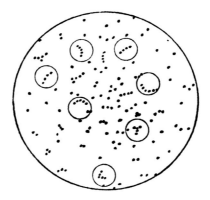

Fig. 53.   Cold welding of shot pellets. Existence of local strings and clusters of pellets in pattern diagrams, as in small circles, indicates cohesion through cold welding over part of their course. (See Balling and crypto-balling below.)

If a gun is to shoot at its best, it must be loaded with best-quality shot, that is, shot that is as nearly as possible perfectly round, and of uniform size and density. For the improvement of patterns, the very best shot is nowadays plated with copper or nickel. This has the effect of inhibiting the 'cold-welding' or sticking together of the pellets, whereby strings and clusters of them may fly together over part of their course, giving a certain characteristic defect in patterns chiefly recognisable in those thrown by high pressured cartridges. (See fig. 53)

Balling and crypto-balling.   Fig. 54 shows at A an agglomeration of about three dozen game pellets—one of several recovered from the base of an iron target used for testing. This unpleasant object is not only indicative of unhealthy conditions in the gun-cartridge combination concerned, carrying the implication of bad patterns, but it could also be highly dangerous. Burrard quotes a classical case in which a man had his jaw broken and some teeth carried away as a result of being struck by balled pellets in a charge of game shot fired from no less than 133 yards away. The agglomeration that caused the wound appears to have included about a third of the total charge.

I myself have had the entire charge from a reputable British cartridge of superseded design travel as a single projectile, so that it punched a clean hole through my pattern plate. I shudder to think of what might have happened if that charge had been fired in the air, in the ordinary way of sport, and had ultimately struck someone far out of normal shot-gun range. One hears more frequent but less lurid accounts of birds being blown to pieces at full sporting distances—no doubt through the balling of part of the charge.

I believe that there is a widespread impression that balling is a modern trouble, brought about by the higher pressures of modern smokeless ammunition, and perhaps by the decline in the quality of the wadding used since best quality felt became prohibitively expensive. But that is not so: it was well-known in the old days, even with flintlock guns. In experiments carried out by the *Field* in 1889 on old muzzle-loaders, both flint and percussion, balling frequently occurred. The reasons are fairly reliably known, and are significant in the modern context, as will be seen.

There appear to be three causes of balling, which may operate singly or in combination. The first is cold welding, whereby the pellets, or

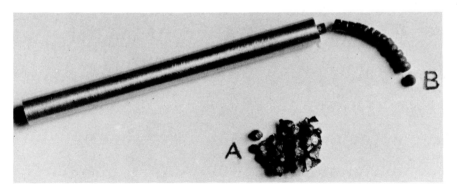

Fig. 54. Balled shot (A), and cold welded pellets (B)

some of them, may be squeezed into effective welding contact by the pressure to which they are subjected when the charge is undergoing its maximum acceleration. Ordinary welding—that is, smith's welding—is brought about by a combination of heat and hammer-induced pressure. But the greater the pressure available, the lower the temperature at which welding can be effected, provided only that the oxide film can be broken, or dispersed by fluxing. With the lead pellets in a shotgun, the necessary conditions for cold welding of a not very efficient sort, but efficient enough to cause trouble, can be attained. Long shot columns and high pressures, as in small-bore magnums, afford the predisposing conditions. Journée gives ·79 inch and about $3\frac{1}{4}$ tons per sq inch as the safety limits.

With the help of a bench vice, and the small steel cylinder and ram shown in the photograph, I have had no difficulty in cold welding lead pellets into cohesive strings, as at B.

The second cause of balling is the escape of hot powder gases past the wad, which may fuse the outside parts of some of the pellets so that they become soldered together. Excessive pressures, inefficient wadding and nitro-glycerine based powders, which involve high temperatures, are all operative here.

What may possibly rank as a third cause is barrel friction. There are reasons for thinking that when there is conspicuous leading because of the roughness of old and neglected barrels, or the finer, transverse striations of new ones, there may be some melting of the charge where friction with the barrel wall is greatest. Whether or not this is independently capable of inducing balling, it could certainly add to any possibility otherwise arising.

So far, I have considered balling as being largely attributable to factors arising from the cartridge—chiefly high pressures and inefficient wadding. But the gun must not be forgotten, because a cartridge that will ball in one gun will not necessarily ball in another.

Dominant considerations here are the size of the bore and the degree of choke. Other things being equal, the gun most likely to ball is an old one, carrying little or no choke, and with a bore diameter in the higher reaches of the appropriate proof category. Such guns are indeed often wonderful game-getters, but they are nonetheless highly dependent on efficient wadding for their effective performance. The gun which I mentioned just now as having thrown its entire charge as a ball was such a gun. The wadding used on that occasion was the old Eley 'Vacuum' wadding, which lacked the obturating power to cope with the situation. But the same gun, when loaded with felt wadding, was a splendid performer.

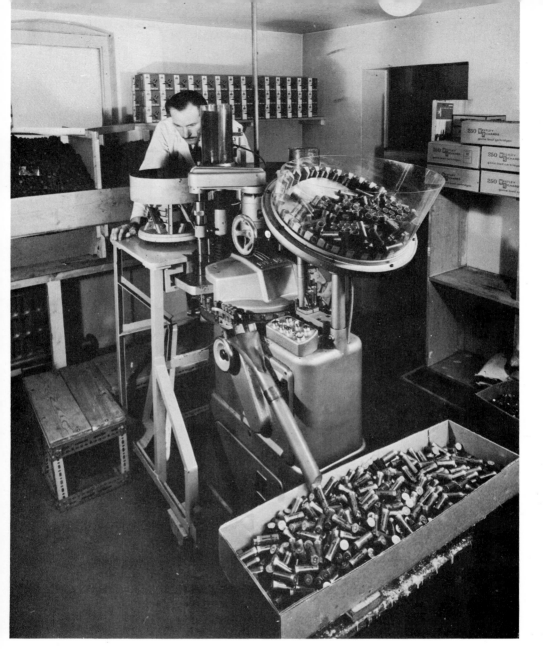

Fig. 55. An automatic loading machine which checks its own operations continuously for correct powder volume, presence of wads and position of the total wad column, and stops in the event of any error (Westley Richards)

Choke is important in this context because a charge that has already balled before it reaches the muzzle may be broken up again as it passes through the constriction. This is the crypto-balling I have previously referred to, which is worthy of more attention than it receives. It implies the existence of bad conditions in the cartridge which never manifest themselves in choke-bored guns, but which are capable of doing so in cylinders.

The cartridges designed for small-bore magnums are particularly suspect, since they not only develop pressures that are higher than normal, or more sustained, or both, but also involve long shot columns. The modern skirted plastic wad with protective shot cup, which excludes any gas leakage that may take place from access to the pellets, and eliminates friction between them and the barrel wall, is valuable in avoiding balling through pellet fusion in these cartridges, but it clearly does nothing to prevent the cold welding to which they are especially subject.

In view, therefore, of the danger and the inferior patterns associated with balling, all shooters should be quick to notice any symptoms of it, and particularly those who use vegetable felt wads in old cylinder guns, loose in the bore, or small-bore magnums carrying little choke, or short cartridges in long chambers.

Cartridge manufacture. In recent years improvements in factory-loaded cartridges have been responsible for a big reduction in the amount of loading undertaken by individual gunmakers. These

Fig. 56.　Testing Eley cartridges in a pendulum gun

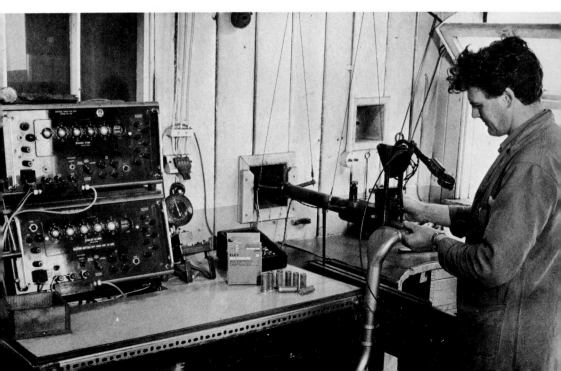

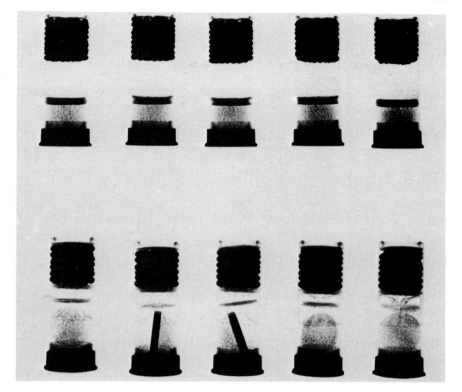

Fig. 57. X-rayed cartridges: upper row correct, lower row defective (IMI)

improvements are not merely those attributable to better and more uniform components, but to refinements in production technique. Chief among these are a scientific sampling and continuous testing of finished cartridges for pressure and velocity, whereby deviations from established standards, such as those that might be caused by slight variations in powder from batch to batch, are at once detected and corrected or compensated. To these measures must be added visual inspection at each appropriate stage as well as X-ray inspection of the finished product, all of which have been responsible for some impressive attainments in consistency as well as quality of performance.

Loads (general). For many years our loads were more or less standardised. They had been arrived at by fully two centuries of experience, which had taught us the charges of shot required to deal effectively

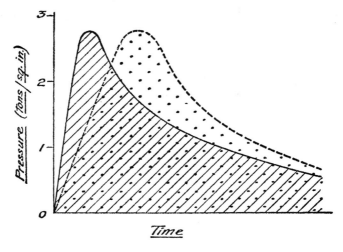

Fig. 58. Effect of progressive powders. Solid curve is pressure curve of normal powder; dotted curve that of progressive powder. In the case of the latter, pressure rises more slowly and is more sustained, but peak shows no increase

with the various kinds of game met with in this country and the best-sized bores from which to fire them. For example, the standard load for general game shooting was $1\frac{1}{16}$ oz., which might be reduced to 1 oz. or increased to $1\frac{1}{8}$ oz. according to circumstances and the taste and fancy of the shooter. For pigeon shooting (meaning, originally, live pigeon shooting from traps) we used $1\frac{1}{4}$ oz.; and for wildfowling $1\frac{1}{2}$ oz. These loads have been found to go best in $2\frac{1}{2}$-inch, $2\frac{3}{4}$-inch and 3-inch 12-bores respectively. Larger and smaller loads had similarly been arrived at for other kinds and conditions of shooting, ranging from the 3 oz. allotted to the 4-bore to the $\frac{9}{16}$ oz. assigned to the 28-bore.

But in recent years, a range of slow-burning or progressive powders has become available, enabling larger charges of shot to be handled by a given bore without increasing the peak pressure. The way these powders work may be seen from fig. 58, in which the solid curve represents the rise and fall of pressure with a normal powder when plotted against time. The area enclosed by the curve, indicated by cross-hatching, is a measure of the *momentum* imparted to the charge of shot. Now, with a progressive powder, we might get a curve like that shown by the dotted line, indicating a pressure that rises more slowly but is more sustained. It will be noted that the peak pressure is $2\frac{3}{4}$ tons as

a

b

Fig. 59. Relative appearance, accurately to scale, of a mallard at the maximum effective range of a full choke with (a) $1\frac{1}{16}$ oz. and (b) $1\frac{1}{4}$ oz. of shot. In practice, lacking any opportunity for comparison, it would be difficult to recognise the difference

before; but the area enclosed by the curve, shown stippled with dots, is appreciably greater. So, therefore, is the momentum imparted to the shot charge; and since momentum equals *Weight** multiplied by *Velocity*, the effect could be a greater velocity imparted to the same shot load, or a larger shot load propelled with the same velocity. It is the latter that we are considering.

This process of increasing the weight of shot that can be handled by a given gun without increasing the peak pressure is useful in enabling a larger load to be used to meet the needs of a special occasion, for the sake of which the extra recoil may be tolerated. A good example is that provided by Eley. *Maximum* cartridge loaded with $1\frac{3}{16}$ oz. of shot, but suitable for firing in an ordinary $2\frac{1}{2}$-inch chambered 12-bore normally used with $1\frac{1}{16}$ oz. But things have gone much further than that, particularly in America, where 3-inch, 20-bore magnum cartridges are now being loaded with as much as $1\frac{1}{4}$ oz. of shot and corresponding 12-bores with $1\frac{7}{8}$. As I am dealing separately with the magnum

* I have used the expression 'weight' instead of 'mass' herein as being more generally comprehensible, though less correct scientifically

principle in Chapter 10, I am only concerned here with the cartridge aspect of these heavy American loads. Some of them set up working pressures substantially in excess of those for which our guns are designed, and should not be used without consulting the makers of the gun in question as to their suitability. In any event they may cause excessive recoil unless used in guns of appropriate weight, or in a type of self-loading weapon which reduces the recoil otherwise felt by the shooter.

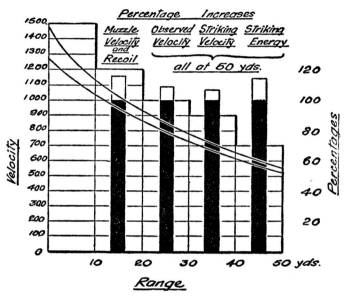

Fig. 60.   High-velocity and normal cartridges compared

But apart from these considerations, many shooters who take to these heavy loads are disappointed with them. The reason, I have no doubt, is that they expect too much of them. They fail to recognise sufficiently clearly that the shotgun is fundamentally a short-range weapon, and that nothing can make it otherwise. They accept, say, 50 yards as their greatest possible reach with a standard, $1\frac{1}{16}$ oz. load; but when they adopt a 'Maximum' cartridge, loaded, perhaps, with a modest $1\frac{3}{16}$ oz. they expect a disproportionate increase in range, and are quite likely to fire at birds 60 to 70 yards away. Disappointment is inevitable: their increased load has not increased their effective range to any appreciable extent, as a study of fig. 59 and the diagram on page 56 should make clear.

Standard loads. The standard loads for the more popular gauges using Nobel-Glasgow powders are set out in Chapter 8 (Home-loading and Reloading).

High-velocity loads. As applied to shotgun cartridges, 'high-velocity' is an inexact term. At one extreme, it can be nothing more than an advertising slogan, applied to a cartridge giving an observed velocity, as defined on page 54, of perhaps 1,050 feet per second, corresponding to a muzzle velocity of, say, 1,270; and at the other to a really high-velocity cartridge giving corresponding figures of 1,150 and 1,475, these latter being about the highest practicable values for medium shot.

Fig. 60 gives a graphic comparison between two such cartridges. The two curves show the respective velocities at all points of the range with No. 6 shot, and the relative figures of muzzle velocity, striking velocity and energy at 50 yards. It will be seen that, for the $9\frac{1}{2}$ per cent increase in observed velocity there is a 16 per cent increase in muzzle velocity and therefore in recoil; but only a 7 per cent gain in the striking velocity at 50 yards. Owing, however, to the fact that energy is proportional to the square of the velocity, the gain in energy at this range is 14 per cent. Most high-velocity cartridges, as sold, would show a good deal smaller gain than in this somewhat extreme case.

Since, as I have already explained, patterns normally fail before velocity, I have some difficulty in attaching solid advantages to high-velocity loads, more especially as they tend to impair patterns, particularly those thrown by open-bored guns. I have indeed seen some deplorable results with this combination.

Nevertheless, some eminent manufacturers claim that with the right powder, careful loading and the right gun, pattern quality *can* be preserved, when a high-velocity load may possibly justify the use of smaller shot, thus maintaining adequate pattern density and pellet energy at a longer range than normal; but, for my own part, I would by no means take the fulfilment of these prerequisite conditions for granted: I would not be prepared to accept a substantial increase in recoil for an advantage that the pattern plate might well prove to be evanescent. The wildfowler in particular, with his relatively large shot, must seek range in the various means for maintaining pattern density rather than in any enhancement of normal velocities.

New developments. Although, for the economic and other reasons already indicated, the paper-cased cartridge is likely to be with us for a long time yet, the trend of modern developments may repay brief consideration.

The plastic case shows every indication of remaining the normal standard case of the future. Improvements are likely to take place chiefly in the field of manufacturing technique, and possibly in the use of alternative or modified materials. I have already referred to the possibility of our having biodegradable plastic cases for the avoidance of the litter problem.

Two cartridges already or recently on the market exemplify these trends. The first is the Winchester 'compression-formed' cartridge shown in fig. 52. This has a polyethylene case made in one piece by an ingenious process in the course of which the molecular structure of the material is so modified as greatly to increase its tensile strength. The metal head could probably be dispensed with in conventional guns, but is retained out of consideration for the severe duty imposed on the rim by the claw-type extractors of repeaters.

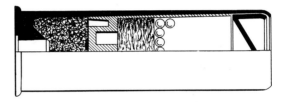

Fig. 61.   The Wanda Cartridge. Half-section showing the one-piece polycarbonate case and special plastic top wad. The over-powder wad is an Alcan 'Flite-max'—a combination plastic and fibre wad incorporating a protective shot cup. (This cartridge is no longer in production.)

The Wanda cartridge (fig. 61), made by the Wanda Cartridge Company of Houston, Texas, broke new ground by using a straight injection moulding of polycarbonate plastic. The natural strength of this material, which, incidentally, is transparent, enables the metal head to be dispensed with, but makes it impracticable to use a turnover or crimp to seal the case, which was therefore closed by a specially shaped plastic plug or top-wad. It was claimed that this closure device did not interfere with patterns. The Wanda cartridge is no longer in production, but is still notable as indicating future possibilities.

In recent years, the ever-rising cost of cartridges and the growing popularity of clay pigeon shooting have been responsible for a great increase in home-loading, hitherto neglected in this country; and although there are signs that the more serious competitive shooters are reverting exclusively to factory-loaded ammunition, there is still a premium on the cartridge case with the best reloading potential. Conventional crimp or rolled turnovers may thus be marked for extinction, as in the Wanda case, though by what means cannot at present be foreseen. There are several possibilities.

The boom in clay pigeon shooting also focuses attention on any way of improving the quality and consistency of patterns and shortening the shot-string. One of the means to this end is hard shot of the highest degree of uniformity and of the utmost resistance to deformation in its course up the barrel. We already have machine-made shot and shot plated with resistant metals, and the scope for future improvement would appear to lie chiefly in reducing the cost of these refinements.

Another possibility I have suggested* is that the advent of the plastic case with skived mouth and skirted plastic wad might justify the abolition of the chamber cone and the re-introduction of the chamberless gun, as designed for use with the old, all-metal 'Perfect' cases, now no longer made. The abolition of the cone should help to reduce pellet-deformation, and would confer some incidental advantages. This suggestion could well form the subject of further experiments.

Lead poisoning of wildfowl. The serious amount of lead poisoning among wildfowl in the USA, caused by their picking up lead pellets on heavily shot-over marshes, has provoked the long-threatened legislation to ban lead shot on the main flyways. Soft iron or steel shot is represented as affording an adequate substitute, but impressive evidence has been urged against it, chiefly on the grounds that the main menace to wildfowl by shooting comes from wounding, and that iron or steel shot, being ballistically inferior to lead, would increase it. It would also cause damage to guns, and materially increase the cost of their ammunition. (See also Chapter 23.)

Imported cartridges—a warning. The pressures developed by British cartridges are regulated to conform to the appropriate standards of British proof, which in turn have been laid down in due relation to the guns and loads evolved by our home gun trade to meet the needs and preferences of British sportsmen. But this is not the case with some imported cartridges, which the prudent user will therefore avoid unless they are offered with explicit assurance (preferably printed on the carton) as to their suitability for use in British and Continental guns of clearly defined proof status.

---

* 'Doing Away with the Cone', by Gough Thomas, *Shooting Times*, July 20, 1968, and 'Case Non-Proven', May 3, 1969

CHAPTER EIGHT

HOME-LOADING AND RELOADING

In the early days of breechloaders it was commonly assumed that the sportsman would need or wish to load his own cartridges, and guns were often sent out with the necessary equipment in the case. It comprised dippers for powder and shot, a combined de-capper and re-capper, a hand-rammer and a turnover machine. By these simple means, satisfactory black powder cartridges could be turned out.

When the breechloader had become thoroughly established, practically every gunsmith loaded cartridges on his premises, if necessary according to the individual requirements of his customers. At the same time, many shooters continued to load their own.

But the advent of smokeless powder and the rise of the big sporting ammunition manufacturers produced a change in this situation. The new powder was more tricky to load—no longer could it be safely entrusted to an apprentice or undertaken by a slapdash amateur. Accordingly, many sportsmen gave up home-loading.

So did many gunsmiths, who found it paid them to let the big manufacturers load their cartridges—still bearing the gunsmith's name and brand, but probably of better and more uniform quality than he himself had ever produced.

Things progressed in this way until the end of the last war, when the boom in clay pigeon shooting, and the American influence that accompanied it, brought about a sharp revival of interest in home-loading. There was also an economic urge. Cartridge prices had risen steeply and were continuing to rise, and clay pigeon shooters had great appetites for ammunition. Besides, new and improved loading equipment—mostly American—was coming on to the market. And so the present home-loading revival set in, and has since prospered. In addition to providing a source of economical practice ammunition, many have found that home-loading becomes an interesting and self-justifying hobby. Any intelligent person, with the equipment and components now available, can turn out safe and satisfactory shotgun ammunition, provided that he carefully and consistently follows the instructions freely available.

Precautions. Cartridge loading requires a place where all equipment and components can be set up or set out in familiar order, and where the work can proceed without interruption or distraction. This as a rule means a corner of an amateur workshop—a place where there is likely to be a portable electric fire, and where soldering, brazing, grinding and other operations involving movable sources of heat, flame and sparks are carried out. It is also a place where many a man most enjoys a quiet pipe or cigarette. The hint should be sufficient, and the precautions taken should, so far as possible, be proof against any momentary forgetfulness.

Powder should be stored in the smallest convenient quantities and in the original containers. Black powder needs special care, partly to exclude moisture and partly because it is much more readily inflammable than nitro, and is the more dangerous stuff to have about. Loose powder should never be allowed to lie on the loading bench, which should be kept scrupulously clear and clean.

The powder used should always be fresh—not old, recovered or of uncertain origin, which may have suffered deterioration through improper storage. Fresh powder has a somewhat pleasant smell, derived from alcohol, ether or acetone. But powder undergoing deterioration has an irritating, acrid odour.

Caps should be treated with great respect. Powders burn: caps detonate, and if one of a tin or jar full of loose caps were accidentally set off the result could be lethal.

There is also danger in the use of unsuitable caps. With a fixed normal load of smokeless powder and shot in a 12-bore gun the French Ammunition Society (SFM) obtained pressures ranging from 1·9 tons to 3·75 tons merely by using caps of increasing strength. And in an outstanding recent case in this country, an intelligent and otherwise cautious home-loader, simply by using the wrong cap, attained pressures of over 5 tons as against the $3\frac{1}{4}$ tons which represented the safe limit.

Equipment. The modern home-loader who requires to load and reload crimp-closed plastic cases with smokeless powders will need one of the popular loading machines, as advertised in the sporting press. Unless the machine has facilities for varying the powder and shot charges, he will also need the appropriate 'bushings' or measures which

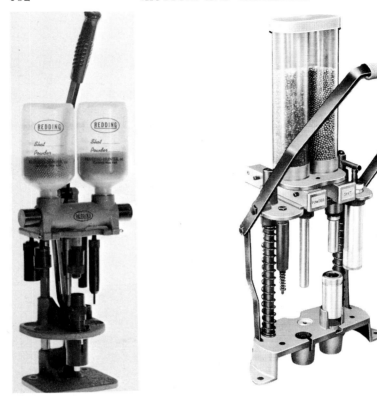

Two popular loading machines—Fig. 62, the Redding Model 16, and Fig. 63, the Lyman

Fig. 64.   The Lyman 'Ohaus' beam balance

fit inside it, and which determine the charges it delivers. A highly desirable, not to say indispensable, addition is an apothecary's balance for checking the powder charges at intervals, or one of the new beam balances made for the purpose.

Incidental equipment, such as containers for components, should be provided and so organised as to facilitate orderly and progressive working according to a set routine, thus enlisting the aid of habit and reducing the risk of error through absentmindedness.

Procedure. The object here assumed is the production of safe and consistent ammunition of a certain type having well-established characteristics—not the working up of experimental loads or the pursuit of some real or imaginary advantage that has hitherto eluded the regular manufacturers. To attain this object the home-loader must stick to the book. He must recognise that *any* departure from recommended loads and components may have unpredictable results, particularly as affecting the danger-element of pressure, which he is not ordinarily equipped to measure. For example, a given charge of powder and shot may give significantly different pressures in cases, outwardly similar, but of different internal dimensions, as determined by the type of base wad employed (see figs. 51 and 52). Pressure may also be seriously affected by what might appear to be innocent changes in the nature or dimensions of the wadding column, or, as explained, in the type of cap.

So if a home-loader is using, say, Eley cases of a certain type, he must not regard himself as free to use any others that he may acquire, without having sample loads tested for pressure and velocity.

Another point: charges are properly determinable by *weight*, whereas the loading machine measures them by *volume*. But the weight of a given volume may change—for example, by the vibration of the machine, or by the amount of powder in the container. Both factors will affect the extent to which the powder packs down in the bushing. If a charge is thrown from a nearly empty container, and care is taken to avoid vibration, it may be found to be a full grain lighter than one thrown by the same bushing when the container is full, and the powder slide is moved with a jerk. Hence the need for checking the weights thrown.

The machine should thus be used in a regular manner. If the user makes a habit of tapping the slide after moving it to receive powder, he should *always* tap it, and in the same way.

Coming now to reloading, the first step, and an important one, is to examine critically the available cases.

The state of the base wad must be visually checked, and cases in which any part of it is missing should be rejected. So should any showing signs of splits, cracks or burns, or fractured or deformed heads, or heads that are not tight on the tubes. Cases should not be used if the tubes are deformed, or if the mouths are too frayed or weakened to form good, firm crimps or turnovers, or if the base wads are wet.

The actual reloading operation involves eight stages—(1) decapping; (2) re-capping; (3) charging powder; (4) seating wads; (5) charging shot; (6) starting crimp; (7) crimping, and (8) resizing.

It is especially important to check that the re-capping operation has been properly carried out and that the cap is firmly seated in the chamber, and yet flush with the cartridge head. If it protrudes, there is a danger that it may be set off by the closing of the gun. If it is loose— if it goes in without resistance—the case must be discarded. For the rest, these operations will require to be performed in accordance with the instructions issued by the manufacturers of the machine. These should be read in conjunction with the notes issued by Imperial Metal Industries (Kynoch) Ltd. for the reloading of Eley cartridges and reproduced by permission at the end of this chapter. They include all the loads likely to be required for normal use.

Requests for information on special loads should be addressed to Eley, PO Box 216, Witton, Birmingham B6 7BA.

TABLE 7.   Black Powder Loads

		drams powder	oz. shot
12-bore	$2\frac{1}{2}$ inch (Standard)	3	$1\frac{1}{8}$
	$2\frac{1}{2}$ inch (Light load)	$2\frac{3}{4}$	1
	$2\frac{1}{2}$ inch (Long range)	$2\frac{3}{4}$	$1\frac{1}{4}$
	$2\frac{3}{4}$ inch (Long range)	3	$1\frac{1}{2}$
	3 inch (Long range)	$3\frac{1}{4}$	$1\frac{3}{4}$
10-bore	$2\frac{5}{8}$ inch (Long range)	3	2
	$2\frac{7}{8}$ inch (Long range)	$3\frac{1}{4}$	2
8-bore	$3\frac{1}{4}$ inch (Long range)	5	$2\frac{1}{2}$

Notes:
(1) All the above loads are suitable for sound guns of the appropriate gauge and chamber length as normally proved for black or smokeless powder.
(2) The shot size for the long-range loads should not be smaller than No. 4 for the 12-bore and No. 1 for the 8- and 10-bores.
(3) The chamber lengths shown for the 8- and 10-bores are the only ones for which Eley cases are now available.

Black powder loads.   As already indicated, black powder, though more inflammable than nitro, is more tolerant of variations in associated components and treatment, and detailed loading schedules are not required.

For 12-bore and smaller shotguns the powder should be TS2, and for larger bores TS6. A police permit is required to buy black powder.

Paper or plastic cases may be used, primed with the ordinary 1B Eley 'Surefire' cap.

Wads may be of felt or vegetable felt, such as the Eley 'Kleena', loaded with an $\frac{1}{8}$-inch over-powder card. There is no critical wad pressure; the wad column should merely be firmly seated on the powder. A normally tight crimp or turnover is necessary.

As I am never asked for black powder loads below 12-bore, but often for larger gauge, I give the selection in Table 7 as likely to be most useful. Except for the first two, which are general purpose loads, they are all wildfowling loads.

Checking results

The home-loader would be well advised to confine himself, if possible, to one line of cartridges, whether it be for trap or skeet, or for field shooting or wildfowling. And having settled down to a steady type of production, he would be wise to send samples to the Birmingham Proof House for tests. This would reveal any undesirable characteristics and provide an invaluable guide to future operations. The cost of such tests is very reasonable, and even if the ammunition is above reproach, the reassurance is well worth the money.

The following notes by Eley give all the necessary information and instructions for this purpose. I have included loading tables both for the new Nobel-Glasgow Series 80 powders and for the superseded Series 60, since considerable stocks of the latter are likely to remain in the hands of home-loaders and others. *It should be particularly noted that the Series 80 powders have 11–14 per cent greater volume for a given weight, and therefore bushings hitherto used for the Series 60 powders must be changed, otherwise charges will be too light.*

Conversely, it would be dangerous to use Series 80 bushings with Series 60 powders, as charges and pressures would then be excessive.

Readers using American powders and components should refer to the 'Lyman Shotshell Handbook' published by the Lyman Gun Sight Corporation, Middlefield, Connecticut, USA, which gives a large range of tested loads using this material.

RELOADING ELEY SHOTGUN CARTRIDGES

These notes on the reloading of shotgun cartridges are offered as a guide and the Eley Ammunition Division of IMI can accept no responsibility for the performance of cartridges not loaded at their factory.

IMPORTANT

A new series of powders, the 80 series, is replacing the 60 series. The new powders, while of similar weight, are substantially greater in volume compared with the previous powders.

This means that dispensing bushes suitable for the 60 series will need to be replaced or opened up to increase the volume metered. If in doubt please consult your gunmaker.

During the changeover period, as there is no visual difference between the two types of powders, reloaders are advised to mark clearly the respective bushes—to prevent any possibility of using an 80 series bush with 60 series powders, which would produce a reload having too large a charge of powder and result in dangerously high pressures.

Components

(1) CASES intended for reloading should be examined carefully for soundness of head and tube and any showing signs of weakness should be discarded. Paper cases with damp tubes and waterproof cases with wet base wads must be rejected.

(2) POWDER must be kept away from heat and open flame and the container should be kept closed when not in use and stored in a cool dry place.

(3) CAPS should be selected to match the powder used. In the recommended loads tabulated overleaf it is essential that Eley Surefire caps are employed to match the Nobel-Glasgow propellant.

(4) ELEY-KLEENA WADDING is ideal for reloading. The wad diameter suits both paper and plastic fired cases and ensures perfect obturation (gas-seal) and freedom from barrel leading.

Reloading techniques

(1) CASE TRIMMING, if required, should be carried out, to the overall lengths shown in the tables.

(2) DECAPPING AND RECAPPING are simple operations and should not present any difficulty to the reloader. The decapping tool should freely enter the cap chamber without distorting or enlarging the flash hole.

Eley cases with coppered cap chambers are made so that they may be reprimed with either Eley Surefire caps or with battery pocket primers. If the recommended loads with Nobel-Glasgow powders are being used Eley Surefire caps are essential, and it may be necessary to support the cap chamber flange when decapping these cases to ensure that the cap chamber is not removed.

(3) POWDER charges must be accurately weighed out. If the propellant is loaded by volume it is recommended that the charges are checked frequently by weight to ensure the minimum variation from the desired ballistic level. The temptation to 'put an extra pinch in to give a good velocity' should be resisted.

(4) The OVERPOWDER CARD should be carefully inserted to avoid tilting but should not be rammed.

(5) WAD insertion into fired plastic cases is made easier if the case mouth is opened slightly with a tapered plug. If this is done the reloader will find the plastic cases are easier to wad than the paper cases which tend to delaminate on the inside edge at the mouth and form an obstruction to the wads.

About 50 lb. ramming should be applied to the complete wadding column when it is in the cartridge and before the shot is inserted. With the prescribed wadding column this should leave $\frac{1}{2}$ inch free length of case after the shot charge has been inserted for crimping for a paper tube and $\frac{13}{32}$ inch free length for a plastic tube. For a rolled turnover closure $\frac{9}{32}$ inch of the tube should remain after a $\frac{1}{16}$ inch card has been placed over the shot charge for both paper and plastic cases.

(6) CRIMPING a plastic tubed cartridge is simplified if a 'crimp starter' is used to press the plastic folds into position before the conventional coned re-crimping die is used.

Re-crimping paper case cartridges and re-closing paper and plastic cases with a rolled turn-over should present no difficulties.

Care should be taken to avoid loose shot or free space in the cartridge and any looseness should be taken up by adjusting the length of the wadding column.

(7) RESIZING cartridges after loading is recommended especially for plastic cartridges to reduce the excessive step between the tube and the head. This operation will also smooth out any shot bulges which may have occurred when the crimp was consolidated.

Performance

For consistent cartridge performance and also for the higher velocity levels a factory loaded product is essential. Nevertheless, with care and attention the reloader can achieve adequate results with medium power cartridges using the recommended loads.

If, however, it is suspected that the reloaded cartridges are showing a tendency towards weak shooting and this is confirmed by the presence of unburnt powder in the barrel, the performance can often be improved by increasing the strength of the closure. This may be achieved by varnishing the crimp in a paper case, or by increasing the ramming on the wadding column and deepening the crimp closure on a plastic case. Similar techniques may also assist in maintaining the ballistic levels of paper and plastic cartridges with rolled turn-over closures.

Laboratory reports on hand loads

The Birmingham Proof House is equipped and willing to test and report on hand loaded shotgun cartridges from any source. Reports normally cover pressure at 1 in. and 6 in. from the breech, velocity over 20 yards and recoil. Reports can be given (if specifically requested) on shot patterns at 40 yards. One cartridge of each loading is broken down and report issued as to the load, components and turnover resistance or pull. (A loading check is essential to safeguard valuable laboratory equipment.) Submitters are asked to advise the loads used quoting type and weight of powder and weight of shot.

The cost of such reports at present is £3.15 for up to eleven cartridges of one gauge and chamber length, and 15p each for extra cartridges of the same gauge and chamber length. It is recommended that not less than six and preferably eleven cartridges of each loading

SERIES 80 POWDER

TABLE 8. Recommended loads for PAPER cartridges—primed with Eley Surefire Caps

Gauge and Chamber length (inches)	*Actual case length (inches)*	*Type of closure*	*Shot charge (ounces)*	*Powder*		*Wadding thickness—in inches*			
				Type Nobel-Glasgow	*Charge (grains)*	*Overpowder card*	*Main Wad Kleena*	*Undershot card*	*Overshot card*
12G $2\frac{3}{4}$	$2\frac{3}{4}$	Crimped	$1\frac{1}{4}$	No. 82	$29\frac{1}{2}$	$\frac{1}{8}$	$\frac{1}{2}$	$\frac{1}{11}$	—
12G $2\frac{1}{2}$	$2\frac{3}{4}$	Crimped	$1\frac{3}{16}$	No. 82	27	$\frac{1}{8}$	$\frac{3}{8}$ (2)	—	—
12G $2\frac{1}{2}$	$2\frac{9}{16}$	Rolled	$1\frac{3}{16}$	No. 82	27	$\frac{1}{8}$	$\frac{3}{8}$ (2)	—	$\frac{1}{16}$
12G $2\frac{1}{2}$	$2\frac{3}{4}$	Crimped	$1\frac{1}{8}$	No. 82	29	$\frac{1}{8}$	$\frac{3}{8}$ (2)	—	—
12G $2\frac{1}{2}$	$2\frac{9}{16}$	Rolled	$1\frac{1}{8}$	No. 82	29	$\frac{1}{8}$	$\frac{3}{8}$ (2)	—	$\frac{1}{16}$
*12G $2\frac{1}{2}$	$2\frac{3}{4}$	Crimped	$1\frac{1}{8}$	No. 80	$24\frac{1}{2}$	$\frac{1}{8}$	$\frac{3}{8}$ (2)	—	—
12G $2\frac{1}{2}$	$2\frac{3}{4}$	Crimped	$1\frac{1}{16}$	No. 80	26	$\frac{1}{8}$	$\frac{3}{8}$ (2)	$\frac{1}{11}$	—
12G $2\frac{1}{2}$	$2\frac{9}{16}$	Rolled	$1\frac{1}{16}$	No. 80	26	$\frac{1}{8}$	$\frac{3}{8}$ (2)	—	$\frac{1}{16}$
12G $2\frac{1}{2}$	$2\frac{9}{16}$	Crimped	1	No. 80	25	$\frac{1}{8}$	$\frac{1}{2}$	$\frac{1}{11}$	—
12G $2\frac{1}{2}$	$2\frac{9}{16}$	Rolled	1	No. 80	26	$\frac{1}{8}$	$\frac{3}{8}$ (2)	—	$\frac{1}{16}$

* Trapshooting load

SERIES 80 POWDER

TABLE 9. Recommended loads for PLASTIC tube cartridges—primed with Eley Surefire Caps

Gauge and chamber length (inches)	*Actual case length (inches)*	*Type of closure*	*Shot charge (ounces)*	*Powder*		*Wadding thickness—in inches*			
				Type Nobel-Glasgow	*Charge (grains)*	*Overpowder card*	*Main Wad Kleena*	*Undershot card*	*Overshot card*
12G $2\frac{3}{4}$	$2\frac{3}{4}$	Crimped	$1\frac{1}{4}$	No. 82	$30\frac{1}{2}$	$\frac{1}{8}$	$\frac{3}{8}$ (2)	—	—
12G $2\frac{3}{4}$	$2\frac{3}{4}$	Rolled	$1\frac{1}{4}$	No. 82	$30\frac{1}{2}$	$\frac{1}{8}$	$\frac{3}{8}$ (2)	$\frac{1}{11}$	$\frac{1}{16}$
12G $2\frac{1}{2}$	$2\frac{3}{4}$	Crimped	$1\frac{3}{16}$	No. 82	$29\frac{1}{2}$	$\frac{1}{8}$	$\frac{3}{8}$ (2)	—	—
12G $2\frac{1}{2}$	$2\frac{9}{16}$	Rolled	$1\frac{3}{16}$	No. 82	$29\frac{1}{2}$	$\frac{1}{8}$	$\frac{3}{8}$ (2)	—	$\frac{1}{16}$
12G $2\frac{1}{2}$	$2\frac{3}{4}$	Crimped	$1\frac{1}{8}$	No. 82	29	$\frac{1}{8}$	$\frac{3}{8}$ (2)	$\frac{1}{11}$	—
12G $2\frac{1}{2}$	$2\frac{9}{16}$	Rolled	$1\frac{1}{8}$	No. 82	29	$\frac{1}{8}$	$\frac{3}{8}$ (2)	—	$\frac{1}{16}$
*12G $2\frac{1}{2}$	$2\frac{3}{4}$	Crimped	$1\frac{1}{8}$	No. 80	$24\frac{1}{2}$	$\frac{1}{8}$	$\frac{3}{8}$ (2)	$\frac{1}{8}$	—
12G $2\frac{1}{2}$	$2\frac{3}{4}$	Crimped	$1\frac{1}{16}$	No. 80	27	$\frac{1}{8}$	$\frac{3}{8}$ (2)	$\frac{1}{8}$	—
12G $2\frac{1}{2}$	$2\frac{9}{16}$	Rolled	$1\frac{1}{16}$	No. 80	27	$\frac{1}{8}$	$\frac{3}{8}$ (2)	—	$\frac{1}{16}$
12G $2\frac{1}{2}$	$2\frac{9}{16}$	Crimped	1	No. 80	$25\frac{1}{2}$	$\frac{1}{8}$	$\frac{3}{8}$ (2)	—	—
12G $2\frac{1}{2}$	$2\frac{9}{16}$	Rolled	1	No. 80	$25\frac{1}{2}$	$\frac{1}{8}$	$\frac{3}{8}$ (2)	$\frac{1}{11}$	$\frac{1}{16}$
16G $2\frac{3}{4}$	$2\frac{3}{4}$	Crimped	1	No. 82	25	$\frac{1}{8}$	$\frac{3}{8}$ (2)	—	—
16G $2\frac{3}{4}$	$2\frac{3}{4}$	Rolled	1	No. 82	25	$\frac{1}{8}$	$\frac{3}{8}$ (2)	—	$\frac{1}{16}$
16G $2\frac{1}{2}$	$2\frac{3}{4}$	Crimped	$\frac{7}{8}$	No. 80	$21\frac{1}{2}$	$\frac{1}{8}$	$\frac{3}{8}$ (2)	$\frac{1}{8}$	—
16G $2\frac{1}{2}$	$2\frac{9}{16}$	Rolled	$\frac{7}{8}$	No. 80	$21\frac{1}{2}$	$\frac{1}{8}$	$\frac{3}{8}$ (2)	—	$\frac{1}{16}$
20G $2\frac{3}{4}$	$2\frac{3}{4}$	Crimped	$\frac{7}{8}$	No. 82	$20\frac{1}{2}$	$\frac{1}{8}$	$\frac{3}{8}$ (2)	—	—
20G $2\frac{3}{4}$	$2\frac{3}{4}$	Rolled	$\frac{7}{8}$	No. 82	$20\frac{1}{2}$	$\frac{1}{8}$	$\frac{3}{8}$ (2)	$\frac{1}{11}$	$\frac{1}{16}$
20G $2\frac{1}{2}$	$2\frac{9}{16}$	Rolled	$\frac{3}{4}$	No. 82	$20\frac{1}{2}$	$\frac{1}{8}$	$\frac{3}{8}$ (2)	—	$\frac{1}{16}$

* Trapshooting load

SERIES 60 POWDERS

TABLE 10. Recommended loads for PAPER tube cartridges—primed with Eley Surefire Caps

Gauge and chamber length (inches)	Actual case length (inches)	Type of closure	Powder Type (Nobel-Glasgow)	Powder Charge (grains)	Shot charge (ounces)	Overpowder card (inches)	Wadding thickness in inches Main wad Kleena (inches)	Wadding thickness in inches Undershot card (inches)	Overshot card (inches)
10G $2\frac{7}{8}$	$2\frac{7}{8}$	Rolled	No. 62	38	$1\frac{7}{16}$	$\frac{1}{11}$	$\frac{3}{8}$ (2)	$\frac{1}{11}$	$\frac{1}{16}$
10G $2\frac{5}{8}$	$2\frac{5}{8}$	Rolled	No. 62	32	$1\frac{5}{16}$	$\frac{1}{11}$	$\frac{3}{8}$ (2)	$\frac{1}{11}$	$\frac{1}{16}$
12G 3	3	Crimped	No. 62	32	$1\frac{3}{8}$	$\frac{1}{11}$	$\frac{3}{8}$ (2)	—	—
12G 3	3	Rolled	No. 62	32	$1\frac{3}{8}$	$\frac{1}{8}$	$1\frac{1}{2}$ (2)	—	$\frac{1}{16}$
12G $2\frac{3}{4}$	$2\frac{3}{4}$	Crimped	No. 62	32	$1\frac{1}{4}$	$\frac{1}{11}$	$1\frac{1}{2}$	$\frac{1}{11}$	—
12G $2\frac{3}{4}$	$2\frac{3}{4}$	Rolled	No. 62	31	$1\frac{1}{4}$	$\frac{1}{8}$	$\frac{3}{8}$ (2)	—	$\frac{1}{16}$
12G $2\frac{1}{2}$	$2\frac{3}{4}$	Crimped	No. 62	27	$1\frac{3}{16}$	$\frac{1}{8}$	$\frac{3}{8}$ (2)	—	—
12G $2\frac{1}{2}$	$2\frac{9}{16}$	Rolled	No. 62	27	$1\frac{3}{16}$	$\frac{1}{8}$	$\frac{3}{8}$ (2)	—	$\frac{1}{16}$
12G $2\frac{1}{2}$	$2\frac{3}{4}$	Crimped	No. 62	29	$1\frac{1}{8}$	$\frac{1}{8}$	$\frac{3}{8}$ (2)	—	—
12G $2\frac{1}{2}$	$2\frac{9}{16}$	Rolled	No. 62	29	$1\frac{1}{8}$	$\frac{1}{8}$	$\frac{3}{8}$ (2)	—	$\frac{1}{16}$
*12G $2\frac{1}{2}$	$2\frac{3}{4}$	Crimped	No. 60	$24\frac{1}{2}$	$1\frac{1}{8}$	$\frac{1}{8}$	$\frac{3}{8}$ (2)	—	—
12G $2\frac{1}{2}$	$2\frac{3}{4}$	Crimped	No. 60	26	$1\frac{1}{16}$	$\frac{1}{8}$	$\frac{3}{8}$ (2)	$\frac{1}{11}$	$\frac{1}{16}$
12G $2\frac{1}{2}$	$2\frac{9}{16}$	Rolled	No. 60	26	$1\frac{1}{16}$	$\frac{1}{8}$	$\frac{3}{8}$ (2)	—	—
12G $2\frac{1}{2}$	$2\frac{9}{16}$	Crimped	No. 60	25	1	$\frac{1}{8}$	$1\frac{1}{2}$	$\frac{1}{11}$	$\frac{1}{16}$
12G $2\frac{1}{2}$	$2\frac{9}{16}$	Crimped	No. 60	$26\frac{1}{2}$	1	$\frac{1}{8}$	$\frac{3}{8}$ (2)	$\frac{1}{11}$	$\frac{1}{16}$
12G $2\frac{1}{2}$	$2\frac{9}{16}$	Rolled	No. 60	$26\frac{1}{2}$	1	$\frac{1}{8}$	$\frac{3}{8}$ (2)	—	—
16G $2\frac{3}{4}$	$2\frac{3}{4}$	Crimped	No. 62	25	1	$\frac{1}{8}$	$\frac{3}{8}$ (2)	$\frac{1}{11}$	$\frac{1}{16}$
16G $2\frac{3}{4}$	$2\frac{3}{4}$	Rolled	No. 62	25	1	$\frac{1}{8}$	$\frac{3}{8}$ (2)	—	$\frac{1}{16}$
16G $2\frac{1}{2}$	$2\frac{1}{2}$	Crimped	No. 60	20	$\frac{7}{8}$	$\frac{1}{8}$	$1\frac{1}{2}$	$\frac{1}{8}$	$\frac{1}{16}$
16G $2\frac{1}{2}$	$2\frac{9}{16}$	Rolled	No. 60	20	$\frac{7}{8}$	$\frac{1}{8}$	$1\frac{1}{2}$	$\frac{1}{11}$	$\frac{1}{16}$
20G $2\frac{3}{4}$	$2\frac{3}{4}$	Crimped	No. 62	22	$\frac{7}{8}$	$\frac{1}{8}$	$\frac{3}{8}$ (2)	—	—
20G $2\frac{3}{4}$	$2\frac{3}{4}$	Rolled	No. 62	22	$\frac{7}{8}$	$\frac{1}{8}$	$\frac{3}{8}$ (2)	—	$\frac{1}{16}$
20G $2\frac{1}{2}$	$2\frac{3}{4}$	Crimped	No. 62	21	$\frac{3}{4}$	$\frac{1}{8}$	$\frac{3}{8}$ (2)	$\frac{1}{11}$	—
20G $2\frac{1}{2}$	$2\frac{9}{16}$	Rolled	No. 62	21	$\frac{3}{4}$	$\frac{1}{8}$	$\frac{3}{8}$ (2)	—	$\frac{1}{16}$

SERIES 60 POWDERS

TABLE 11. Recommended loads for PLASTIC tube cartridges—primed with Eley Surefire Caps

Gauge and chamber length (inches)	*Actual case length (inches*	*Type of closure*	*Powder*		*Shot charge (ounces)*	*Wadding thickness in inches*			
			Type (Nobel-Glasgow)	*Charge (grains)*		*Overpowder card (inches)*	*Main Wad Kleena (inches)*	*Undershot card (inches)*	*Overshot card (inches)*
12G $2\frac{3}{4}$	$2\frac{3}{4}$	Crimped	No. 62	31	$1\frac{1}{4}$	$\frac{1}{8}$	$\frac{3}{8}$ (2)	—	—
12G $2\frac{3}{4}$	$2\frac{3}{4}$	Rolled	No. 62	31	$1\frac{1}{4}$	$\frac{1}{8}$	$\frac{3}{8}$ (2)	$\frac{1}{11}$	$\frac{1}{16}$
12G $2\frac{1}{2}$	$2\frac{3}{4}$	Crimped	No. 62	$30\frac{1}{2}$	$1\frac{3}{16}$	$\frac{1}{8}$	$\frac{3}{8}$ (2)	—	—
12G $2\frac{1}{2}$	$2\frac{9}{16}$	Rolled	No. 62	$30\frac{1}{2}$	$1\frac{3}{16}$	$\frac{1}{8}$	$\frac{3}{8}$ (2)	—	$\frac{1}{16}$
12G $2\frac{1}{2}$	$2\frac{3}{4}$	Crimped	No. 62	$29\frac{1}{2}$	$1\frac{1}{8}$	$\frac{1}{8}$	$\frac{3}{8}$ (2)	$\frac{1}{11}$	—
12G $2\frac{1}{2}$	$2\frac{9}{16}$	Rolled	No. 62	$29\frac{1}{2}$	$1\frac{1}{8}$	$\frac{1}{8}$	$\frac{3}{8}$ (2)	—	$\frac{1}{16}$
*12G $2\frac{1}{2}$	$2\frac{3}{4}$	Crimped	No. 60	$24\frac{1}{2}$	$1\frac{1}{8}$	$\frac{1}{8}$	$\frac{3}{8}$ (2)	$\frac{1}{8}$	—
12G $2\frac{1}{2}$	$2\frac{3}{4}$	Crimped	No. 60	27	$1\frac{1}{16}$	$\frac{1}{8}$	$\frac{3}{8}$ (2)	$\frac{1}{8}$	—
12G $2\frac{1}{2}$	$2\frac{9}{16}$	Rolled	No. 60	27	$1\frac{1}{16}$	$\frac{1}{8}$	$\frac{3}{8}$ (2)	—	$\frac{1}{16}$
12G $2\frac{1}{2}$	$2\frac{9}{16}$	Crimped	No. 60	$25\frac{1}{2}$	1	$\frac{1}{8}$	$\frac{3}{8}$ (2)	—	—
12G $2\frac{1}{2}$	$2\frac{9}{16}$	Rolled	No. 60	$25\frac{1}{2}$	1	$\frac{1}{8}$	$\frac{3}{8}$ (2)	$\frac{1}{11}$	$\frac{1}{16}$
16G $2\frac{3}{4}$	$2\frac{3}{4}$	Crimped	No. 62	25	1	$\frac{1}{8}$	$\frac{3}{8}$ (2)	$\frac{1}{11}$	—
16G $2\frac{3}{4}$	$2\frac{3}{4}$	Rolled	No. 62	25	1	$\frac{1}{8}$	$\frac{3}{8}$ (2)	—	$\frac{1}{16}$
16G $2\frac{1}{2}$	$2\frac{3}{4}$	Crimped	No. 60	$21\frac{1}{2}$	$\frac{7}{8}$	$\frac{1}{8}$	$\frac{3}{8}$ (2)	$\frac{1}{8}$	—
16G $2\frac{1}{2}$	$2\frac{9}{16}$	Rolled	No. 60	$21\frac{1}{2}$	$\frac{7}{8}$	$\frac{1}{8}$	$\frac{3}{8}$ (2)	—	$\frac{1}{16}$
20G $2\frac{3}{4}$	$2\frac{3}{4}$	Crimped	No. 62	21	$\frac{7}{8}$	$\frac{1}{8}$	$\frac{3}{8}$ (2)	—	—
20G $2\frac{3}{4}$	$2\frac{3}{4}$	Rolled	No. 62	21	$\frac{7}{8}$	$\frac{1}{8}$	$\frac{3}{8}$ (2)	$\frac{1}{11}$	$\frac{1}{16}$
20G $2\frac{1}{2}$	$2\frac{9}{16}$	Crimped	No. 62	$20\frac{1}{2}$	$\frac{3}{4}$	$\frac{1}{8}$	$\frac{3}{8}$ (2)	$\frac{1}{11}$	—
20G $2\frac{1}{2}$	$2\frac{9}{16}$	Rolled	No. 62	$20\frac{1}{2}$	$\frac{3}{4}$	$\frac{1}{8}$	$\frac{3}{8}$ (2)	—	$\frac{1}{16}$

* Trapshooting load

be submitted for test. Reports will normally be issued within four days of receipt of cartridges.

Cartridges must not be sent through the post. They may be sent by passenger train or road carrier clearly labelled 'Ammunition Class 6 Division 1—Safety Cartridges—Not Liable to Explode in Bulk'.

Cartridges should be addressed to the Laboratory, The Birmingham Proof House, Banbury Street, Birmingham, 5.

Plastic wads.   The loads set out in Tables 8 to 11 may be used with plastic-skirted wads such as the Eley Monowad or the new British Plaswad. Pending specific pressure tests, however, powder charges associated with such wads should be reduced by 10 per cent.

Owing to the vagaries of home-loading, all information in this chapter is given without responsibility.

CHAPTER NINE

CLAY PIGEON GUNS

The increasing popularity of clay pigeon shooting requires special consideration of the guns used for the three main divisions of this sport, namely:

(1) Trap or Down-the-Line (DTL), including Olympic Trench
(2) Skeet
(3) Sporting

All guns used for these competitive sports have certain requirements in common. Thus, they must be efficient from every point of view, because a single bird lost may lose a major competition. They must accordingly throw the best quality, the most suitable and the most consistent patterns of which the available ammunition is capable, and must deliver them to the right place. The guns should be well fitted and well balanced, and should point easily and naturally, and should not harbour any feature of form or function likely to irritate the shooter or distract his attention, whether consciously or subconsciously. Several of these points are elaborated later, or in other chapters.

Type of gun.   For informal or non-competitive shooting, any ordinary 12-bore game gun can be used. For trap, at least one well choked barrel is desirable, and for skeet, the reverse. For sporting clays, the ordinary game gun has a claim to be regarded as the proper weapon.

For serious competitive work, including 'sporting', the British shooter appears to have decided overwhelmingly in favour of the over-and-under (O/U). The reason for this is not entirely clear, since Continental live-pigeon trapshooters, engaged in a similar but even more exacting sport, favour the side-by-side. But I have examined this question elsewhere* and will not pursue it now.

* See *Gough Thomas's Gun Book*, A. & C. Black, Ltd., London

The reasons usually given for the popularity of the O/U are that it prints its second or top barrel pattern somewhat higher than it does the first or bottom one, which is advantageous for second shots at rising birds. In addition it is considered to be more 'pointable'. American shooters still seem to favour the pump or slide-action, perhaps because it provokes a vigorous recovery of direction after the first shot. This, like the high-shooting second barrel of the O/U, may compensate for a natural tendency to shoot low with the second shot. But the O/U and the self-loaders are also favoured in the US, though the latter have much declined in favour here.

The normal gun for trap and skeet in this country is thus a 12-bore over-and-under with $2\frac{1}{2}$- or $2\frac{3}{4}$-inch chambers, adapted for firing the standard $1\frac{1}{8}$ oz. load.

The trap gun usually has 30-inch choked barrels. For protection against recoil, it is of full weight—$7\frac{1}{2}$ to $8\frac{1}{4}$ lb. Since the gun is shouldered before calling for the bird, the stock is longer and straighter than that of a game gun, with a high, level comb for accurate positioning of the shooter's aiming eye.

The rib is raised, knurled and ventilated, often with a mid-sight in addition to the normal foresight. The triggers may be double or single. If the latter, the gun usually has a pistol grip or half-pistol.

The gun for skeet is similar to the trap gun except that it has shorter open-bored barrels, 26 inches or more in length. It is often the same gun, fitted with an alternative pair of barrels.

Borings.   The trap gun is usually bored half to full choke in the bottom barrel and full in the top one.

The skeet gun is usually bored true cylinder and improved cylinder, or improved cylinder in both barrels.

Continental guns now bear 'star markings' indicative of the degree of choke in their barrels at the time of proof. These markings are as follows:

* = 0·9–1·0 mm.	(full choke)
** = 0·7–0·8 mm.	(three-quarter choke)
*** = 0·4–0·5–0·6 mm.	(half choke)
**** = 0·2–0·3 mm.	(improved cylinder)
CL =	(true cylinder)

It should be particularly noted, however, that *these markings are dimensional indications only*, and convey little or no assurance that the patterns thrown by a given cartridge will be of corresponding density. Now that there are several inexpensive clay pigeon guns on the market it is important that their performance should not be taken on trust. Some Continental guns, for example, are over-choked, and actually give closer patterns when some of the choke is removed.

Some shooters take it for granted that the best boring for a trap gun is full and full; but, as I have pointed out elsewhere, they may find, especially if they are naturally quick but in one of the lower handicap groups, that they can do better with a more open-bored first barrel, and with No. 8 shot rather than No. 7.

Single-barrelled trap and skeet guns can, of course, be fitted with replaceable choke tubes or collet-type variable chokes, though not with muzzle brakes under CPSA rules; but the performance of these devices, particularly the latter, should be checked. (See page 79 'Variable chokes'.)

Mean point of impact. The serious trap or skeet shooter must infallibly check his patterns and their mean point of impact (MPI) in relation to the point of aim. The normal O/U prints its top barrel pattern, say, 6 to 9 inches above that of the bottom barrel. But this distance varies from gun to gun, perhaps to an extent sufficient to prejudice performance. It may be unduly exaggerated, or it may be reduced to nothing. It may even go into reverse—that is to say, the barrels may cross-shoot in the vertical plane. The only feasible remedy for any abnormality here is eccentric choking, not normally practised by the English gun trade.

Over-and-under guns also need checking for lateral deviation of the MPI, particularly if they are cast-off. Cases have come to my notice in which the deviation is sufficient to affect results. The cure is to remove the cast-off and to restore fit by a slight reduction of the comb height, which enables the shooter's head to lean over sufficiently to restore the alignment of rib and eye.

Holding the pattern. Some expert clay shooters value their guns according to whether or not they 'hold the pattern'. The implication is that, in the course of a round of shooting, the density or quality of the patterns may deteriorate.

What actually happens, or may happen, is that when one barrel only of a double gun is repeatedly fired, whereby it becomes much warmer than the other, unequal thermal expansion causes the whole barrel assembly to warp, whereby the MPI may shift sufficiently to affect results. The direction of shift will be away from the hot barrel.

Even with sustained accuracy of pointing by the shooter, the target may thus no longer be caught by the dense central part of the pattern, but by the thinner outer zone, thus giving the impression of a deterioration of pattern quality. I examine this point further in Chapter 22.

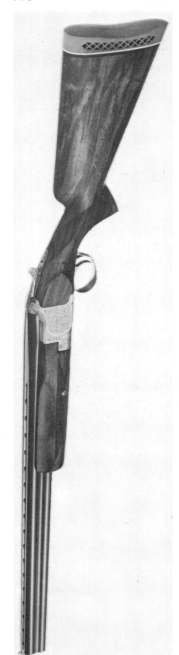

Fig. 65. An FN Browning over-and-under trap gun. This celebrated model is perhaps the most widely favoured of all double-barrelled guns for clay pigeon shooting

Fig. 66. An SKB over-and-under trap gun. This BSA-sponsored Japanese weapon is a strong challenger to European models

Triggers and trigger pulls.   The triggers of the clay pigeon gun may be double or single. Here the strong arguments in favour of the double trigger either largely do not apply or are invalidated by the single trigger's capacity to promote greater accuracy with the second shot. (See also SINGLE TRIGGERS, Chapter 2.)

The weight of the trigger pulls is a matter for individual preference, though a light pull, if the shooter is happy with it, is advantageous. The quality of the pulls should be above reproach—clean, crisp and totally free from drag.

In this country, triggers are invariably of the normal 'pull' variety, though the merits of the release trigger*, briefly referred to on page 35, are believed to be gaining recognition abroad. The release trigger has the effect of cutting out the sudden access of nervous and muscular tension immediately preceding the shooter's decision to fire, and the alternative name by which it is known—the relaxation trigger—may well have some special significance for the competitive shooter.

In a two-triggered trap or skeet gun, various combinations of normal and release triggers are possible. For example, Perazzi offer release/ release or release/pull—the latter a fascinating arrangement, as can be realised even by going through the necessary motions without a gun.

Testing and appraisal of patterns.   I have previously stressed the importance of checking patterns. There is no room in the mind of a competitive shooter for any doubt or distrust of his gun's performance. But valid conclusions on patterns cannot be drawn from tests carelessly or ignorantly performed. In *Gough Thomas's Gun Book* I have gone fully into the testing of guns for pattern and can now only emphasise the need for tests to be *properly* performed and *correctly* interpreted.

A shooter could almost certainly score higher with an imperfect gun in which he has blind confidence than he could with a somewhat better one which he distrusts on a false appraisal.

---

* See 'The Release Trigger' by Gough Thomas, *Shooting Times*, November 22, 1969

CHAPTER TEN

MAGNUM GUNS

The term 'magnum' is nowadays loosely applied to any shotgun normally firing a heavier load than that previously associated with the calibre
concerned.

There is, of course, nothing new about the magnum principle. In
the muzzle-loading days the shooter was free to increase his load according to circumstances, and up to the limit of his ability to stand recoil.
But although he did not hesitate to take advantage of this flexibility
to meet the needs of special occasions, he learned to prefer for general
shooting the more moderate charges from which our own notions of
standard loads were in due course derived.

The breechloader with its fixed ammunition naturally substituted
certain rigidities for this flexibility, and to meet the special needs for
which the muzzle-loader provided so easily we have long had variants
of the common $2\frac{1}{2}$-inch cartridges, such as those with $2\frac{3}{4}$- and 3-inch
cases, each carrying its appropriately increased load. But, as I explained
in Chapter 7, with the development of progressive powders this process
has gone much further, especially in America. There, all bores have
been promoted one or even two stages in recent decades. Their standard
case in the medium bores used to be $2\frac{5}{8}$ inches: it is now $2\frac{3}{4}$. The standard
load for a 12-bore used to be $1\frac{1}{8}$ oz. of shot. Later, the same charge was
loaded into 16-bore cases, and, later still into 20-bore, and so on through
the range. As much as $1\frac{7}{8}$ oz. is being crammed into the 3-inch, 12-bore
case.

These magnum guns have attracted many devotees. When compared
with the larger bores firing the same charges, they possess the advantages of superior lightness, elegance and fast-handling quality, and
there can be no doubt that the very word magnum has a powerful
psychological appeal.

A clear challenge.   As made by a leading English gunmaker, the 20-
and 16-bores, firing 1 oz. and 1⅛oz. of shot respectively, but weighing
anything up to half a pound less than the corresponding 2½-inch 12-
bore, are sufficiently attractive to present the latter with a clear challenge, and to provoke the question as to whether it should continue
to be regarded as the proper gun for firing standard British charges,
or whether it is not out of date.

The case against the small-bore magnums, which I myself have more
than once argued in the *Shooting Times*, is based on two considerations:
first, that, charge for charge and velocity for velocity, they must weigh
the same as the corresponding 12-bore if they are not to exceed its recoil;
and secondly, that their longer shot-columns expose more pellets to
abrasion and deformation in their course up the barrel, which is bound
to impair patterns and diminish their efficiency by increasing 'stringing', or the elongation of the shot charge in flight.

Nevertheless, because of the popularity attained by these highly-
charged little guns in the USA and the foothold they have gained in
Europe, particularly in France, I felt some years ago that the time was
ripe to review the whole issue. I accordingly addressed enquiries on
the subject to our leading gunmakers and ammunition experts and to
eminent authorities in France, Belgium and Spain, with several of
whom I had subsequent discussions. Easily the best case for the chal-
lengers is that put forward in a pamphlet published by the French gunmaker and magnum specialist, M. Kerné, who attributes a lower
sensible recoil to the magnums by virtue of the progressive powder
they employ.

But after carefully considering all the evidence placed at my disposal,
including the results of the recoil experiments described in Chapter 16,
and taking special note of certain features in the evidence of Kerné,
I came to the conclusion that *the verdict must go to the 2½- or 2¾-inch 12-
bore as being still the supremely effective weapon, in the hands of the average
shooter, for firing the standard game charges favoured in this country.* I am satisfied that the small-bore magnums do not, in general, throw such good
patterns, and that their lighter weight has to be purchased by some
loss of velocity or increase in recoil, or both.

I have latterly been reinforced in this conclusion by evidence from
the USA—from which country, incidentally, most of the eulogistic
references to small-bore magnums, especially the 20-bores, seem to
come. Some writers there presumably have guns of that gauge which
have been worked up to an exceptional standard of performance, higher
than that of the average 12-bore. But if we want a general answer to

the question posed, we must consider the normal standard of performance for both gauges.

From this point of view, the dice are undoubtedly loaded against the 20-bore. In a gun of this gauge, the area of the base of the charge on which the gas pressure operates is some 30 per cent smaller than that in a 12-bore. It follows that to accelerate a given charge to the same velocity over the same length of barrel requires a pressure in the smaller gauge which is higher or more sustained or both. In the case concerned, it will undoubtedly be both. An analysis of 39 tested $1\frac{1}{4}$ oz. loads for 12- and 20-bore guns given in the Lyman Shotshell Handbook—an independent source—gives an average maximum pressure of 9200 LUP (equivalent to about $3\frac{1}{4}$ tons in English proof-testing apparatus) for the 12-bore as against 9960 ($3\frac{1}{2}$ tons) for the 20-bore.

This higher pressure in the smaller gauge cannot fail to cause more compressive deformation of the pellets at the rear of the charge, and a corresponding increase, both in the wild-flying and relatively ineffective specimens in the fringe of the pattern, and in the length of the shot string. Pellet abrasion against the barrel wall would also be considerably greater if protective shot-cups were not used.

And even with this higher pressure, the muzzle velocities are not equal, for that of the 12-bore averages 1255 feet per second as against 1187 for the 20-bore, a reduction of over 5 per cent with the smaller gauge.

So, with the 20-bore firing a charge of somewhat inferior ranging power at a somewhat lower muzzle velocity, the prospect of its attaining the full performance standard of the 12-bore—let alone exceeding it—is by no means rosy. It is only likely to do so in a particular case on grounds of its greater suitability for the shooter concerned.

How then is the success of the magnum to be accounted for? I believe there are several reasons, namely:

(a)   The more walking and less shooting a man does in the course of a day's sport the more he will be willing to buy lightness at the expense of recoil. The average American, we are told, fires only about 50 cartridges a year. We are also told that the average *chasseur* in France spends much of his time 'marching and countermarching' and greatly values a light and well balanced gun. Under these conditions, the small-bore magnum might well be justified.

(b)   In the hands of a one-gun man pursuing different kinds of sport, a small-bore magnum can provide the flexibility of the old muzzle-loader—a light charge for dogging or walking-up birds shootable at easy range, and a heavy charge for an occasional shot at wildfowl.

(c)   The large-bore magnum, the 12, enables the shooter to fire the heavy charges needed for duck and goose shooting in certain circumstances without resorting to a larger bore, which may not be available, or legally permitted or within his purse.

(d)   An American sceptic, whose views I quote without comment, attribures even greater importance than I have suggested to the psychological appeal of the magnum. To his countrymen, he says, it is a virility symbol.

But a pointed question remains: has the small-bore magnum achieved an *enduring* success? I am told by a reliable informant that there are distinct signs in America of a return to the lightly loaded 12-bore for game shooting. Time will tell.

CHAPTER ELEVEN

SELF-OPENING GUNS

As indicated in Chapter 3, the culminating development of the sporting gun, as intended for use against live game, was undoubtedly the side-by-side hammerless ejector with self-opening action. This is the type chosen by our leading English gunmakers to demonstrate their highest skill, and the one that commands the top prices in the gun markets of the world. The recent appearance on the British market of medium-priced imported guns of this type justifies their special consideration.

It must be admitted that the advantages of the self-opening principle are most apparent and most attractive to those who shoot driven game in a big way, and are accordingly most appreciative of anything that increases the general facility with which the gun can be used in active shooting, as more particularly affecting its rate of fire.

For all that, it would be a mistake to underrate self-opening guns on the grounds that they have nothing to offer the rough shooter, or the man whose sport is conducted on a modest scale. On any occasion when rapid fire may be required, for however brief a period, the self-opener, *properly used*, is a joy. Unless a shooting man's opportunities are singularly limited, such occasions will come his way. Even the solitary rough shooter has his moments of intense activity, as when one of the fraternity succeeded in manoeuvring three full coveys of partridges into a small patch of good holding cover; or when another, a Crown Licensee in the New Forest—a breed of sportsman normally prepared to walk all day for a single pheasant—flushed thirteen from a small clump of bushes. And on innumerable other occasions of a more common sort—at a pigeon roost or a coot-shoot, for example—opportunities for making a memorable bag may be notably increased by the possession of a self-opener.

Fig. 67.   An easy-opening boxlock of superior quality—the Churchill 'Hercules'

Apart from these considerations, a self-opening gun, other things being equal, is more durable than one of the ordinary kind. That is because its internal mechanism is continuously and strongly urging it to open, so that all clearances and any slack in the bolting arrangements are taken up before firing. The hammering effect, by which any loose-ness in the action of a gun tends to develop rapidly, is thereby largely prevented, and the gun lasts longer in service—probably very consider-ably longer—than it would do if it were not a self-opener.

There is a final point which I would not underrate; it is the aesthetic appeal of a perfected mechanism—one which, as in this case, instantly performs a full cycle of operations at the command of a mere finger pressure or the like. One does not have to be mechanically minded to be sensitive to its appeal.

The self-opener's gain in fire-power is admittedly not overwhelming, and is, moreover, dependent on proper usage—a point to which I will return in a moment; but it is nevertheless real, demonstrable and occa-sionally valuable. And throughout all varieties of use, all vicissitudes of opportunity, the aesthetic pleasure remains.

Using the self-opener.   I have already hinted that, in order to get the best out of a self-opening gun, it must be properly used. The point arose clearly in the case of a Kentish sportsman when he acquired a Purdey, which, of course, is the archetype of all self-openers. From sheer force of habit, he manipulated this gun just as he did his old, familiar non-self-openers, pressing the lever with his right thumb, holding the barrels throughout in his left hand, and loading with his right. Not surprisingly, he found no gain in speed or fire-power.

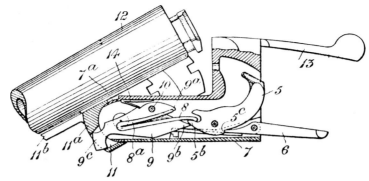

Fig. 68.   The Smith easy-opening action (from the original patent drawing)

My own method of using a self-opener, which is decidedly quicker, is to lower the gun to my side immediately I have fired and to press the lever with my right thumb. While I am doing this, and while the gun is opening, my left hand is on its way to my left-hand side jacket pocket, or to the left-hand side of my cartridge belt, to gather fresh cartridges. These I load simultaneously, provided that they come out the right way up, which, of course, they always do with a belt. For speed, I prefer a spring-clip belt, with the clips opened out if necessary, so that they do not grip the cartridges unduly. From such a belt, I break

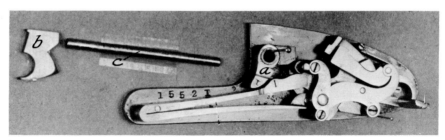

Fig. 69.   The Purdey self-opening action. In this action, both limbs of the mainspring act on the hammer or tumbler, the lower limb tending to fire the gun and the upper tending to restore the hammer to the cocked position. As the upper limb has the greater mechanical advantage it is always operative unless it is depressed by the cam *b* which rotates with the barrels and operates on the compressor *a* by means of the push-rod *c*. The reaction of the upper limb of the mainspring on *a* and thence on *b* tends at all times to throw the gun open

out two cartridges between my left fingers and thumb, position them on the edge of the chambers, and then tilt them over until they fall in. When I am in practice, I can do this with impressive efficiency, which, in company, does something to offset the inevitably less favourable impression created by my subsequent performance.

Those who use a self-opener on grand occasions, but an ordinary boxlock on rough days, would be well advised to preserve the knack of using the former to the best advantage by using the latter, so far as possible, in the same way, more especially by persisting in the left-hand loading drill.

A disadvantage frequently alleged against self-opening guns is the effort required to close them after firing both barrels, involving, as it does, the simultaneous recompression of both mainsprings and ejector springs. It is pointed out that the work involved in manipulating an ordinary gun is more evenly distributed, inasmuch as the mainsprings are recompressed by opening and the ejector springs by closing it. That is true, but the superior fire-power of the self-opener remains. It derives from the fact that it leaves the left hand free to be seeking fresh cartridges when, with an ordinary gun, it would be otherwise engaged. The effort required to re-close a self-opener after firing (which is a two-handed operation in either case) is admittedly disconcerting at first to

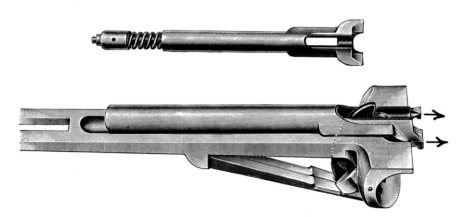

Fig. 70. The Holland & Holland self-opening mechanism. A spring-loaded plunger with a forked end (top) fits in the fore-end of the gun (bottom) and presses against the upper edge of the knuckle of the action, as indicated by the arrows, thus throwing the gun open whenever the locking bolt is withdrawn

anyone not used to these guns, but it is no more than that, and any
sense of effort quickly disappears with the acquisition of a simple
knack.

Self-opening actions.   As noted in Chapter 2, some guns are self-
openers before they are fired, but not after. These are not true self-
openers. The distinction rests on whether, when both barrels have been
discharged, the force of the mainspring (as in the Purdey) or of some
auxiliary spring (as in the Holland & Holland and Lancaster 'Twelve-
Twenty actions) is freely available for throwing open the gun, and
whether it is adequate for that purpose. Some guns, such as the Westley
Richards 'Connaught' or the Churchill 'Hercules', which, like several
others, use the Smith action (British Pat. No. 372035/32), are more
accurately described as easy-openers.

The Purdey gun, as I said, is the archetype of self-openers, the action
(invented by F. Beesley) having been introduced in 1880. Its principle
has been widely misdescribed, but may be understood from fig. 69. The
Holland & Holland action is totally different in that it depends on an
auxiliary spring (see fig. 70) accommodated in the fore-end. This
action has the advantage of being potentially applicable to a boxlock,
though, so far as I am aware, it has never been so applied.

The only boxlock self-opener of which I am aware is that covered
by my British Pat. No. 417743/33, of which a few specimens, made
by Westley Richards, may still be found. It is shown in fig. 71 and
may be seen to resemble the Smith easy-opening action (fig. 68).
Mechanically, however, it is fundamentally different, in that the mainspring rests on the action body, and is not, as in the Smith action,
accommodated within the cocking lever. Because of this, it requires no
auxiliary spring and gives a strong self-opening effect with rebound
action. It was favourably commented on by Burrard, and with modern
production facilities could, it appears, advantageously be revived.

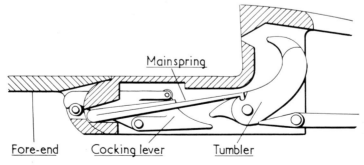

Fig. 71.   The author's self-opening, rebounding, boxlock action

CHAPTER TWELVE

SPECIAL GUNS

It is my purpose in this chapter to consider, not those guns intended for special purposes in the hands of normal users, but those intended for normal purposes in the hands of special users. These include boys, women, elderly shooters and those suffering from some disability.

In the present case, boys must come first, because they represent the largest category.

The choice of a suitable gun for a boy is no easy matter. It is, moreover, one which is beset by unique pitfalls, in that he is growing, and that what suits him today may not suit him a year hence. For this reason, there is often a tendency to treat his needs too lightly, and to let him start his shooting with a totally unsuitable weapon. This may do him both physical and psychological harm, and get him into bad habits that may prove hard to eradicate later.

Many parents and others seem to think that a boy's prime need is a light gun, and give little consideration to any other requirement. But a light gun, unless charged with an appropriately light load, can recoil painfully, especially if, as in the case of many boy's guns, it is not a good fit. By these means, a boy can easily form the fatal habit of flinching. A $2\frac{3}{4}$-inch chambered 20-bore, for instance, weighing perhaps under $5\frac{1}{2}$ lb., but firing commercial cartridges loaded with an ounce of shot, can easily give rise to recoil trouble.

Sometimes boys are started on a ·410 bore, in the vague belief that it is well to start at the bottom; but the very limited range of these guns, imposed by the light charges they employ, and the improbability of their making patterns of fair quality, can combine to engender a lack of confidence which may continue to impair performance long after the young shooter has graduated to a more adult weapon.

But I must beware of being too specific. A boy, in the present context, may be anything from, say, 10 to 17 years old, and individuals of any given age vary greatly in strength, stamina and general physical development. For all these variables, two fixed principles need to be observed: the gun must not be so heavy that the boy comes to regard it, even subconsciously, as a tiresome burden; and it must not be so loaded or ill-fitted that it causes him to suffer painful recoil. (It should be emphasised that badly fitting guns are a major cause of recoil trouble with boys.)

Subject to these points, I consider that the sooner a boy can take to a light and lightly loaded 12-bore, the better. Conversely, if he is really not capable of handling anything better than a ·410, there is a case for deferring his introduction to adult forms of shooting until he can happily use a gun firing an effective game charge. A short-barrelled 6 lb. 12-bore, firing three-quarters of an ounce of No. 7 shot (such as in the Eley 'Trainer' cartridge), makes an admirable combination for many boys.

The late N. M. Sedgwick, when editor of the *Shooting Times*, made the point that it is inadvisable to start boys on single-barrelled guns, because of their tendency to encourage an aiming or 'poking' technique and to give rise to difficulty when switching later to an ordinary double barrel.

Much the same general considerations arise in the choice of a gun for a girl or woman; but for all their latterly much vaunted superior biological toughness, their muscularity on the whole is (fortunately) below the masculine level, whilst their tendency to bruise is conspicuously above it. Even more care should therefore be taken about the fit of their guns, which should always have a soft and well-rounded recoil pad.

The veteran shooter. The man who, maybe, has shot all his life with a 6¾ lb. 30-inch-barrelled 12-bore may well find, as he passes the grand climacteric, that he could shoot more happily if he made some concessions to his declining strength and stamina. Such men, I notice, often contemplate stepping down to a 16-bore, but I regard that as a mistake, if only because of the ever-contracting choice of ammunition. A better adjustment can usually be made by taking to a short-barrelled 12-bore weighing around 6 lb. Such a gun, firing a 1 oz. load, is fully effective against ordinary game; and Churchill's assertion, when he was campaigning in favour of his 25-inch-barrelled guns, that their fast-handling quality made up for any theoretical disadvantage, was, in my opinion, justified. Many middle-aged and elderly men have found these guns a boon, though a minority, missing the inertia of their long barrels, cannot get on with them. They should be adopted only after trial, preferably under the supervision of a good coach to check the fit, more especially in view of the changes that take place in physique and eyesight with advancing years.

The disabled shooter.   In view of the wide range of disabilities from which sportsmen suffer, I can only deal briefly with one or two of the main categories under which they fall.

The loss, or partial loss, of the sight of one eye, provided it is not the dominant one, has little effect on performance; but if it is the normal aiming eye, the shooter must either resort to a cross-eyed stock or learn to shoot from the other shoulder. This latter expedient, be it noted, is nothing like so difficult as may at first appear. A few, brief practice sessions are usually sufficient to dispel any impression that the thing is impossible, and even to engender a conviction that it can be done.

The loss of the left hand or arm (in the case of a right-handed shooter) is not inconsistent with first-class shooting, as exemplified by the late Lord Gough, who, I was assured by a relation, did indeed shoot brilliantly after the loss of his left arm. I myself suffered this disability temporarily some twenty years ago, when I continued to shoot with my usual $6\frac{3}{4}$ lb. 12-bore with far better success than I would have thought possible.

To minimise the handicap, I would suggest a short-barrelled $2\frac{1}{2}$-inch 20-bore, with a pistol grip, a single trigger and a butt-plate with a pronounced toe. This, I consider, would help the correct placement of the butt in the shoulder. But the butt-plate should be detachable to facilitate experiment.

There remains the question of manipulation. It is one thing to shoot one-armed with a gun once it is at the shoulder, but another to undertake the entire management of one's weapon throughout a shooting day. Things that would help would be a full-length carrying case and a cartridge belt.

My own loading technique, which could probably be bettered, is to press the top-lever and to allow the gun (if a self-opener) to open by itself, and to eject the spent cartridge or cartridges. The right hand is then freed by holding the barrels between the thighs, and the stock between the upper arm and the side, when the hand can easily reach new cartridges from the belt and transfer them to the breech. This does not even need practice. The gun can readily be closed by pressing the muzzles down on the knee, slightly raised for the purpose, but keeping the toes on the ground. A non-self-opener can be broken open against the calf of the leg without at any time getting in front of the muzzles.

A common and more generalised disability arises from the onset of arthritis in the relevant joints. This may create a need for the lightest possible gun and one with minimum recoil—two conflicting requirements. They can only be reconciled by a compromise affecting range and power. A 2-inch 12-bore weighing about $5\frac{3}{4}$ lb. might make an acceptable solution in some cases, or a $2\frac{1}{2}$-inch 20-bore of about the same weight.

Inasmuch as all off-the-shelf guns, other than certain repeaters, are made for right-handed shooters, left-handedness must be accounted a minor disability in this context. The direction of movement of the top lever is adapted to the right-handed user, and in a good quality gun the triggers are cleverly set so as to fit the fingers of the right hand. Still, left-handed men often use right-handed guns without marked disadvantage, though the ideal solution is a gun correctly adapted to the shooter.

CHAPTER THIRTEEN

THE SHOTGUN BARREL

The barrels of a shotgun are its heart and soul, or, to change the simile, its engine room. There is hardly a single constructional or dimensional element of the barrels which is not capable of significantly affecting the gun's performance from one viewpoint or another.

Considered first by reference to an ordinary side-by-side gun, the barrels comprise the basic tubes; the ribs and (unseen) packing pieces by which they are assembled; the lumps, hooks or bites by which they are secured to the action; the 'loop' which holds the fore-end in place; the twin extractors with their stop-pin; and finally the foresight. Over-and-unders have their corresponding parts.

The barrels proper. These are normally, but not always, smooth-bored, and may regrettably be chromium plated internally (see Chapter 28). The exteriors are blued by one or other of several chemical processes. At the muzzle end, the bores are usually constricted or choked to a greater or lesser degree (see Chapter 6); and at the breech end they are enlarged to form chambers for the reception of the cartridges. The chambers taper down to the bore proper over a short length known as the 'cone' or 'lead', or in America as the 'forcing cone'. The extreme breech ends of the chambers are recessed to accommodate the rims of the cartridges.

The barrels are usually of alloy steel, though many survive in service that are made of 'damascus'—a composite steel and iron material made by an intricate welding process. The single barrels of a few repeaters are made of high-duty aluminium alloy, and in one—the superseded Winchester M50—it consists of a thin steel liner wound with bonded glass fibres.

The steel favoured for the barrels of good quality modern English guns, and several of the better ones of foreign make, is a 3 per cent

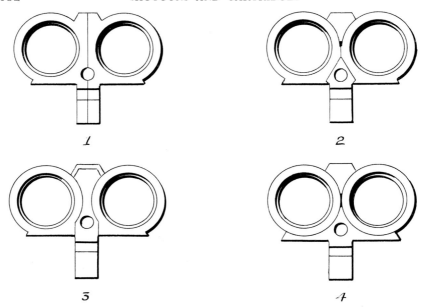

Fig. 72.   Methods of assembling shotgun barrels—(1) chopper lump;
(2) brazed lump; (3) through lump; and (4) entablature lump

nickel steel, corresponding more or less approximately to En 21 (British Standard 970/55). This steel has an ultimate tensile strength of 45–50 tons per sq. inch.

In view of the large numbers of damascus barrels that have survived or been resuscitated because of the current shortage of good, used English guns, it should be said that the best damascus barrels rival the best steels of their period; that good damascus is superior to the lower grades of steel; but that owing to the range of quality in both kinds, old guns, whether damascus or steel, should on no account be used with modern smokeless ammunition unless they have been duly nitro-proved.

The lumps.   The lumps may be forged integrally with the barrels ('chopper' or 'demibloc' lumps) or may be brazed thereto in one or other of several ways (see fig. 72). All these methods are acceptable, but the chopper variety are strongest and are to be preferred. They are occasionally united by shallow dovetails instead of by brazing.

Another variety, favoured on the Continent for guns of all grades, is the 'monobloc', in which the lumps are an integral part of a solid

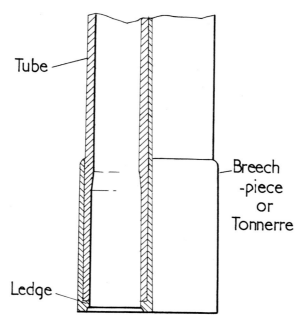

Tube

Breech
-piece
or
Tonnerre

Ledge

Fig. 73. Monobloc barrel assembly. The illustration shows the best application of the Monobloc principle, but the outline of the *tonnerre* is more frequently faired into that of the barrel without visible joint

breech-piece or *tonnerre*, into which the plain tubes are forced and soft-soldered. Owing to the latitude in design and choice of material permitted by this system (which is not to be confused with sleeving) it is arguably the best of all methods of assembling the barrels of a double gun (see fig. 73).

Barrel assembly.   As already indicated, the barrels of most double guns are united by packing pieces and ribs, which can be soft-soldered (English practice) or hard-soldered (Continental practice). The former is preferred here as avoiding the slight distortions attributed to the latter, which are stated to interfere with the 'viewing' process, as being part of proof.

Some barrels are 'ribless'—that is, they are not united except, of course, at the breech ends and (usually) at the muzzle. The purpose is (a) to improve forward lightness and balance (Alexander Martin); (b) to enable the barrels to be independently changed (Bretton); and (c) to avoid warping by differential expansion (Remington 3200).

When the last mentioned purpose is principally in view, the muzzle ends are joined by a slip-ring or the like, so that they are free to expand independently. But it should be noted that normal assembly tends to reduce warping by facilitating heat transfer from the more heated barrel to the other.

Rifled barrels. On the Continent, shotgun barrels are occasionally rifled with a slow twist of one turn in about 90 calibres. Such barrels make wide-spreading patterns of superior quality with small shot, and are intended for short range shooting (e.g. woodcock in covert). One such gun, presumably typical, is stated to have given a spread of 53 inches at 22 yards—nearly twice that of an improved cylinder. With an ordinary game load of No. 8 shot, which would have adequate striking energy within that distance, the pattern density would be sufficient to put three pellets in a woodcock with fair reliability. Many—probably most—of these birds are shot at considerably shorter distances in woodland, as are other species of game.

The chamber. Much importance attaches to the form and dimensions of the chamber (see fig. 74). It must be large enough to accommodate inevitable variations in the diameter of different cartridges, and must also be slightly tapered to facilitate extraction. But any excess diameter is objectionable as tending to promote the splitting of paper cartridge cases, especially if they are unduly dry. In the case of over-and-under guns, with their limited arc of engagement between the extractor and the cartridge head, chambers at the upper limit of tolerance must be recognised as tending to provoke the overriding of the cartridge rim by the extractor—that most provoking and incapacitating mishap, which, in the absence of a suitable screwdriver, can put an end to a day's shooting.

In view of the importance of chamber dimensions to the safe and proper functioning of the gun and cartridges, British and Continental proof authorities specify them, with appropriate tolerances. In this country, they are laid down in our joint proof authorities' Rules of Proof, 1954; and on the Continent they are defined by the International Proof Commission (CIP).

For 12-bore guns, the British and Continental figures are as follows. I have converted the latter to inches.

But apart from these purely mechanical considerations, the size of the chamber exerts considerable influence on ballistics. In an ordinary 12-bore game gun, increasing the mean diameter of the chamber by 5/1000 inch reduces the maximum pressure by about $\frac{1}{4}$ ton, and the muzzle velocity by about 30 feet per second, with a proportionate reduction in recoil. But an excessive increase, especially with a slow

| | Chamber length | Underhead dia. (ins.) | | Forward dia. (ins.) | |
		Max.	Min.	Max.	Min.
British	2½ in	·822	·812	·810	·800
	2¾	·823	·813	·810	·800
	3	·825	·815	·810	·800
CIP	2½				
	2¾	·817	·813	·803	·799
	3				

burning powder, may give rise to imperfect combustion, as evidenced by muzzle flashes and blown patterns.

Undue depth of the rim recess, by permitting a free runback of the cartridge case, may seriously increase sensible recoil. There is some possibility that a smooth, oily chamber, in association with a plastic cartridge, may enhance this effect.

A concluding point of potential importance concerns the accuracy of the chamber. Chambers are often hand-reamed, and if the reamer is not fitted with a frontal guide, the chamber axis may run out of coincidence with the bore axis. This may be spotted by eye in the finished gun, when the dark ring visible at the end of the chamber may be seen to be of non-uniform depth. The effect on patterns is conjectural, but may well be adverse. What is worse, the consequent weakening of the barrel wall on one side may be a source of serious danger.

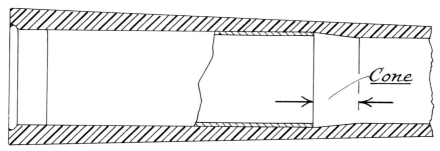

Fig. 74. Typical 12-bore shotgun chamber and cone

The cone or 'lead'. Fig. 74 shows, accurately to scale, a typical cone as formed in the barrel of a 12-bore gun, and its function is to afford the shot charge a smooth transition from the cartridge case to the bore.

I may say straight away that the cone does not perform this function with total success. To the extent that it does succeed, it may contribute notably to the performance of the gun; but if it fails, it can have a hurtful influence, reducing the ballistics of the charge, damaging the patterns, and even giving rise to those dangerous clumps of pellets previously described as 'balling'. So, the cone, unseen and unthought of, as it usually is, is far more important than some of those features of a gun which engage the attention of the average shooter, and its variations and vagaries are accordingly worth a little study.

It will be seen from the drawing that the shot charge and the wads, in their transition from the cartridge case to the bore, encounter in the cone a temporary enlargement of their passage. The pellets, like a jammed mass of people emerging from a narrow alleyway, will at once spread and tend to fill the enlargement, only to be confined again as they enter the bore. Inevitably, they will suffer some damage in the process. The wad, if it is a good wad, with a powerful tendency to convert the thrust of the powder gases into a lateral thrust against the barrel wall, will also tend to spread and fill the enlargement, and thus prevent any escape of the gas around it. And the gas itself, most certainly filling the increased space available, will undergo a slight reduction in the pressure and temperature that it would otherwise register. Some loss in the efficiency of combustion, however unimportant it may be, will thereby be incurred.

With these considerations in mind, the suggestion at once arises that it would be best to cut out the cone entirely, and to arrange for the cartridge case to butt hard up against a rectangular step at the end of the chamber. By these means, the charge would pass smoothly from case to bore without check, and without having to jump any gap. But this, unfortunately, is not practicable. Cartridges cannot be manufactured to the precise standard of length required for such an arrangement, and a gap would have to be left between the case mouth and the step to accommodate the inevitable variations.

Things would at once go wrong. The sharp step, thus exposed, would slice the tops off the passing pellets, and do more damage than a normal cone. Even a cone, but one that is too short, will do this, and I have recently seen a fired case the open end of which is adorned with a necklace of lead sliced from the charge in this manner.

The question then arises, why not a really long cone—five or six inches maybe—by which the pellets would be gently eased back into the bore? Such cones have been strongly advocated, notably by that doyen of American shotgunners, Elmer Keith. They would certainly lower ballistics (Journée lost 33 ft./sec. of muzzle velocity by lengthening cones from about $\frac{3}{8}$ inch to $1\frac{1}{4}$ inch), but might well achieve a net gain with high-pressure cartridges by the improvement of patterns. Superior patterns are worth more than marginal values of muzzle velocity.

Years ago, it was the practice of many of our best gunmakers to bore their guns with what could fairly be regarded as a prolonged extension of a normal cone. This was a tapered entrance—perhaps 9 or 12 inches long—from the cone to the bore proper. In a high-class specimen which I have measured, the bore diameter immediately in front of the cone is ·738 inch tapering down to ·730 inch at 10 inches from the breech.

But long cones rely absolutely for any merit they possess on the high quality of the wadding. If the wad does not expand adequately immediately on its emergence from the case, a long cone will invite gas to escape past it, and if any considerable amount does so, bad patterns, accompanied by serious balling, are almost inevitable. Here, two of the virtues of the modern full plastic wad stand out conspicuously; the skirted wad provides an efficient gas-seal, and any gas that does escape is prevented by the shot-cup from invading the pellets.

It is not surprising that, with all these conflicting considerations, there is no unanimity in the gun trade as to what constitutes the best length of cone. In this country, we appear to favour about $\frac{3}{8}$ inch to $\frac{1}{2}$ inch for ordinary 12-bores, and with cones of this sort there is no conspicuous disadvantage attached to Eley's use of *suitably loaded* $2\frac{3}{4}$ inch cases for $2\frac{1}{2}$ inch-chambered guns. But if these guns have short cones, such as those of the famous French 'Robust' model made by Manufrance, the excess case length, constricted in the cone, may give rise to unduly high pressure and increased recoil.

Before the last war, there was a vogue for chamberless guns for wildfowling. These guns, associated with the name of Dr Heath, were designed to use thin brass cases of the same overall diameter as the bore proper, so that there was not only no chamber, but no cone, and no limitations on case length. As mentioned in Chapter 7, I have advocated that, with the thin-walled plastic cartridge and the full plastic wad, we could advantageously revive the principle, using 16-gauge cases for a 12-bore gun.

In conclusion, there appear to be subtle possibilities of modifying the regulation of a gun by performing minor operations on the length and shape of the cones. But if so, these are craft secrets of individual barrel regulators.

Barrel length. With modern smokeless ammunition, and within proper limits, there is little to choose between long and short barrels on the score of ballistics. Thus, a 28-inch-barrelled 12-bore gun firing a standard game charge of No. 6 shot would show a gain of only 1

per cent in striking energy at 40 yards if the barrels were increased
to 30 inches, and a loss of only 5 per cent if they were reduced to 25.

These variations are submerged in those normally experienced from
round to round in the cartridges giving the average results quoted, and
the choice of barrel length can therefore safely be regulated by other
considerations, including weight, recoil, pointability and balance. The
chief merit of the longer barrels is their steadying forward weight and
inertia, which some men find beneficial, as discouraging any tendency
to check their swing. On the other hand, short barrels generally shoot
higher than long, which is normally advantageous.

Sleeving—a new appraisal
It is now several years since I wrote at any length on the practice of
renewing the barrels of shotguns by the sleeving process*, and in view
of its prevalence nowadays it is opportune to review it.

Several questions are commonly asked about sleeving. Why is it that
guns which have been sleeved do not command anything like such good
prices as do those with original barrels, or with barrels which have been
renewed *in toto*, even when this has been done by some anonymous
repairer; and to what extent is this market appraisal reflected in the
practical qualities of the sleeved barrels themselves? Are they functionally inferior? Are they less durable? Or have safety margins been unduly encroached upon?

I welcome these questions because of their obvious general interest.
Also, I must confess to a slight feeling of personal responsibility in the
matter, for I believe (perhaps quite unjustifiably) that the modern practice of sleeving was instigated by my suggestions, made some 25-odd
years ago.

There is no doubt about the widespread nature of the practice. There
are now some half-dozen gunmakers or repairers in Birmingham alone
who regularly undertake sleeving, following on Westley Richards' eminent example; and of all the British shotgun barrels passing through
the Birmingham Proof House last year, some 57 per cent were sleeved.
When we consider that the remaining 43 per cent included new barrels
as fitted to new guns, it is clear that sleeving has become more than
a method of rebarrelling: rather it has become *the* method, for better
or worse.

A cautious approach.   When in 1955 the attention of the proof authorities was first drawn to the sleeving technique, their responsibility for
securing the safety of the public caused them to approach the question
of proving sleeved barrels with great circumspection, and in a

* *Gough Thomas's Gun Book*, pp. 106–109

memorandum issued in May 1956, and in revised form in January 1960, they fairly set out all the considerations that could be urged against the practice. They even took the extreme precaution of requiring that the separate components of every sleeving job should be submitted for their approval prior to assembly, and only relaxed this precaution in the light of accumulating experience.

There is no doubt that that experience has been overwhelmingly favourable, which is not only a testimony to the soundness of the practice, but also to the standards of the firms who regularly engage in it. It is, indeed, as necessary as it has ever been to avoid attempting it in unsuitable cases, and when it is carried out, to do the work with precision. It would seem that these requirements are being fairly met.

As for the prime question, it can be said outright that sleeved barrels are not *ipso facto* functionally inferior to the originals. They can be better or worse: it is all a matter of boring, weight, length and balance, and possibly of the kind of rib chosen.

As for durability, this is theoretically determined by the grade of steel selected by the repairer for his new tubes. But the durability of a gun in service is so largely a matter of the kind of treatment it receives, and so little dependent on the grade of steel used for the barrels, that the point is largely an academic one so far as sleeving jobs carried out by established repairers are concerned.

Safety is a more pointed question. It involves consideration of the initial strength, the possible effect of fatigue, and the sustained resistance of the sleeving joint.

The initial strength is taken care of by proof. Sleeved barrels have to withstand the same proof pressures as normal ones, and are stamped accordingly.

Concern for fatigue originally focused on the step in the tube where it joins the original breech end. Sudden changes in the cross-section of mechanical parts under stress are always suspect as sources of potential fatigue failure, and I remember originally insisting that this step should be fully 'radiused' to avoid any abrupt change of section. But the change is in any case very slight, and there has now been sufficient experience to remove any apprehension of fatigue, or of failure of the generous soldered joint between the sleeve and the breech-piece.

Why then does the sleeved gun make a relatively poor showing in the used gun market? Undoubtedly some of the early prejudice against sleeving still survives. It was widely regarded as a dubious expedient for rescuing from the scrapheap ancient weapons of advanced decrepitude. Distinguished gunmakers long rejected it; yet as a means for restoring good guns, the barrels of which have suffered damage from accident or neglect, sleeving must now be regarded as a thoroughly respectable process, offering better intrinsic value for money than is the case with new barrels. Still, if funds will run to it, it is always better to have a good gun rebarrelled to the original standard, if only from the investment viewpoint.

Incidentally, the practice of using the original rib, bearing the original maker's name, on new barrels supplied by another maker is much to be deprecated unless the words 'Rebarrelled by ...' are added.

CHAPTER FOURTEEN

THE SHOTGUN ACTION

It is profitable to consider what happens to the action of a shotgun when it is fired, because some of the points that come to light can justly affect the appraisal of individual weapons.

I should make it clear that by the action of a shotgun, I mean the more or less solid mass of metal into which the barrels hook, and which includes the standing breech. Also, that I am not concerned with what goes on in the mechanism housed, or partly housed, in the action, but literally, as stated, with what happens to the mass of metal itself. It will be easiest to consider this in relation to an ordinary Anson & Deeley boxlock—besides, all I want to say will apply equally to sidelocks unless otherwise indicated.

Before I go any further, we had better think of what the action consists, and how the barrels are attached to it. There is the flat, horizontal part, called the 'bar', in which are formed slots to accommodate the lugs or lumps projecting from the underside of the barrels. The foremost lump hooks over a stout transverse pin in the corresponding slot, and this pin constitutes the hinge about which the barrels turn when the gun is opened. When it is closed, the barrels are locked in position by a sliding bolt which engages with a square notch in the rearward lump. There may be some supplementary fastening in the shape of a cross-bolt or a doll's-head, but for the moment I want to confine myself to those actions which are not so reinforced.

A hammer blow.   When the gun is fired, a high gas pressure is set up in the chamber, which rapidly accelerates the shot charge. This pressure acts in all directions: it acts to the rear against the standing breech, and forwards on the shot charge. It also acts laterally—or, rather, radially against the barrel wall. But it should be noted that *it does not act forwards on the barrels*, tending to separate them from the

141

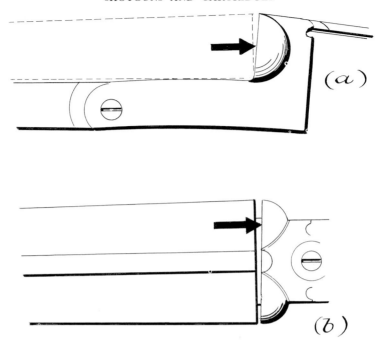

Fig. 75.   Flexure of shotgun action at instant of firing—(a) shows the bending of the bar, and (b) the gape of the breech

breech, except to the slight extent arising from its action on the sloping shoulder where the chamber diameter reduces to that of the bore. In a chamberless gun, there would be no such forward action; and in the case of an ordinary 12-bore game gun, developing a maximum pressure of 3 tons per square inch, the total forward pressure acting on the barrels is only about a third of a ton.

The main effect to be considered, therefore, is the hammer blow delivered by the gas pressure to the standing breech. This causes the gun to recoil; and since the barrels are attached to the action, they too have to recoil. They are, in fact, dragged back by the hinge pin acting on the forward lump, which has to overcome both their inertia and the incidental gas pressure last explained.

The net effect, and the main effect, of these forces—the rearward pressure on the standing breech, and the forward reaction against the hinge pin—is to flex the action as shown in a highly exaggerated fashion in fig. 75. If the action is sufficiently strong to absorb this flexure without exceeding its elastic limit—if the nature, amount and disposition of the metal is adequate—all should be well. The action will recover its original form directly the stress of firing is relieved, and will be ready to repeat the performance indefinitely. But note that word 'should', for all may not be well, as I hope to show in a moment.

A vital operation. So far we have only considered the action as if it were that of a single-barrelled gun, whereas in a double-barrelled gun things are more complicated. This arises from the fact that the forces and resistances involved do not all act in the same vertical plane. Thus, when the right barrel is fired the action receives a complex twisting to which fig. 75 affords no more than a clue. It would seem that the right-hand side of the standing breech goes back further than the left, as shown, and that the right-hand side of the bar is correspondingly more flexed. Conversely, when the left is fired.

The upshot of all this, bearing in mind that the action can only develop its strength by flexing, is that it must be free to flex, and in the complex manner indicated. If it is in any way restrained from flexing in any part, stress will be transferred to whatever offers the restraint, with what may be unfortunate consequences. This underlines the importance of the work carried out by the 'jointer'—the man who fits the barrels to the action—on whose skill largely depends the capacity of the gun to stand up to long service without shooting loose.

Room to breathe. It might be thought that the jointer's terms of reference are simple, and that his task is simply to fit all the parts concerned as closely as possible together—the hook to the hinge-pin, the lumps to the slots, the bolt to the bite, the flats of the barrels to the flats of the action, and the breech-ends of the barrels to the standing breech. But that is not so; indeed, I believe that if a gun were jointed in this manner it would probably be found 'off the face' after proof, and would be failed on that account. The reason would be that the jointer, by not allowing certain small but significant clearances where long experience has shown them to be necessary, had denied the action the flexure needed to develop its strength, and had thereby transferred undue stresses to parts not adapted to resist them.

In practical terms, the needs of a well-jointed gun are these: the forward lump must fit the hinge-pin and its own slot as closely and accurately as possible. The rear lump, however, must 'clear the smoke' on each side—that is to say, it must have a small but appreciable side clearance. So must its forward curve, where it is 'jointed on the circle' into the bar.

Again, the flats of the barrels should not touch the flats of the action, except possibly just at the foot of the standing breech. Yet I have known men, who should have known better, to mark a gun down because there was a glint of daylight visible between these flats.

But there should be no daylight between the breech ends of the barrels and the standing breech. There, the correct prescription is the closest possible fit. All these points can be checked by visual inspection.

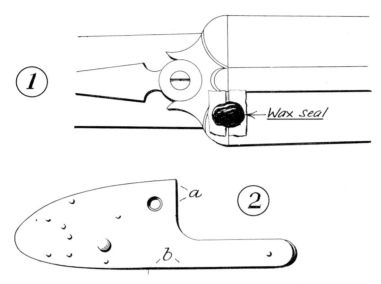

Fig. 76.   Demonstrating the flexure of the shotgun action

Demonstrations.   At this stage it is necessary to examine the value of the top extensions frequently applied to reinforce the junction between barrels and action, but before doing so, I would like to point out how the elastic movements or flexures of the action body, which I have just described, may be made visible—or, rather, may be shown to have taken place. These movements are chiefly the bending of the action bar under the impact of the hammer-blow delivered to the standing breech by the gas pressure suddenly developed in the chamber, and the consequent gaping at the breech.

To demonstrate the bending of the bar, place a tiny pellet of plasticine half way along the flat of the action and to one side. Then close the gun, when the pellet will be flattened to a thickness representing the clearance between the barrel and action flats. Check the diameter of the flattened pellet and then fire the gun. If the gun is tight and sound, and if it has been well and properly jointed, it will be found that the diameter of the pellet has increased, showing how the bar, by bending upwards in the way illustrated in fig. 75 has taken up the clearance left for this purpose by the jointer.

Again, to demonstrate the gaping of the breech, apply two little strips of surgical tape to the breech-end of one of the barrels and to the bump of the breech respectively (fig. 76) so that the strips lie edge to edge. Now load the gun and apply an ordinary sealing-wax seal to the junction. If the gun is then fired, the seal will be found to have broken along the line of junction between breech and barrels. (The purpose of the surgical tape, incidentally, is not merely to provide a bite for the seal, but also to afford it a cushion to prevent its being broken by mere shock.)

In sidelock guns, evidence of the elastic movement of the standing breech and of the bending of the bar may often by found on the edge of the right-hand lock-plate, this being the one corresponding to the barrel most often fired. Bright rubbing spots may be found at points *a* and *b* in fig. 76, though they may be missing unless the lock-plate is particularly well fitted and the gun much used.

The role of the top extension. Coming now to top extensions, these may be divided into three categories: (1) those that merely hold the standing breech up to the breech ends of the barrels; (2) those that merely reinforce the under-barrel bolt in holding the barrels down to the bar of the action; and (3) those that combine both functions. The first category is best represented by the plain doll's-head. Examples of the second category are the Purdey 'secret-bite' and the various forms of plain screw-grip, whilst the third is exemplified by the Greener cross-bolt (fig. 77).

Since all these extensions, with the exception of the inoffensive Purdey, may fairly be charged with impeding rapid loading, and menacing, in varying degrees, the hands and fingers of the person cleaning the gun, their utility may well be called into question. It requires consideration in the light of the 'minute but significant flexures' undergone by the action body, as already described.

It would seem that category (2) extensions—the holding-down kind—are hard to justify in the light of the fact that the ordinary under-barrel bolt has an enormous reserve of strength. The tendency of a drop-down gun to throw open on discharge is, in fact, so slight that there is no difficulty in holding the gun closed without any kind of fastening. So, at least, it is reliably stated. I myself have never tried to prove it; but I have fired an ordinary 12-bore secured with nothing more than two turns of half-inch cellophane tape, which were evidently adequate

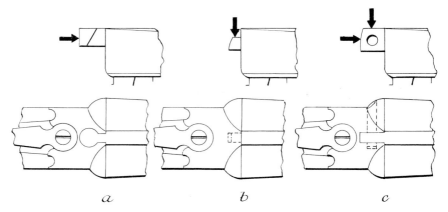

Fig. 77. Basic types of top extensions—(a) the doll's head; (b) the Purdey 'secret' extension; and (c) the Greener cross-bolt. Theoretically (a) reinforces the bar of the action; (b) reinforces the under-barrel bolt; and (c) both bar and bolt

without any help from the hands. There is the further fact that if this kind of extension is adopted, it is unlikely that both it and the under-barrel bolt will fit equally well: one or other of them will be doing the work, and the likelihood is that the extension will be the passenger. In neither case is the bar relieved of the bending stresses which tax it at its weakest point—at the foot of the standing breech.

Doubtful efficiency. The typical category (1) extension—the doll's head—if perfectly fitted and strong enough, would, on the contrary, relieve the action of all stress. By holding the standing breech tightly up to the barrels it would prevent the action undergoing any flexure— or contributing any of its strength!

What happens in practice is that, however well the doll's-head may be fitted initially, it is not adequate to undertake the whole of the duty thus thrown upon it. It accordingly quickly develops clearance sufficient to allow the standing breech to spring back, and the bar to bend, until they have developed more or less their normal, elastic resistance, and undergone more or less their normal stress.

This may be demonstrated by taking any well-used gun that is fitted with a doll's-head and performing my sealing-wax experiment.

The foregoing remarks, in combination, apply fairly to category (3) extensions, such as the cross-bolt. I should be surprised if any cross-bolted gun that had seen considerable service failed to break its seal.

The upshot of all this, in my opinion, is that the action body of a drop-down gun should be designed, as it well can be, to withstand the whole of the pressure acting on the standing breech, and with an adequate factor of safety. Better an external bolster, which can be neatly contrived, than a top extension of doubtful efficiency.

CHAPTER FIFTEEN

BOXLOCK OR SIDELOCK?

I find that the old arguments about the relative merits of boxlock and sidelock actions have been strongly revived and intensified in recent times, by the availability of many imported sidelocks in the medium price range.

Before the last war, when imported sidelocks were a rarity, prevailing opinion was much influenced by Burrard, who came down heavily in favour of the sidelock. In particular, he insisted that sidelocks are inherently stronger than boxlocks—an opinion which cannot be sustained on any fundamental grounds, though it is one that is often quoted. As the general question is one which frequently exercises the minds of prospective gun buyers casting acquisitive glances at moderately-priced Continental sidelocks, it is opportune to review it.

There is no doubt as to which of the two main types of shotgun actions stands higher in general esteem—it is the sidelock, and for reasons that are not hard to seek. Up to the time when the shotgun had become a hammered, central-fire weapon, all guns within the main stream of evolution were sidelocks. But with the introduction by Westley Richards of the Anson & Deeley boxlock in 1875, the stream divided, and never became united again. In the main stream, evolution continued. Hammers disappeared, ejectors were developed and perfected, and the modern type of sidelock gun finally emerged as the normal production of our best makers.

But the boxlock remained a thing apart until the original patents expired, whereupon gunmakers everywhere eagerly adopted the design, not only because of what were at that time its proven merits, but because its basic simplicity enabled important economies to be made in production costs. Even the makers of best quality guns, though adhering strictly to the sidelock principle for their top-grade weapons, frequently offered cheaper grades in boxlock form. And so it came about that the sidelock acquired the *cachet* of the thoroughbred, and the boxlock that of the workhorse. The distinction, for all its occasional falsity, was fostered by the sidelock's unmistakably elegant appearance.

A broad comparison. But when we come to assess the broad merits of these two actions, we must not be deceived by appearances, nor must we be misled by the fact that the highest class materials and workmanship are generally to be found in the one type as opposed to the other. We must, in short, consider what are the inherent merits of the two designs. These are generally accepted to be as follows.

The outstanding merit of the boxlock is its simplicity, which, with materials and workmanship of a given standard, yields a cheaper gun. The parts are few and robust, and repairs can be effected anywhere in the world. Functionally, the gun compares, or can be made to compare, on equal terms with most sidelocks.

The advantages usually attributed to the sidelock are superior balance, better trigger pulls, and better access to the lockwork for cleaning and lubrication.

I do not think it necessary to contest this common assessment, nor, without taking my toe off the ground of practicality, do I think it bears much elaboration. However, I would say a word for the self-opening facility and rebounding locks normally found only in sidelock guns. The rebounding principle, in particular, is of undeniable practical value, as anyone would testify who has ever been plagued by a gun that is prone to stay striker-bound and unopenable when birds are streaming over.

For the rest, I would only say that a well balanced boxlock can be better balanced than a poorly balanced sidelock; that good boxlock trigger pulls can be better than indifferent sidelock trigger pulls; and that it is so easy to maintain a boxlock in good condition that the superior access afforded by sidelocks represents only a marginal advantage.

A question of safety. But more fundamental issues than these are sometimes brought into the comparison. They are concerned with the safety of the guns and with their capacity for hard and sustained service.

Safety has two aspects—the strength of the gun to resist the normal stresses and strains of shooting, and the security of the mechanism against inadvertent discharge. So far as the strength of the barrels is concerned, the two types of gun are, of course, on all fours; but when we consider the action itself, this is no longer the case. The weakest part of a shotgun action is at the foot of the standing breech, and action bars can and do occasionally crack at this point, chiefly under abuse.

It is almost certainly true that the majority of cracked actions are boxlocks, but this cannot be regarded as evidence of a fundamental weakness of boxlocks as a type, but of the weakness of individual guns, as arising out of poor design, inadequate dimensions, inferior material, bad manufacture or, maybe, incorrect heat treatment. It must be remembered that, regarded in the mass, boxlocks are the cheaper guns and sidelocks the more expensive ones; and the former, even with everything else equal, would tend to accumulate more faults. It must also be remembered that the heaviest duty ever imposed on a drop-down action was probably that of the ·600 bore double cordite elephant rifle, proved for a 14-ton service pressure, for which the celebrated makers, W. J. Jeffery & Co., chose, not a sidelock action, but a boxlock.

The power to endure. As for the safety of the two types of guns against inadvertent discharge, the *regular or conventional sidelock* scores in that it is always fitted with an intercepting safety, which is designed to catch the hammer in the event of its being jarred free of the sear, as by a blow or fall. But sound boxlock guns, in a reasonable state of adjustment, are so far from being prone to inadvertent discharge that intercepting sears are seldom fitted, even in the most expensive kind. It is worth noting that some cheap sidelocks, not conforming to my underlined description, also carry no intercepting sears.

Fig. 78. The Greener 'Empire' action, famous for its simplicity. It is here shown assembled on the outside of the action body to which it belongs.

Coming finally to the question of durability in service, there is a widespread impression among the most experienced sportsmen that sidelock guns stand up best to hard wear and tear and heavy loads. I believe this to be true, but I regard it as evidence of the superiority, not of the sidelock system, as such, but of best-quality guns, among which sidelocks predominate. A boxlock, correctly designed, of equally good materials and workmanship, and closely and correctly jointed (see Chapter 14), will assuredly last as long as a sidelock.

Variant boxlocks

So far, in writing of the boxlock, I have been thinking almost exclusively of the classical Anson & Deeley type which widely predominates. But, as indicated in Chapter 2, there are variants, which, if foreign guns are included, are too numerous to particularise. (Some of these foreign guns, incidentally, are incorrectly described as Anson & Deeleys.) The best known variant forms in this country are (or were, for they are no longer made) the Greener 'Empire' (fig. 78), 'Facile Princeps' and 'Unique' actions. A more modern variant is the easy-opening Smith action, incorporated in boxlocks made by several firms, including Westley Richards and Churchill, Atkin, Grant & Lang.

So far as I am aware, there is no true self-opening boxlock now made in this country, but one is described in Chapter 11.

CHAPTER SIXTEEN

WEIGHT AND RECOIL

The basic principle involved in the recoil of guns was laid down by Sir Isaac Newton three centuries ago. According to his Third Law of Motion, the momentum of the recoiling gun is always equal to the momentum of the issuing charge. And since momentum is *Weight × Velocity*, the principle may be expressed as follows:

The weight multiplied by the velocity of the recoiling gun equals the weight multiplied by the velocity of the issuing charge.

From this it follows that:

$$\text{Velocity of recoil} = \frac{\text{Wt. of charge}}{\text{Wt. of gun}} \times \text{Velocity of charge}$$

(*Note:*   In working out practical examples all weights must be in the same units; and the weight of the charge must include the weight of the wads and, say, 50 per cent of the weight of the powder.)

In a work as comprehensive and recent as Burrard's *The Modern Shotgun*, this is the only aspect of recoil considered, it being laid down that the acceptable limit of recoil in a sporting gun is a velocity of about 16 feet per second.

But the recoil of a firearm supported by a shooter and braced against his shoulder cannot be disposed of so simply: it is necessary to consider what I will call (1) the dynamic recoil and (2) the sensible recoil, using the word 'sensible' in accordance with its primary meaning, which, according to my dictionary, is 'capable of being perceived by the senses'.

(1)   The dynamic recoil is the recoil determined by Newton's law already explained. The weight and velocity of the shot charge

being settled, the gun's recoil is decided by its weight, provided it has a solid breech and no muzzle brake, in which case, to keep the velocity of recoil down to Burrard's 16 feet per second it is usually necessary that the gun should weigh about 96 times the shot charge, or 6 lb. of gun to every ounce of shot.

But if the gun has a moving breech, like those of the recoil-operated automatics, an appreciable portion of the energy of the recoil is absorbed by friction in the barrel-braking system, the actual amount being variable and dependent on lubrication, as many users of long-recoil automatics who have been too free with the oil-can have found to their cost.

Dynamic recoil in single-barrelled guns is also affected by whether or not a muzzle brake is fitted. These brakes work by permitting a substantial part of the high velocity gas following the shot charge up the barrel to escape sideways through slots formed near the muzzle. The diversion of this gas sideways sets up strong reactive forces on the forward edges of the slots, thus tending to throw the barrel forward, and partly counteracting the pressure on the breech which initiates the recoil. (See fig. 80.) These brakes, incidentally, can introduce unpleasant blast effects.

(2) The sensible recoil, or recoil as felt by the shooter, can be defined as the net effect of the dynamic recoil on his physical and nervous organisation. This is the aspect of recoil which really matters. For a given dynamic recoil the sensible recoil can vary considerably. For example, a shooter firing an ill-fitting gun, which kicks his face and bruises his arm, might find the recoil from a given charge intolerable, but not so if the gun were made to fit him snugly by a mere alteration of the stock or the addition of a recoil pad. The particular system of springs used for absorbing and utilising the recoil of self-loading weapons, and the energy absorbed in the mechanism, may similarly have an important influence on sensible recoil.

More subtle effects are produced by different powders, giving different rates of burning. These powders may be loaded successively into the same gun to give the same velocity to the same charge, thus producing the same dynamic recoil, in terms of final momentum. But not the same sensible recoil, because the final momentum will be attained at different rates, and a sensitive shooter may for this reason pronounce one powder decidely unpleasant and another quite the reverse. The difference may well correspond to that between severe gun-headache and complete freedom from it, and may be likened to the difference between a blow from a hammer and one of equal momentum from a soft rubber mallet.

An old fallacy

It is widely believed that the slow-growing momentum of recoil imparted to a gun by a progressive or slow-burning powder produces less sensible recoil than a quick-burning powder, other things being equal. This belief has been completely undermined by rigorous and prolonged scientific experiments, and must, it seems, now be discarded as a popular fallacy. It has been much fostered by the fact that earlier 'sweet-burning' powders, such as the old Amberite, gave somewhat low ballistics.

The more modern approach to the reduction of sensible recoil was first brought to my notice by a famous Birmingham gunmaker. He was developing a special-purpose gun, the recoil of which was excessive, yet he was barred from reducing the weight or velocity of the projectile or increasing the weight of the gun. He found his solution in the use of an ultra-quick-burning propellant. It might be thought that this would give an abnormally painful hammer blow, but in fact the blow was too quick for the shooter's nervous system to appreciate.

It is a matter of common experience that sensation does not follow instantly on stimulus: there is an appreciable time-lag, which is why we intuitively snatch a splinter out of a wound instead of drawing it out gently. We know that if only we can be quick enough, the splinter will be gone before the pain has time to develop. Indeed, if the stimulus, however violent it may be, is only sufficiently transitory, it may fail completely to awaken pain. 'I never felt anything of it at the time,' is the common experience of those who suffer grave and painful injuries from very sudden happenings.

This, then, is the explanation of how the Birmingham gunmaker arrived at his solution. Nevertheless, it is a hard principle to demonstrate. It cannot be demonstrated by firing one or two cartridges, differently loaded, in cold blood, for even the frame of mind in which a gun is fired can have a big influence on sensible recoil. Who has not noticed the curiously heavy recoil when a familiar gun loaded with a familiar cartridge is fired deliberately at a mark? Yet the recoil of the same gun and cartridge fired in the course of sport may seem light and pleasant. To demonstrate the influence of rate of burning on sensible recoil requires a prolonged course of scientifically controlled experiments, such as those carried out by Eley when they were developing their modern range of powders and ammunition. These were the experiments I have already mentioned. They involved the firing of many thousands of cartridges by a team of nine experienced shots of varying build, shooting under a wide variety of conditions with guns of different types, weight and boring. The cartridges were all loaded to give the same velocity to the same shot charge, though by means of powders of various rates of burning. The shooters did not know what they were firing, but were merely required to give marks for recoil. They were unanimous in assigning the lowest recoil to the cartridges loaded with the fastest-burning powder, the dynamical effect of which was checked throughout by electric accelerometers built into the stocks of the guns, and their conclusions have since been widely confirmed.

To summarise, therefore, the dynamic recoil, hitherto regarded as the sole measure of recoil in practical shooting, is now seen merely as its broad determinant. In fixed-breech guns, and in the absence of a muzzle brake, it is settled by their weight in relation to the weight and velocity of the charge. In moving-breech guns it may be modified, as, for example, by the frictional-braking of the recoiling barrel. The effect of the dynamic recoil on the shooter, or the sensible recoil, which, as I have said, is the recoil that really matters, is in turn modified by a number of factors, chief among which are gun-fit and the rate of burning of the powder. It follows that the recoil-sensitive individual and particularly the gun-headache sufferer may find relief in one or other of several ways—not merely or necessarily in a lighter charge or a heavier gun, or in a better fitted stock or a recoil pad, but possibly in a faster-burning powder, or even, if the conditions of his sport admit of his using such a weapon, in a pump gun fitted with a muzzle brake or a gas-operated repeater.

In the USA various proprietary 'recoil reducers' are advertised, the best known being the Edwards. This is a sealed device, and the working

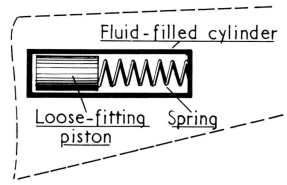

Fig. 79.   An American-type recoil reducer

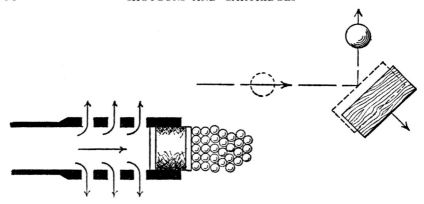

Fig. 80.   Principle of muzzle brake. Ball deflected from wooden block on floor exerts reaction on block causing it to move as shown. Sideways deflection of barrel gases through slots of muzzle brake exerts similar reaction on slots' forward edges, thus reducing recoil

principle is not disclosed. It takes the form of a metal cylinder which is inserted in a hole drilled lengthways in the butt of the stock, and it may be inferred that it works partly by absorbing some of the recoil energy, as by a damped internal inertia weight, and partly by the dead-weight it adds to the gun. Inevitably, these devices materially disturb a gun's balance, for which reason, presumably, they do not appear to have gained any foothold in this country.

Pathological cases
There remain the cases of guns, apparently normal in every respect, which recoil painfully with standard ammunition. This may arise from some vagary of boring such as an enlargement immediately in front of the chamber cone, caused, for example, by allowing a polishing lap to dwell unduly at the end of its travel.

Perhaps a more familiar cause is an undue clearance (i.e. headspace clearance) between the cartridge head and the standing breech. Theoretically, if a cartridge case had a free run back before it hit the standing breech, the kinetic energy it would acquire, and duly impart to the breech by impact, would be greater than would have been imparted by the same pressure acting directly on the breech during the same brief interval, and in the ratio of the gun weight to the case weight—say, about 400 times greater. This takes no account of the wave pressure set up by the following gases.

In practice, frictional and other losses greatly reduce this figure, but enough may remain to increase recoil to an intolerable extent; whilst the following wave pressure, if the gun is badly 'off the face', may split the cartridge rim and permit a large escape of gas. In *Gough Thomas's Gun Book* I have given practical examples and details of effective cures, including the soldering of thin circular 'shims' to the breech face. I have also explained an apparent paradox arising from the effect of slow *versus* fast-burning powders.

The importance of weight

To be both safe and suitable for firing a given load or cartridge, an ordinary fixed-breech gun must not only have been proved to an appropriate pressure level, but it must also have sufficient weight to protect its user from excessive recoil. Not all modern guns conform to these requirements.

For example, many 12-bore game guns, weighing 6½ lb. or less, nowadays have 2¾-inch chambers, and if they have been made on the Continent they may have been proved to 900 kg. per sq. cm. or more. They are thus officially safe to use with such a cartridge as the Eley 2¾-inch Magnum loaded with 1½ oz. of shot. But the recoil of such guns with such a cartridge would be intolerable—they might be safe, but they would certainly not be suitable.

What a man can tolerate in the way of recoil depends on several factors—the robustness of his constitution, his weight (a tough light-weight can often stand more recoil than a heavyweight, and theoretically should be able to do so), his degree of habituation, the fit of his gun, and the number of shots he may require to fire in close succession.

Recoil may be measured in terms of the momentum or speed of recoil of the gun, or, more appropriately, its kinetic energy or energy of movement. For average conditions, Burrard gives 15·4 ft./sec. as a fair limit for the speed, which corresponds to a 6½ lb. 12-bore firing a standard British game cartridge. For corresponding conditions, Journée has suggested an energy limit of 4 kilogram-metres, or about 29 ft.-lb. I have suggested 24 ft.-lb., which ties in fairly well with the Burrard figure, and is about right for trapshooting.

But the average shooter has no means for measuring the velocity or energy of recoil, and can best rely in the first instance on the old rule that with fixed-breech guns there should be 6 lb. of gun to every ounce of shot. It should never be forgotten that a light gun needs a light load; that a magnum load needs a magnum gun; and that the accelerated deterioration inevitably suffered by a gun that is persistently over-loaded cannot be avoided by adding any kind of passenger weight to the stock, or any sort of recoil pad. The shooter's shoulder may thus be relieved, but not the gun.

CHAPTER SEVENTEEN

. BALANCE

I must now pick up a point involved in the choice of a gun which I could not deal with adequately in Chapter 3. It is so important in my view as to deserve a chapter to itself.

In these days, when the highest quality conventional guns are out of the reach of the average sportsman—out of the reach indeed, of most men whose fathers and grandfathers went to Purdey, Boss or Holland for their guns as a matter of course—there is some likelihood that a generation may grow up to whom fine balance in a sporting gun is a source of pleasure of which they have had no adequate experience. That would be a pity, for as I have previously said, it is hard to overrate the value of balance, or the pleasure and economy of effort with which it enables a gun to be used in the field.

So far as the mere transporting of a gun is concerned, weight, of course, is practically all that matters. It is when a gun comes into action—when it is raised and swung here and there on to swiftly-moving marks—that the virtue of good balance really stands out.

What then is balance, meaning good balance? There are many who believe that the balance of a gun is determined by the point at which it balances, see-saw fashion, when poised on the edge of the forefinger. Others believe that it is a mysterious and altogether indefinable quality that somehow attaches itself to the costly productions of famous gun-making firms. But the subject can neither be comprehended nor dismissed so simply.

A dynamic quality
Properly regarded, balance is bound up with movement and energy. A clue to its real nature is to be found in an expression for which I believe we are indebted to the Americans—'a fast-handling gun'. Such

158

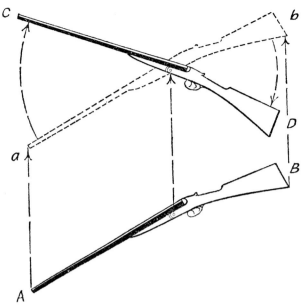

Fig. 81. Composite gun movement resolved into components. Movement of gun from, say, carrying position A-B to firing position C-D is
same as if movement were executed in two stages, i.e. from A-B to a-
b, without change of direction, and thence to C-D by rotation about
point of balance. Energy required for executing first stage is proportional
to weight only of gun; that required for second stage is proportional to
gun's moment of inertia

a gun is one that, with a minimum expenditure of energy on the part
of the user, can be swung quickly and easily from one position to another, and more particularly from the carrying position to the shoulder.
Now, for the purposes of analysis, this single movement can be regarded
as a combination of two movements—one being a change of position
without change of direction, and the other merely a change of direction
(see fig. 81); and the science of dynamics teaches us that the amount
of energy we have to put into the first of these movements—the change
of position—is proportional simply to the weight of the gun, while that
absorbed by the second—the change of direction—is proportional to
the way in which the weight is distributed fore and aft. Whether the
weight is dispersed towards the end or concentrated towards the middle
makes no difference to the amount of energy required to change the

position, but it makes a world of difference to that required to change the direction.

Balance, therefore, is not determinable by any static test, but rather by the amount of energy demanded from the shooter in the active use of the gun, and by the way in which the effort is distributed between the hands. By reference to simple dynamical principles, it may be shown that this energy is in turn largely determined by what is called the gun's *moment of inertia* as measured about the point of balance—an engineer's expression, which takes into account not only the weight but also the way in which it is distributed. If, with two guns of the same weight, and balancing at the same point, one has its weight more concentrated between the hands, it will have a lower moment of inertia than the other. For that reason, it will be better balanced and faster-handling, and will make less demand on the energies of its user in the process of active shooting. It will also be proportionately more pleasant to use. Viewed this way, balance and its index—the moment of inertia—may be seen to represent, possibly, the difference between hard work and pleasant exercise, between fatigue and buoyancy; and between missing and clean kills at the end of the day.

There is a further point. The moment of inertia of a gun varies according to the point or axis about which it is measured. It is least if measured about the point of balance, and it is important that this point should fall naturally about half-way between the hands. The reason for this is that when one attempts to change the direction of a gun by a relative movement of the hands, it tends to turn about the point of the least moment of inertia; and it is clearly desirable that the point about which the gun *tends* to turn should be the same as that about which one is trying to *make* it turn. If these two points are materially separated, the gun will feel unresponsive or even at odds with its user, and a gun that is conspicuously muzzle-heavy (or, for that matter, butt-heavy, like some automatics with inertia-weights in the stock) can give this feeling strongly and unpleasantly.

Good balance defined
Summing up, therefore, good balance and fast handling are attained by a gun which is as light as it can be, having due regard for recoil; which has the lowest possible value for its least moment of inertia; and which realises this value at a point about mid-way between the hands.

But this is not quite all, for the muscular sensations to which these purely mechanical properties give rise combine in the brain of the user with tactile sensations derived from the shape, smoothness and fitness to the hand of the parts of the gun actually handled. So, to complete the total effect of a finely balanced gun, it is necessary to specify that the external shape shall be elegant, with fluent lines and well finished surfaces, conformable to the hand and pleasant to the sense of touch.

With guns in which the natural disposition of weight is either forwards, or unduly dispersed, such as in the various repeaters, all this is difficult if not impossible of attainment. With guns in which the disposition of weight is more central, such as boxlock doubles, the prescription can be filled with due care in design and construction. With sidelocks, it is easier, though more costly. It is perhaps easiest of all with guns of the Darne type, because of the naturally rearward disposition of weight. There is no excuse for even a cheap gun of this kind not being well balanced.

The prescription I have given for a well balanced gun merely puts into semi-technical language what generations of gunmakers have found out empirically. Over the years, they have lightened their guns by taking advantage of smokeless powders to reduce barrel lengths and lighten them forward; they have hollowed-out stocks, and in some cases they have cleverly brought the mass of metal around the breech closer into the right hand. By so doing, they have not only got rid of weight, but have much reduced the moment of inertia and thereby improved balance and fast-handling quality.

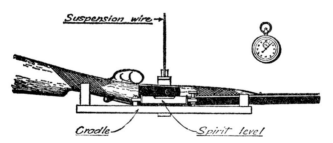

Fig. 82. Apparatus for measuring balance (moment of inertia) of gun

Measuring balance

It is instructive to leave generalities and to get down to some figures. There is no difficulty in measuring the moment of inertia of a gun. I use for this purpose a kind of torsion balance—a simple device consisting of a gun-cradle fitted with a spirit level and suspended from a ceiling by a high-tensile steel wire, which is carefully fixed at both ends in rigid attachments (see fig. 82). The gun being secured in the cradle and

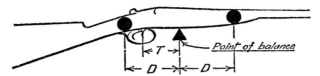

Fig. 83.   Equivalent distribution of weight. Black spots represent positions where half-weights of gun could theoretically be concentrated without altering 'feel' or balance

adjusted by the help of the spirit level so that its point of balance coincides with the axis of the wire, it is made to oscillate gently and freely in a horizontal plane, whereupon the time taken to perform a given number of oscillations is taken with a stop watch. Having calibrated the wire and the empty cradle beforehand, the moment of inertia of the gun can be readily calculated. Further, if we know its value for a particular gun, we can work out where the weight is effectively concentrated, and can thus assess the skill that has gone into the designing and building of it in this most important respect. I think it will be clear that if the total weight of the gun were divided equally in two, there would be two points, equidistant from the point of balance, where the half-weights could be effectively concentrated without altering the 'feel' or balance in any way. The black spots in fig. 83 represent the half-weights concentrated in this manner; and in view of the gunmaker's constant endeavour to centralise the weight, it will be realised that a large value for the distance D is bad, and implies a gun that is lumpish and inert, while a short distance is meritorious and indicates a lively one. The distance T should preferably not exceed about $4\frac{1}{4}$ inches. If it is much more than that the gun will begin to feel heavy forward and, for reasons previously explained, at odds with its user.

As a first exercise, I chose an historical sequence of four top-quality, London-made, double-barrelled guns by celebrated makers as being likely to reveal the best kind of performance attainable at their respective dates. Their particulars are set out below.

Gun No.	Type	Date	Bore and Chambers	Barrels	Weight (lb.)
1	ML (Manton)	1830	16	29 in. twist	$6\frac{1}{4}$
2	Hammer	1875	$12 \times 2\frac{1}{2}$	30 in. damascus	$6\frac{3}{4}$
3	HE	1900	$12 \times 2\frac{1}{2}$	30 in. steel	$6\frac{3}{4}$
4	HE	1948	$12 \times 2\frac{1}{2}$	27 in. steel	6 lb. 3 oz.

In like order, these guns gave the results set out in Table 12. (The units, by the way, in which the moments of inertia are measured are what is known as gravitational or 'g' units; but that need not concern us here because we are only considering the results comparatively.)

TABLE 12. Balance Data—Best Guns

Gun No.	Actual Moment of Inertia in g units × 1000	Moment of Inertia as per cent of No. 1	D (ins.)	T (ins.)
1	181	100	11·5	6
2	151	83	10·3	5
3	136	75	9·7	$4\frac{1}{2}$
4	99	55	8·6	$4\frac{1}{4}$

This is a notable record of improvement. It will be seen that over the period in question, weight has been centralised and brought back, while the moment of inertia has been reduced by no less than 45 per cent. The energy required to manipulate the modern gun in active shooting should thereby be reduced in much the same proportion. Practical handling entirely confirms this conclusion and the high importance I have attached to balance in this chapter. It is indeed hard work handling the old Manton; but the modern 12 seems to leap into action almost by itself. The last mentioned gun, in fact, is probably the best balanced 12-bore in its class I have ever handled. The intermediate guns have just the intermediate qualities the figures would suggest.

By way of comparison, I measured corresponding values for the following $2\frac{3}{4}$-inch bore, 12-bore Continental guns, namely (5) a low-priced model Darne, (6) an Italian long-recoil automatic, (7) a popular Belgian boxlock, and (8) a well-known Italian over-and-under. These guns gave the results set out below.

TABLE 13. Balance Data—Other Guns

Gun No.	Actual Moment of Inertia in g units × 1000	Moment of Inertia as per cent of No. 1	D (ins.)	T (ins.)
5	126	70	9·7	$3\frac{1}{4}$
6	136	75	9·5	$5\frac{1}{2}$
7	141	78	10.0	$4\frac{7}{8}$
8	151	83	10.0	5

As might have been foreseen, the Darne came best out of this selection, though its moment of inertia was higher than expected. The secret of its handling quality evidently lay largely in its forward lightness, as indicated by its abnormally low value of $3\frac{1}{4}$ inches for T.

The rest of the guns were without this redeeming feature; but as they all had $2\frac{3}{4}$-inch chambers, they were not strictly comparable with the English guns from a technical point of view. They were nevertheless representative of guns commonly being bought here today to fire the same standard $2\frac{1}{2}$-inch cartridge, and may thus be taken, not unfairly, to illustrate my original point, by showing how far certain popular guns fall short of the standards of balance, liveliness and fast-handling that have been attained by the best guns hitherto made in this country.

There is one concluding point on balance generally, and that is that the best balanced guns go beyond what some regard as the optimum in fast-handling quality: they prefer a slower gun as being steadier and less likely to encourage checking the swing. This, of course, is a legitimate personal preference and one that might be entertained in relation to a particular kind of shooting only. The fastest-handling guns show at their best at such sport as partridge driving or rabbit, pigeon or woodcock shooting in covert, and the slowest-handling types are least disadvantageous, or, it may be, positively advantageous, for duck flighting or the like.

Shooters should recognise that the optimum compromise between fast-handling quality and steadiness is something personal to each shooter, and is not properly determinable by any fashionable trend in weight or barrel-length.

CHAPTER EIGHTEEN

PROBLEMS OF VISION

Good shooting at game or clays is the result of correct muscular response to visual stimuli. There are usually two of them—(a) the shooter's view of the target, and (b) his simultaneous view of the gun. The first is obviously indispensable, but not the second, for it is possible to shoot fairly well from the hip, with the gun unsighted. Even when it is shouldered in the ordinary way, the shooter's view of it may be totally subconscious. The extent to which he relies on seeing it depends as much on the kind of sport in which he is engaged as it does on his personal idiosyncrasies. A good shot at driven partridges, for example, would almost certainly insist that he is totally unconscious of seeing his gun at the instant of shooting; whereas a trapshooter, shooting with gun up and using a quasi-aiming technique, would almost certainly admit to being fully conscious of his.

The master eye. One thing on which both these shooters would agree would be the importance of either aligning the gun with the master eye, or of dimming or closing it if it is on the wrong side.

I take it that all readers will be familiar with the theory of the master eye as usually set out, so I must say straightaway that I believe that that theory, as commonly understood and recited in shooting books, is either incorrect or is over-simplified to a misleading extent. I once overheard an experienced sportsman explaining the matter to his companion in the following terms. 'Everybody knows,' he said, 'that one half of the brain lags behind the other. If you're right-handed, it is the left-hand half that lags, and that is why the right eye is the master—it is connected to the leading half of the brain. If the left eye is the master, the wires must be crossed.'

This explanation, reasonably interpreted, would probably pass muster pretty widely in shooting circles. Yet it is basically untrue: the eyes are not exclusively connected to the respective sides of the brain. The optic nerves, I am instructed, proceed first to a sort of transfer junction called the chiasma; and if, say, the right-hand vision centre of the brain is damaged, it is not the sight of the right eye that is alone affected, but the right-hand half of the field of view of *both* eyes. Clearly, then, the lagging of one half of the brain (whatever that may mean) cannot account for the existence of a master eye.

A firm denial. Where the popular conception of eye-mastery often goes wrong again is in assuming that the dominance of one eye is due to some specific condition, and that it is accordingly irreversible. Of course there *may* be a specific condition in the shape of a functional defect in the non-master eye—it may even be totally blind, which puts all argument out of court! But the popular conception does not suppose the existence of any functional defect: even with two perfect eyes, it is assumed that there is some specific condition, whether in the eye itself, or in the brain, or in the nerves connecting them, that assures the dominance of the master.

My professional friends firmly deny this. They assure me that there is nothing in eye-mastery, apart from some functional defect, that could be revealed by an autopsy. One ophthalmologist, who is also a shooting man, is so far sceptical about conventional master-eye doctrine as to quote the famous rustic at the Zoo—'I don't believe there ain't no sich animile.'

But as shooting men, I think we have to admit that there is such an 'animile', even though it is not so solid and immovable as the hippopotamus in question. Indeed, in the absence of a specific condition, it is often reversible, especially in young and adaptable people. In *Gough Thomas's Gun Book* I describe experiments in which reversal was easily procured in two young subjects simply by making them look with the appropriate eye through a large peepsight, which evidently acted as a command to that eye to take charge. Similarly, the presentation of a gun beneath either eye has a strong tendency to make it take over the task of pointing; though in a mature shooter with a firmly settled bias this by itself is clearly not enough to prevent the opposite eye from taking charge. But it *can* be prevented by the old trick of dimming or winking it, and I would like to look a bit more closely at this trick.

An easy choice. A strongly right-handed man, who has been shooting from his right shoulder for years, and with both eyes open, is sometimes told, when he goes to a shooting school to find out why his performance is declining, that his left eye is, or has become, the master. He is accordingly faced with the need (a) to learn to shoot from his left shoulder; (b) to have a gun with a cross-eyed stock; or (c) to wink or dim his left eye. As an alternative to (c), he may be advised to use one of those handguards with an upturned flap, or even to wear spectacles with some partial obscuration of the left-hand lens.

At one time I used to look with favour on these devices, but I have now come to regard them as mistaken. This is because, when we have both eyes open, we have a strong instinct to dodge, or to sweep out of the way, any close object that interferes with our binocular vision. All fixed obstructional devices, therefore, generate some degree of irritation or frustration, which is not conducive to the relaxed frame of mind in which the best shooting is done.

On the other hand, the dimming of one eye immediately before some decisive act, though truly a form of visual obstruction, seems entirely natural. My theory is that this is because it is no more than an easy adaptation of the protective instinct that causes us to reduce our eyes to mere slits in a variety of critical situations.

Another great advantage of the dimming technique, apart from its independence of all gadgets, is that it may, and I believe often does, cause the mastery to switch to the appropriate eye, so that in time it may be discontinued.

It would be a mistake, incidentally, to lump dimming with regular one-eyed shooting, or with the use of any of the obstructional devices mentioned. These cause a total loss of binocular vision with its great advantage of depth-perception. Dimming does not. The eye can be left wide open until the very last moment, and then closed only sufficiently to inhibit its tendency to take charge. The timing and extent of the closure are well worth practising.

Idiosyncracies. In view of the vital rôle of eyesight in shooting, it needs to be recognised that there are considerable differences between men blessed with normal vision. I have deliberately said 'vision' and not 'eyesight' because I want to exclude all the common defects for which spectacles may be prescribed, as well as all eye ailments falling in the province of an ophthalmologist. The variations I have in mind, indeed, appear to reside in the brain rather than in the eyes themselves, and are matters of much subtlety.

Not all men see the same things or see them in the same way. Depth-perception undoubtedly varies between individuals, and so does the relative impact on the consciousness of things in the central and the marginal parts of the field of view. It is for this reason, I consider, that some men attach exceptional importance to the kind of rib on a gun. For the same reason, some may benefit unexpectedly from having their guns so fitted as to give a generous view of the rib, so that the bird has accordingly to be taken floating well above the foresight.

Again, the advantages of shooting with both eyes open mean more to some men than to others. Captain Bogardus, the self-styled 'Champion Wingshot of the World', certainly shot like a wizard, but he tells us that he always took deliberate aim, and presumably closed one eye. Only recently, I have learned that some men, shooting with both eyes open, lose sight of an oncomer when it is blotted out to the aiming eye by the muzzle of the gun, notwithstanding that it remains fully and clearly in the field of view of the other eye, and in the right relation to the barrels. I find this astonishing, but I have to accept it as a fact.

Training for mastery.   I am indebted to D. McCorkindale for drawing my attention to the possibility of deliberately training one eye to become dominant, or to resume dominance after it has yielded ascendancy to the other, as even mature men with two good eyes sometimes discover when their shooting has gone off. This training or rehabilitation can be done by simply *concentrating* with the required eye on all occasions when one remembers to do so. This does not mean closing or dimming the other, which must be carefully avoided, but merely performing a mental switch. This may sound difficult, but I find that after a very little practice, it becomes quite easy. Strangely enough, it is easiest in darkness or if both eyes are closed, when one can clearly feel the mental switch. Insomniacs can practise it at night!

The objection at once arises, 'If you look at a distant object which appears practically the same to both eyes, how do you know when you are concentrating with one eye as opposed to the other? I would offer two replies to that. First, the mind, or whatever may be the right name for the higher cognitive faculty which translates the nerve impulses from the eyes into vision, has no doubt of the matter. Secondly, and more practically, if one makes the conventional test for mastery after a single sustained session of such practice, it will probably be found that mastery has at least temporarily switched. If the eyes are both more or less equally free from any specific defect, I believe therefore that this kind of practice, duly persisted in, may switch or restore dominance to a chosen eye.

A theory.   In the light of all these observations, I have come to the conclusion that, in the absence of any predisposing physical condition, the dominance of one particular eye *is merely a habit*. It is a habit which, like right- or left-handedness, had a survival value in our primitive ancestors, when split-second hesitations arising out of ambidexterity and non-dominance of either eye might have been fatal in a variety of emergencies. It may be a deeply engrained and ineradicable habit, or one that can be overcome, or even reversed, as in the instances, or by the method, I have quoted.

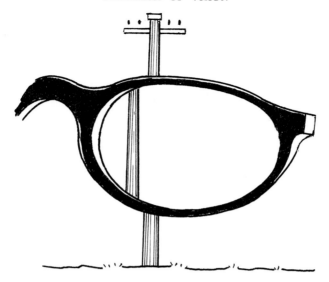

Fig. 84. Displacement of object when seen obliquely through glasses

Finally, I would say that shooters and gun fitters alike should recognise the existence of idiosyncrasies in *normal* vision; that they should try to identify them where they exist; and that they should be prepared to adapt their tactics accordingly, and avoid taking up doctrinaire positions on gun fitting and shooting technique. A budding Bogardus, for instance, may want to close one eye. It *could* be best to let him.

Shooting glasses. These need consideration whether worn for protection from sun and glare, or for protection from fragments of clay targets, or for the correction of eye defects.

It has been pointed out* that when a target is viewed obliquely through any kind of spectacles, as it is when shooting with a normal head position, it undergoes a lateral displacement, and that this may give rise to inaccurate shooting. In my own case, with ordinary glasses, as used to correct long sight, I find that there is a displacement of about 4 degrees, or over 7 feet at 35 yards! This can easily be checked by viewing a tall vertical object, such as a telegraph pole, through that part of the glasses through which the foresight is usually viewed in the act of shooting. The effect is as shown in fig. 84.

* 'Eyesight and Shooting', by G. A. D. Hammond *Shooting Times*, July 18–24, 1974

If the target and the foresight are both viewed through approximately the same part of the lens, they would both undergo the same displacement, and all would be well so far as aiming the gun is concerned. But two disturbing possibilities remain. If the target were first seen *over* the glasses, and then brought within the spectacle frame, it would undergo a *sudden* displacement which would almost certainly disconcert the shooter. The other thing, which is not a possibility but a fact, is that even if target and foresight are both viewed through the glasses, so that they are both displaced equally, the visual and manual pointability of the gun are thus thrown out of accord. (Chapter 20 should make this clear.) Trap-shooters in particular cannot afford to ignore this point. Accordingly, any spectacles used for competitive clay shooting should be of the deeply concave form, whereby the eye looks more or less straight through the glass at all points, and not obliquely through it, as in the case of ordinary spectacles, even those with normal toric lenses. Further, the lenses should be large enough to exclude, so far as possible, vision outside them.

Two minor points in conclusion. Contact lenses have been highly recommended by shooters whose eyes need major correction, especially in rainy weather. Also, a shooter with marked (astigmatic) asymmetry or the condition known as lazy eye may be wise not to persist in trying to shoot with both eyes open.

CHAPTER NINETEEN

STOCKS AND FITTING

There is no doubt that the great majority of shooting men use guns
for which they have never been properly fitted. They are guns which
they inherited, or bought second-hand or ready-made. Sometimes the
stocks have been shortened or lengthened to remedy a gross misfit; less
frequently the bend or cast may have been altered, and by such
adjustments the owner may occasionally have arrived at a good fitting.
But in the majority of cases, the shooter is called on to adapt himself
to a greater or lesser degree to his weapon. Thanks to the flexibility
and infinite adaptability of the species, he usually succeeds in doing
this sufficiently well to shoot satisfactorily, according to his natural
ability, and without any significant discomfort.

Still, there can be no doubt of the added pleasure and proficiency
to be derived from a really well fitting gun—one that 'fits like a glove',
and comes into place sweetly and easily, as though of its own accord,
without obtruding itself in the slightest degree on the shooter's attention. To a man of normal physique, such a fitting is often attainable
by minor alterations to an existing stock, and the requirements of such
a fitting will well repay study. Before I go further, however, I should
draw attention to the dangers of fitting a gun without shooting it.

One of the commonest things to happen in any gun shop is for the
prospective purchaser of a new or second-hand gun to throw it up to
his shoulder a few times to check the length of the stock, and to see
if it 'comes up nicely' to chosen marks. If the buyer is of normal physique, and if the gun is a new one, there is every likelihood that it will
do so. The gunsmith may then invite the buyer to go through the
motions of taking a snapshot at one of his eyes, which he denotes with
his forefinger. He thus checks the shooter for master eye, and observes
whether that eye comes into place at about the right distance above

the standing breech. If the gun survives these tests, it is pronounced a good fit; the deal is concluded; and the buyer goes off with his new treasure, in high expectation of being able to shoot better with it than he has ever shot before.

He may well do so; but on the other hand, he may not. There may be at least two niggers in the woodpile, and the one I am considering now is the possibility that the gun may not shoot accurately to the point of aim. If the gun has been properly fitted, this would have been spotted at the time. The fitter would have noticed that the shooter's snapshots were falling, say, below the mark, indicating a need for some straightening of the stock so as to raise the comb, and thus lift the master eye by an amount sufficient to correct the error.

But in the simple gun-shop routine I have described it is assumed that the gun shoots accurately if and when aimed as a rifle; and this is an assumption that is often not justified by experience.

Inaccuracy in a shotgun, according to its degree, is an insidious thing. Unlike the corresponding fault in a rifle, it is not instantly detectable: indeed, a man may use an inaccurate gun for years without being aware of anything amiss. For all that, it is likely to act as a constant drag on his performance. Birds that should be taken by the centre of the pattern fall into the outer zone; and those that could be successfully killed, if not so cleanly, by the outer zone fall into the wild fringe, where they may be pricked by a chance pellet, or missed altogether.

In all my subsequent references to fitting, therefore, I would like it to be borne in mind that there can be no proper fitting without shooting. Even when a gun has been stocked or altered to try-gun dimensions the shooting check cannot reliably be dispensed with.

Terminology

First, we must be clear about our terminology. In this country, the dimensions of a gun-stock are normally defined by the measurements indicated in fig. 85 opposite, which also gives the names of the parts.

It will be seen that these measurements do not fully define the shape of the stock—for example, the depth from heel to toe, or the length of the comb measured forwards from the heel. Nor is any note normally taken of the thickness of the stock, particularly as affecting the radius of the comb where it comes into contact with the shooter's face. These matters are usually left to established ideas of normality, though note may need to be taken of them in special cases.

Also, there is a dimension known to the Americans as 'pitch', to which they sometimes pay great attention. It is determined by the overall angle between the butt and the line of sight, but does not enter into

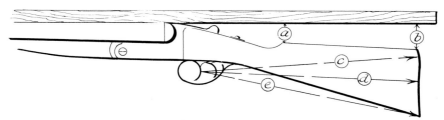

Fig. 85. The measurements of a gun-stock. *a* is the bend to comb, and *b* the bend to heel. *c* is the length to heel, *d* the length to butt, and *e* the length to toe. The lateral deviation of the stock, measured at the butt, is the 'cast': 'cast-off' if it is to the right, and 'cast on' if it is to the left

English parlance. We avoid it by specifying the length of the stock at the three points shown.

Finding the correct stock. It is well known that if a man goes to two expert gunfitters he may collect two different prescriptions for a stock to fit him. Yet it may mean no more than that the two fitters concerned have different ideas of correct shooting posture. One, for example, may advise the shooter that he should face more towards the target than the other, and may prescribe more cast-off in consequence. Both fitters may therefore be right, subject to the shooter duly conforming to the advice given.

But there is something that overrides any such considerations. It is what I would call the principle of minimum adaptation, and leads to the conception of an ideal or natural stock.

Thus, it is agreed that the best results in wing-shooting are attained by instinctively pointing the gun where the shooter is looking, rather than by deliberate aiming. By use and habit, he may have become thoroughly accustomed to a particular gun and shooting posture, and may be able to shoot accordingly with reasonable satisfaction and success. But if the gun requires any adaptation on his part—if he has to rely on doing this or that with his head or limbs or body—he will shoot well only so long as he does these things. They may indeed have become habitual, but under the stress of fatigue or excitement—especially excitement—such acquired habits can and do break down. When that happens, the thing that should be done to ensure proper adaptation may not get done, and the result is an incorrectly mounted gun and a miss.

The ideal is accordingly to leave the shooter free to take up what, for him, is a strictly natural, energetic pointing attitude, and to mould the gun, so to speak, to that attitude. It is the one from which he will have the least possible tendency to depart. What the attitude is may be found by experiment with any intelligent and uninhibited shooter, without a gun and preferably with no idea of the purpose of the experiment. He is asked to pretend to be pointing out something in the distance to a companion, using his left hand if he is right-handed, or *vice versa*. The thing, whatever it is, is fast disappearing, and it is vitally necessary that his companion, who is not so quick-sighted as he is, should be brought to see and recognise it. 'Look!' he should say, 'there it is—there, *there*!'

The result, with a suitable subject, is a delightful demonstration of the ideal shooting attitude—weight on left foot, left shoulder forward, head slightly forward and turned about 25 degrees to the right, and body turned about 45. If a gun could now be moulded to that attitude, it would conform to the principle of minimum adaptation: it would be that person's natural gun stock, not dependent on the acquisition of any special habits for correct mounting.

But the 'moulding' would need to be correctly done. The butt must rest fully and fairly into the shoulder recess. The comb must rest snugly and firmly in the angle between the cheekbone and the jaw; and these conditions being satisfied, the eye must be in line with the rib and just above it. Bend and cast-off are thus determined. The stock must also be of the correct length—not long enough to catch whatever may be the appropriate clothing, and not so short that the thumb or fingers can strike the nose when the gun recoils. (I like to have a clearance of 1 inch between my nose and the tip of my little finger.) Too short a stock can cause or promote bruising of the second finger by the trigger guard. A normal length for an average man is $14\frac{3}{8}$ inches.

A vital measurement.   A measurement of the utmost importance is the drop to that part of the comb which comes immediately below the cheekbone, because that is what determines the height of the gun's backsight, which is the shooter's eye. If the gun delivers its charge truly to the point of aim, the centre of the eye should come about $\frac{3}{16}$ inch above the standing breech. This will cause the gun to print its pattern about 9 inches high at 40 yards—a desirable thing in a game gun— and will normally require a bend to comb of about $1\frac{1}{2}$ inches. If the gun shoots low, the comb *must* be raised—say, to the extent of $\frac{1}{16}$ inch for every 2 or 3 inches by which it is required to raise the mean point of impact of the charge at 40 yards.

Low-shooting guns are commonly cured by straightening the whole of the stock. This is wrong if it raises the butt materially above its correct position in the shoulder. The vertical position of the butt (i.e. the bend

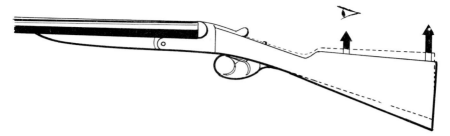

Fig. 86. Curing low-shooting gun by straightening stock

to heel) should desirably be determined by the length of the shooter's neck and the slope of his shoulders, and by nothing else.

If the comb has thus to be raised to cure low shooting, it can be done temporarily and experimentally—or even permanently—by an indiarubber comb-raiser. These are procurable in various thicknesses from any good gunsmith and are stuck on the original comb with a modern adhesive. For a permanent alteration, a well-matched piece of wood can be added to the stock. If a man has an unusually long neck and sloping shoulders, he may require a bend to heel considerably more than the 2 to $2\frac{1}{4}$ inches found on average British guns. In that event, he may tend to suffer from bruised cheek—a condition that can be alleviated or cured by a level comb, or even one sloping slightly upwards to the rear.

American guns often have more bend than English ones, and no cast-off. A man accustomed to an English gun can usually shoot well with an American stock, but he has to adapt himself by leaning his head slightly over to the right in order to get his eye into line with the rib. This he can easily do by virtue of the greater bend; but his eyes are no longer strictly level, which cannot improve his shooting, and there is an obvious and regrettable departure involved from the minimum-adaptation principle which I think is so desirable to follow.

There are several minor aspects of gun fitting, but provided that a shooter has familiarised himself with the basic requirements here described, he will be in a position to pursue the complete satisfaction of his needs in his own way. A critical and observant friend can help to check the fit of an existing gun by noting any difference between the shooter's natural pointing attitude and his attitude when pointing the gun, particular attention being paid to the position of the head.

The grip. The hand or grip of a gun deserves careful attention.

The first requirement of a good, natural grip is that it should be of the right size, and the concensus of opinion among our best gunmakers appears to be in favour of $4\frac{1}{8}$ inches as the proper girth of a straight-handed stock for a 12-bore game gun for use by a man with normal hands. Four guns by different makers which I have recently checked reveal exact uniformity in this particular. (A Japanese O/U of the same bore, incidentally, measures $4\frac{5}{8}$ inches.)

A point here is that it is disadvantageous for a shooter to have a slenderer grip than he strictly needs. Apart from the greater risk of breakage, a slender grip, other things being equal, will cause a gun to shoot low. If, therefore, because of his having unusually small hands, a shooter has to have a slender grip, he should contemplate the need for a straighter stock in order to restore the charge elevation. As for the cross-sectional shape of the grip, this, of course, is usually a moderate oval, the proportions of which can be left to normal practice. Some gunmakers, however, favour a section resembling a rounded diamond, the idea presumably being to enlist the tactile sense against any tendency to cant the gun.

A basic necessity is to have the triggers correctly placed in relation to the natural grip of the gun. By natural grip I mean the place where the hand finds itself when taking hold of the gun unthinkingly with all four fingers. With the hand in this position, it should be possible to curl the forefinger round quite naturally and place the pad of the finger comfortably on the front trigger. This will leave something of a gap between the second finger and the back of the trigger guard. In active shooting, this gap will be partially, but only partially, taken up; but there will be no pressure between the finger and the guard. If there is, no matter how firmly the shooter may grip his gun when firing, there will always be a risk of bruised second finger, which can be a troublesome and painful complaint. The risk can be, and should be, reduced by giving the back of the guard a marked rearward slope.

The advantageous placing of the safety catch and the top lever in relation to the grip is more important than may appear at first sight. This is because, in our conventional guns, they usually *are* advantageously placed. But in some other guns they are not, when we may become acutely, or even painfully, aware of the difference.

Thus, it should be possible to operate the safety catch easily and naturally without disturbing the normal hold of the grip. This would appear to be of some importance to those shooters who walk with their safety catches on, and only throw them off to take a shot, which it should be easy for them to do without disturbing their hold and having to re-settle it before they can pull the trigger.

These are the shooters, I take it, who are most prone to the nasty accident of having their thumbs split by the top lever when the gun recoils. This is a risk which is minimised by a generous distance between the safety catch and the end of the lever, which there usually is in a good conventional gun, but not in all others.

Functional chequering. The only remaining aspect of the grip that requires mention here is that of its surface quality, as determined by the chequering. There is a tendency, which I think is regrettable, to regard the quality of the chequering as being determined by its fineness of grain.

Here we come up against personal preferences, and I can only say that, for secure, non-slipping grip, and one which combines that basic requirement with the happy medium between roughness and smoothness, I would choose a chequering of about 20 lines to the inch, and with pyramids not too sharp, but somewhat flattened. I have a gun with the finest 'powder-grain' chequering, of 30 lines per inch, which, even when it was new and unworn, was too smooth for the best possible effect in my hands.

Variations. The normal two-triggered English gun has a straight 'hand' or grip to facilitate manipulation of the rear trigger; but if a single trigger is used, a pistol grip or, rather, a semi-pistol grip, has considerable attractions.

The normal English fore-end terminates just where most shooters prefer to hold their barrels. Some of the best gunmakers—Purdey's in particular—accordingly make the tip of the fore-end full and round, when it acts as a comfortable handstop, and tends to discourage changes in hold, which are not desirable.

The so-called beavertail fore-end, a broad and clumsy affair, is intended chiefly for the protection of the shooter's hand from hot barrels. Such a fore-end is a sad disfigurement to a good double gun, though a modified version, known as a semi-beavertail, can be pleasant to handle and is not too obtrusive.

Wood. The first requirement of a stock is that it shall be of sound, well-grown and well-seasoned walnut, free from shakes, galls and splits, and straight-grained through the hand or grip. A figured walnut stock is attractive in appearance, but can be less robust than one made of plainer timber, according to how the grain runs at critical points. But a stock so exotic that it cannot be taken into the field without causing its owner acute anxiety is simply a downright nuisance. There is little doubt that the average sportsman who is keen on a good gun pays more attention to the quality of his stock than he does to the quality of his patterns. Yet it is a great mistake to do so.

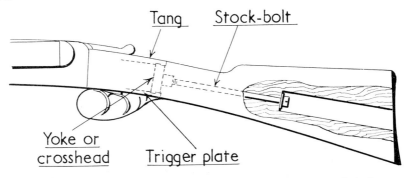

Fig. 87. Attachment of stock to action by means of a stock-bolt

Stock-bolts. Many imported guns, and especially over-and-unders, are nowadays fitted with stock-bolts. These have some marked pros and cons.

A stock-bolt is a long bolt running through the small or hand of a gun stock, and arranged to hold the stock tightly up to the rear face of the action, as shown in fig. 87. It is thus a fixing device as commonly applied to shotguns, but it also serves—or reputedly serves—to strengthen the stock against breaking. In some applications, this is indeed its main function.

English guns have not hitherto used stock-bolts. The common way of fastening the stock to the action is by means of a strong screw—the so-called breech-pin—which passes through the tang or strap and screws into a solid rectangular block forming part of the trigger plate (fig. 88). Birmingham makers usually reinforce this arrangement by another screw—the hand-pin—which binds the tail of the trigger plate to the tail of the tang, as also shown in fig. 88. The end of this screw can be seen behind the safety-catch of Birmingham guns. I regard it as a desirable feature in boxlock guns, though it is unnecessary in side-locks, because the lock-plates themselves usually bind the head of the stock securely to the action.

These mechanical details have a significance for the ordinary non-mechanical shooter, because if they are varied, or not accurately executed, he may find himself with a gun that is loose on its stock.

An example recently came my way. It was a Greener gun—a boxlock with a short tang and no hand-pin, like most of its tribe. There was a conspicuous wobble between action and stock.

In a gun fitted with a stock-bolt, the breech-pin is dispensed with, and the rearward extremities of the tang and the trigger plate are united

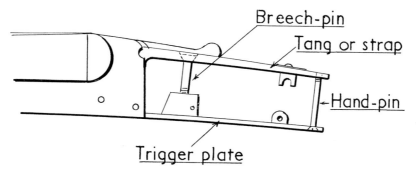

Fig. 88. Normal Birmingham method of attaching stock to action

by a short, stiff yoke or crosshead (fig. 87) into which the stock-bolt screws. If everything has been correctly designed, the bolt not only holds the stock tightly up to the action, but forces its head between confining surfaces which correct any tendency for it to spread and split. If at any time the stock should show a tendency to work loose, through the shrinking of imperfectly seasoned wood or otherwise, it can be corrected by merely tightening the bolt, access to the head of which is obtained by unscrewing the butt-plate.

Bearing in mind its capacity for strengthening the weakest part of the stock, the stock-bolt sounds a very attractive device. It is to be found in several Japanese and Continental guns, though the Spaniards appear to stick conservatively to British practice.

But the stock-bolt is not without its disadvantages. The outstanding objection is that it is a great hindrance to the fit of the gun being adjusted by the familiar process of bending the stock. Good guns last a long time, and often change hands more than once—perhaps several times; and it is more than likely that length, bend and cast will need altering to suit a particular owner. A light stock-bolt could perhaps be bent *in situ*, but it would then tend to become a fixture. Usually the woodwork has to be cut away to accommodate the bolt in its new position. Then, indeed, the stock-bolt earns its description of 'the stocker's curse'.

CHAPTER TWENTY

POINTABILITY

Experienced and critical shooters frequently refer to one gun as being more 'pointable' than another, and the term has become increasingly part of the clay shooter's vocabulary. Yet for all the undoubted fact that pointability is a valuable attribute of a gun, its nature is obscure, and even the shooters who prize it most are seldom prepared to define it intelligibly. Clearly, it is necessary to do so before discussing the subject.

When I asked a well-known clay shooter what he meant by saying that a certain gun was eminently pointable, he replied after some hesitation that the gun seemed to point easily and more or less of its own accord where he wanted it to point. That affords a sufficient clue to the nature of pointability, and so I would say that it chiefly comprises two things, which I call Manual Pointability and Visual Pointability respectively, plus a strong tincture of a dynamic quality which is really part of the subject of Balance (see Chapter 17).

Manual pointability resembles rhythm in music as being the fundamental ingredient. It is based on our ability to point a thing such as an arm and forefinger or a straight stick at a visible object without being able to see the thing with which we are doing the pointing. If, in an otherwise totally dark room, we put up some faintly visible object, such as a luminous watch-dial, we find that we can point our finger at it with complete confidence, which will be justified when someone then switches on the light. Indeed, so remarkable are our innate powers of co-ordination that we can sight an object in broad daylight, shut our eyes, and then point. When we open them, we find that we have usually pointed fairly accurately, but not, of course, so accurately as if we had kept the object in view all the time.

If we repeat the original experiment using, not our arm and fore-finger, but a straight stick, we find that we can do nearly, but not quite so well. And if we use a crooked stick, of which only the forward end is straight (rather like a gun) we normally find that our performance has declined further.

Keeping these points in mind, then, I would say that:

(1) Manual pointability in a gun is that quality, derived from its form and proportions, which facilitates its being directed *manually* to-wards a visible object, the gun itself being unsighted, as in shooting from the hip.

(2) Visual pointability, on the other hand, is that quality in a gun which facilitates its being directed *visually* to an object, without invoking any aid from the shooter's powers of muscular co-ordi-nation, as when laying an ancient cannon.

Pointability, without any qualifying adjective, usually connotes (or should connote) a combination of both manual and visual kinds; and when it is borne in mind that, in shotgun shooting, the target and, of course, the gun, are usually moving, it will be recognised why I admitted some intrusion of dynamic balance into its appraisal by the average shooter. Nevertheless, there is a tendency to use the term as if it referred only to the visual kind—probably because it is the one that is the more apparent, more readily assessed and more easily improved, if necessary.

There is the further point that, owing to the dominance of vision among our senses, visual pointability is more important than manual, and will override it if there is any actual conflict between the two, which there is not in sporting guns.

At the same time, the best shooting is undoubtedly done when the two aspects are maximised in harmony, and are further aided by a favourable dynamic balance.

Visual pointability

In a shotgun, the things that determine visual pointability are the barrel or barrels, the rib and the foresight, and the aim of the discriminating shooter should be to increase the visual impact of the gun to the op-timum value, *which will be the maximum consistent with not attracting his conscious attention to it*. If this optimum is exceeded, as, for example, by fitting an unduly conspicuous foresight, it may induce an aiming or 'poking' technique, to the probable detriment of performance.

It does not follow that the makers of best English game guns have been right in reducing the size of their simple bead foresights to the vanishing point; nor does it follow that performance would benefit from the use of one of the luminous (e.g. fluorescent Perspex) sights on the market. What constitutes the best kind of foresight is undoubtedly a personal matter. Lighting conditions, too, are a considerable factor; but experimenting is easy in this instance and may yield undeniable benefit.

Owing to the fact that plain well-blued barrels can be almost invisible when viewed obliquely against a background of sky, the rib may make an important contribution to visual pointability. In side-by-side guns, the plain hollow rib achieves this by the dark grooves on either side of it. These are usefully accentuated by a high, flat rib, irrespective of whether it is file-cut or effectively knurled. The same applies to the high, narrow Churchill-type rib. (It should be noted that the normal Churchill rib is *high forward*, and, when substituted for an ordinary rib, may noticeably depress the mean point of impact of the charge.)

In single-barrelled guns or over-and-unders, the rib is a well-nigh indispensable aid to visual pointability. Further, lacking the dark grooves which outline the side-by-side rib, it is important that it should be effectively knurled or otherwise treated to ensure that it will not become more or less invisible by reflected skylight just as the gun is coming into position for a shot. Deep, dark, longitudinal grooves, as in the Browning 'Broadway' over-and-under, preserve the pointability of the rib under most lighting conditions.

For the reason already given, the barrel or barrels of a gun cannot by themselves be relied on to afford adequate visual pointability, and a single-barrelled gun or over-and-under without a rib may profit by a more conspicuous foresight than would be appropriate with one. The trap-shooter, with his quasi-aiming technique, usually benefits by adding a mid-sight—a small bead—to the rib of his gun.

Manual pointability

The conditions for realising the best manual pointability are not so easy to define. Some guidance may be found in the universal practice of men from the earliest times when making weapons, tools and implements that have to be pointed or directed towards an object. Unless influenced by incidental requirements, they have invariably chosen a straight shaft of a size that can easily be grasped in a fairly well closed hand. I believe that most men, in the absence of previous familiarity with a gun, would choose something of the proportions of a common broom-handle for pointing, two-handedly and without visual alignment, at a distant object. Of course, a gun of broom-handle form could not be brought to the shoulder in alignment with the eye, but the best degree of manual pointability would probably be realised in a gun approximating as closely as possible to that form. A single-barrelled gun with a small fore-end and a straight 'hand' or grip, or a corresponding English-style side-by-side, comes fairly close to it.

This conclusion is hard to reconcile with the pistol-grip and bulky fore-end of the clay shooter's over-and-under, still less so with the bloated fore-end of the average self-loader, except on grounds of familiarity, and the subservience of manual to visual pointability.

There is a remaining point of some significance in connection with manual pointability. It concerns the 'feel' of the gun, as determined by the roughness or smoothness of the chequering and the shape of the parts handled. If these give rise to unpleasant tactile sensations, manual pointability will assuredly suffer. One example will suffice. I once shot with an over-and-under with a grooved fore-end, the grooves being presumably intended for the comfortable accommodation of the finger tips. Their sharp edges, however, were decidedly irritating to the tips of my fingers, and I could not bring myself to ignore them. Competitive clay shooters cannot afford to submit to any such distracting irritations.

CHAPTER TWENTY-ONE

SIGHTING THE SHOTGUN

We speak of sighting rifles as an operation essential to their correct functioning, but seldom, if ever, refer to sighting a shotgun. Yet this, too, is an essential operation, though it is usually comprehended in the term 'gun fitting'.

Gun fitting, indeed, is largely concerned with adjusting the dimensions of the stock so that when the shooter puts the gun to his shoulder easily, naturally and unthinkingly, his master eye, which takes the place of the backsight of a rifle, will come into the right position above the barrels to ensure a correctly placed shot. The importance of this operation is tacitly acknowledged even by those shooters who insist that they are totally unconscious of seeing anything of their guns in the course of active shooting, for they are frequently the very ones who are most insistent on a correct fit. This is quite understandable, for the barrels, rib and foresight come right into the centre of the shooter's field of vision and are of necessity seen, if only subconsciously; and it may be demonstrated that by what they thus see, shooters are substantially aided in the correct pointing of their guns. But what is the 'right position' for the master eye? It is a question that repays examination.

It can be taken that all conventional guns tend to shoot below the projection of the bore axis. Accordingly, the backsight (that is, the shooter's eye) must be raised to a greater extent than the foresight above the axis of the barrels. To a large extent, this is ensured by the greater diameter of the barrels at the breech end and the corresponding height of the standing breech over which the shooter sights his target. Instinctively, he will raise his eye at least until the standing breech is no impediment to his vision, which means that he will expose the whole of the pupil of his eye above it; and since the pupil in fair daylight is about $\frac{1}{8}$ inch in diameter, the basic line of sight may be taken as running

184

from the centre of the pupil (which will be $\frac{1}{16}$ inch above the stand-ing breech) to the tip of the foresight and thence to the mark.

Is this basic line of sight, then, the line of sight to which the gun should be fitted? The general answer is no, or not necessarily, and for three reasons:

(1)   The elevation of the breech above the foresight may be insufficient to compensate for the gun's natural low-shooting tendency.

(2)   The general tendency of shooters to shoot below the mark, especi-ally when tired, makes it expedient to fit the gun so as to ensure that the pattern centre will be some inches above the mark.

(3)   It is also expedient to improve the gun's visual pointability (see Chapter 20) by giving the shooter a better view of the rib and barrels than is afforded by the basic line of sight, as above defined.

What this comes down to in practice, is that, *provided the superelevation of the breech is sufficient to correct the gun's natural low-shooting tendency*, the eye can advantageously be raised about $\frac{3}{16}$ inch in all. One of our greatest coaches, Percy Stanbury, has expressed this in familiar lan-guage by saying that he likes to see the whole of the shooter's eye (that is, the iris as well as the pupil) above the standing breech. This will raise the charge centre by about 8 inches at 40 yards.

But having thus opened the door to expediency in fitting or sighting the shotgun—having, that is to say, admitted that the best line of sight for practical shooting may differ considerably from what I have defined as the basic line—we can ask ourselves without constraint, what *is* the best line for the best success? The answer must be that it depends on the individual. If we aim a gun like a rifle at a stationary mark, and fix it there in a rest, and then progressively raise our aiming eye more and more above the standing breech, we find ourselves seeing more and more of the barrels, whilst the aiming mark floats higher and higher above the foresight. In this process, visual pointability improves up to a point, after which it declines through lack of obvious correlation between gun and target. At the same time, dependence on manual pointability increases. In the limit, the shooter is, in effect, shooting from the hip. Visual pointability has then practically gone, and depen-dence on manual pointability has become absolute. Clearly, the indivi-dual holds the key to the optimum.

The effect of tension.   In the search for that optimum, there is a con-sideration to which Barney Hartman, the celebrated Canadian skeet champion, has drawn my attention. He points out that an individual's needs in the way of fit vary according to whether or not he is in a state of tension. I am sure that he is right; and adapting the point to my present theme, I would say that a shooter in fast and spontaneous action almost certainly uses a higher line of sight than he does when 'dry' shooting, say, or shooting at a disappearing bird-target on a gunmaker's plate.

An outstanding case in point has recently come to my notice. It concerned a one-gun man who shot game successfully but was no good at all at trapshooting, with its more deliberate technique. But when he fitted a supplementary, superelevated rib to his gun for trapshooting only, he became the star performer at a well-known Continental gun club.

Foresights, ribs and barrels
So far, I have confined myself to what amounts to the correct positioning of the shotgun's backsight, which, in the present context, is where gun fitting stops. But there are other features of the gun involved in the sighting process, namely, the foresight, rib and barrels. They are more appropriately considered in the next chapter.

CHAPTER TWENTY-TWO

PROBLEMS OF ACCURACY

In this chapter I aim to discuss the accuracy of shotguns in the broad sense, as referring to the precision with which they perform all their functions. The subject is of special importance to the trapshooter.

The primary function is, of course, accuracy of fire, and there are three ways in which the accuracy of a double-barrelled shotgun can be rated. They can be more readily distinguished if we imagine it to be firing, not charges of shot, but solid slugs.

We might then be concerned about (a) the ability of each barrel to make a tight group. Or (b) we might be more concerned that the barrels should not shoot apart, or cross-fire. Or (c) we might be most interested in where each barrel shot in relation to the line of sight, as determined by the breech, rib and foresight.

All I can say about the first of these aspects of accuracy is that a shotgun, fired from a rest, does not reliably centre its charge on the same spot from round to round—in other words, it does not make a tight group in the rifleman's sense. This is a matter worthy of more attention than it has so far received. It is most unlikely to be a material factor in game shooting, but the serious competitive trapshooter, with his fully choked gun and his concern for a single dropped bird in a hundred, should recognise it as a possible source of inconsistency with a particular combination of gun and cartridge.

As to (b)—the possibility of the barrels shooting apart or cross-firing—this is a source of inaccuracy which is absent or negligible in side-by-side guns, but a considerable factor with over-and-unders. It arises from the fact that in the former, the force of resistance to recoil makes the same angle to the horizontal irrespective of which barrel is fired (fig. 89). The jump on firing is accordingly the same in each case;

187

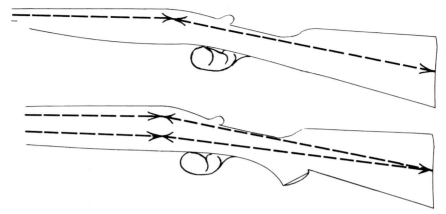

Fig. 89.   Forces of recoil and reaction are at same angle for both barrels
of side-by-side gun (top), but not in over-and-under (bottom)

and if the two barrels have been laid together with the proper convergence, their symmetry in relation to the vertical plane will ensure that
they both shoot to the same mark if there is no cast, or very nearly
so with cast of normal amount.

But in an over-and-under, the resistance to recoil, which acts along
a line drawn from the middle of the butt to the centre of the breech
face of the appropriate barrel, is much less direct for the upper barrel
than it is for the lower. There will accordingly be an increased jump
when the upper barrel is fired, and, for accurate shooting, this has to
be corrected by barrel convergence, which would appear to be a more
critical matter with these guns than it is with side-by-sides, and one
that is not adequately attended to in all cases.

In consequence, most over-and-unders tend to shoot higher with the
top barrel than with the bottom one, sometimes to a very marked
extent. This inaccuracy, however, when present in only a moderate
degree, is widely held to be advantageous when the bottom barrel is
fired first at rising targets, especially if the shooter is tired, and prone
to miss under.

The third source (c) of inaccuracy of fire, as exemplified by the tendency of long-barrelled side-by-side guns to shoot low, is normally
amenable to correction by suitable adjustment of the line of sight. This
can be done by raising the comb, either independently or by straightening the stock (Chapter 19). Some less conventional and more specula-
tive cures are discussed in my *Shooting Facts and Fancies* (Section 11,
Chapter 75).

The accuracy of single-barrelled guns can be seriously affected by the addition of muzzle attachments such as variable chokes. Cause and cure are dealt with in Chapter 6.

Warping of double guns. As previously indicated, when one barrel of a double gun is fired repeatedly, so that it becomes much warmer than the other, the unequal thermal expansion causes the whole barrel assembly to warp, whereby the MPI may shift sufficiently to affect a trapshooter's results. Even with sustained accuracy of pointing by the shooter, the target may thus no longer be caught by the dense central part of the pattern, but by the thinner outer zone, thus giving the impression of a deterioration in pattern quality.

I have calculated that an effective temperature difference of 50° F (28° C) between the two barrels of a 12-bore over-and-under gun would cause the barrel assembly to warp until it conformed to an arc of a circle of about 250 feet radius, and that the MPI would thus shift by some 12 inches at 35 yards. Owing to the broad assumptions involved in such a calculation, however, I would not represent it as affording more than a rough indication of the possibilities. Further, the Winchester company has drawn my attention to the fact that any warping of this sort in over-and-under guns is accompanied by a change in the sight-line, which partly compensates the effect.

Journée, using a double rifle (presumably for the easier observation of results) found that after firing 10 shots from one barrel, the MPI at 109 yards had shifted by 19·7 inches. I myself obtained roughly confirmatory results with a 20-bore over-and-under; but corresponding experiments with two 12-bore guns (an over-and-under and a side-by-side) failed. The net effect with any particular gun *and cartridge* can therefore only be determined by actual trial.

Some gunmakers (e.g. Krieghoff and Remington) have nevertheless been sufficiently impressed by the possibility of warping as a potential source of inaccuracy to provide against it in their basic designs. In the recently introduced Remington 3200, the two barrels are solidly joined at the breech end only. At the muzzle, they are united by a slip ring, which enables either to expand independently of the other.

There would accordingly appear to be some justification on these grounds alone for the practice of many trapshooters using ordinary over-and-unders of always firing both barrels, irrespective of whether they have scored with the first.

Mirage, heat-haze and shimmer. These three sources of inaccurate shooting, which can plague the rifleman and the trapshooter, are variations of the same basic phenomenon. Here I am concerned chiefly with the trapshooter, whose target may dance, or become indistinct, or even momentarily appear to be bodily displaced from its actual position.

Two causes combine to produce these effects: first, the expansion of air when it is heated, whereby it tends to rise as cooler and heavier air flows in beneath it; and secondly, the fact that when light passes from cool air to warm, or *vice versa*, and at an angle to the boundary layer, it undergoes a bending or refraction.

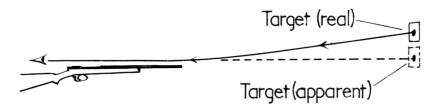

Fig. 90.   Effect of mirage in rifle shooting

When a gun barrel is heated by firing, or by exposure to a hot sun, or both, it heats the air in its immediate vicinity; and the rifleman, shooting with iron sights, and with his line of sight close to the barrel, may find himself viewing his target through a relatively stable skin or layer of hot air. In these circumstances, his bullseye may appear to be displaced bodily downwards (fig. 90). This is the true mirage. It is aided by the fact that the rifleman holds his barrel still, so that, on a windless day, there is nothing much to disturb the more or less adherent layer of hot air immediately adjacent to the barrel. The conditions correspond to those producing the mirage seen by motorists in hot weather—the 'water on the road' phenomenon—when light from the sky may be bent upwards from the road surface into the motorist's eye, in the same way as the light from the target is bent upwards into the rifleman's eye in fig. 90.

The trapshooter, I take it, seldom sees a true mirage. Shooting with a moving gun, and making less use of a deliberate aiming technique, he is more affected by the rising currents of air from the heated barrel, in which hot and cold air, mixed and moving, produce the shimmering or hazy appearance that is so familiar above heated objects.

Though widely recognised as an occasional nuisance and an impediment to top scoring, heat-shimmer does not appear to have attracted the attention it deserves from designers of trap guns or writers on shooting.

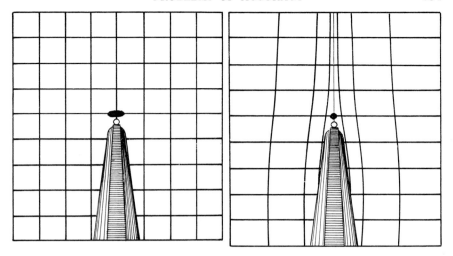

Fig. 91. Clay target and squared background as seen over cold barrel

Fig. 92. Clay target and squared background as seen over hot barrel

In the circumstances, I undertook some simple experiments with curious results. I ruled up a white cardboard target into half-inch squares, with an elliptical aiming mark in the centre corresponding to the apparent size of a clay pigeon at about 30 yards. Pointing at the aiming mark, I fixed an over-and-under gun in a rest, with the fore-end removed, so that the barrels could be conveniently heated by a blow-lamp from below. The appearance of the target was thus as in fig. 91.

I then ran the blow-lamp up and down the barrels from beneath, until they were as hot as they would have been after a quick round of DTL, which was probably about 150° F. All this, I should explain, was done indoors, and in a small room with door and windows closed, so as to have air as still as could conveniently be arranged.

It was then found that the appearance of the target had undergone a marked and systematic change. There was no haze or shimmer, but a regular distortion of the field of view in the neighbourhood of the target, which now presented the appearance shown in fig. 92. It was abundantly clear that, if these conditions could be reproduced in the field, the shooter could be betrayed into significant errors of direction, for the target, and the space to one side of it and immediately above it, had apparently shrunk horizontally to less than half its true value. I estimate that pointing errors of as much as 10 minutes of angle could thus arise. (The effective radius of a full-choke pattern at 30 yards is about 40–45 minutes.)

But in the field, with both gun and air in motion, this regular distortion would be converted into an erratic and variable shimmering, which I had no difficulty in reproducing by swinging the gun sideways in its rest, and by fanning it; and I found it easy to appreciate how disconcerting to the shooter the variable appearance and motion thus induced in the target would be. It seemed fairly obvious that in trying to swing smoothly on a wavering and fluctuating target, a shooter would be likely to fall into larger errors than any regular and steady distortion of the target and its background would provoke.

It is an unfortunate fact that in this matter everything is against the trapshooter, especially if he shoots in hot, still, sunny weather. The over-and-under type of gun which he favours, with its high, narrow rib, concentrates the convection currents into the line of sight, where they cause maximum interference with his clear view of the target. Further, during the brief interval while he awaits his shot with gun mounted and stationary, a well-established column of heated air rises from the barrels, which the low transverse velocity of many of the targets, and therefore the small angular movement on the part of the gun, does little to disperse (see fig. 93a). If, on top of all this, the shooter has been standing about in the sun while awaiting his call, his gun may be hot even before he starts to shoot.

I believe that most trapshooters would accept these facts as being some of the inescapable difficulties of the game; but I hope to show that they can be reduced, and by means that are fully practicable.

I have satisfied myself by further experiments that the best way of avoiding heat-shimmer is to use the broadest acceptable rib, and to keep it as cool as possible. A broad rib tends to divert the rising convection currents to one side and the other of the line of sight, and a cool rib does not set up any convection currents of its own. (It should be noted that a broad rib does not necessarily incur the loss of a narrow sighting line, as I hope to make clear.)

My experiments were made with a 1 inch strip of polished stainless steel applied as a supplementary rib to the normal $\frac{5}{16}$ inch raised and ventilated rib of a Winchester M101 over-and-under. The idea of the polished steel was to reflect radiant heat coming from the barrels. This supplementary rib was merely clipped to the ordinary one; and though no heat-insulating material was interposed between them, there was little effective thermal contact.

The barrels were first heated hand-hot, and the target of ruled half-inch squares, previously described, was viewed over them, in the

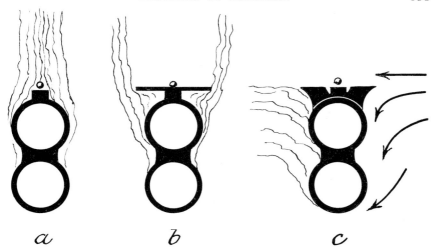

Fig. 93. Convection currents and heat shimmer from O/U barrels—
(a) gun with normal rib; (b) experimental wide rib; and (c) proposed
improved form of rib

ordinary manner, to confirm the results originally obtained. The same
effects were duly noted—a high degree of horizontal distortion of the
space surrounding the target, which, incidentally, appeared to have
shrunk from its true elliptical shape to a round dot.

The temperature of the cooling barrels was then restored, and the
supplementary rib dropped into place. The effect was marked: there
was a distortion-free space above the rib, wider than the rib itself—
perhaps 50 per cent wider—in which the target showed truly and
clearly (see fig. 93b). Although, of course, convection currents would
encroach on this clear space if there were any cross-wind or any swinging of the gun sideways, the initial advantage would presumably
remain, especially if the rib were given the aerofoil shape which I will
describe in a moment.

I believe that these simple experiments serve at least to indicate the
lines on which the ribs for trap guns should be designed for maximum
freedom from heat-haze, shimmer and mirage. I would propose a rib
of the shape shown in fig. 93c (British Prov. Patent No: 15768/71). The
shape of the overhang is significant. Under more or less still air conditions, it would deflect the convection currents outwards and to either
side, as in fig. 93b, but rather better. Under cross-winds, whether natural
or induced by the swinging of the gun, the currents would tend to be
diverted beneath the barrels, as indicated. Pointability could be

preserved, or even bettered, by the two deep grooves shown, imitating those seen more especially in deep-ribbed side-by-side guns, which show up as dark lines under all lighting conditions.

In the absence of a commercial rib of the form described (which could readily be rolled from aluminium strip and adapted to most guns), shooters in climates where heat-haze and shimmer are most troublesome could well try a plain stainless steel strip as shown in fig. 93b. This material is obtainable from any good builders' merchant. The strip disappears when viewed obliquely against a sky background, but visual pointability can be very well restored for experimental purposes by cementing a quarter-inch black linen tape down the middle. The net effect compares very favourably with an ordinary, well-matted rib of the same narrow width.

Mechanical adjustment. The last aspect of accuracy to which I want to draw attention in this chapter, is accuracy of mechanical functioning. Guns that are thoroughly well designed and constructed may yet prove unsatisfactory in service. What is worse, they may be dangerous. The trends of the times, indeed, make the possibility more imminent than ever it was before with guns of fair quality.

The reason is not far to seek. Firms engaged in quantity production rely increasingly on the modern techniques of quality control, and on the vigilance of their factory inspectorate, for the turning out of a product in fair marketable condition. More and more is it the tendency for goods to leave the factory just as they come off the production line: less and less are manufacturers willing to spend costly time and labour in remedying individual deficiencies.

The result, in the case of guns in the popular range, is that the thing most likely to be skimped or neglected is the final adjustment and regulation. No doubt the first thing to be sacrificed is the testing and regulation of the shooting. It is like the road-testing of motor cars. Provided that the barrels have been bored, chambered and rimmed in conformity with the dimensional tolerances laid down, it is probably taken for granted that the shooting will pass muster. So it may, especially if the gun carries considerable choke, even in the right barrel. In any case, no question of safety is involved.

But it is otherwise with the mechanical arrangements of the gun—the breech-locking, percussion, ejection and safety systems. In that department, there are several places where danger may arise from simple lack of adjustment. True, any defect in basic functioning is likely to be picked up at proof. But proof house inspectors are not infallible, and even if they were, it is not the duty of the proof house in any country, so far as I am aware, to carry out overall functional checks.

A fair example of the sort of thing that may happen was provided by a Continental gun of medium quality by a maker of good reputation, which was generally well made. For all that, it had a defect that could easily have given rise to an accident. Thus, the right trigger normally had a pull of about $4\frac{1}{4}$ pounds; but in certain circumstances it could become a hair trigger, pulling off at a mere touch.

This dangerous condition arose from a simple maladjustment. When the safety catch was on, there was a slight clearance between the trigger blade and the safety block, so that the trigger could still yield a trifle to finger pressure. But there was no clearance at all between the blade and the tail-end of the sear which releases the internal hammer. In consequence, if the trigger were pulled when the safety catch was on— as it would be, for example, if the shooter attempted to fire without remembering to put it off—the sear would be partly disengaged from the notch or bent in the internal hammer, and could remain in that state after the safety catch had been thrown off. It did so in the gun in question, which then, as I say, became hair-triggered.

If this condition had been spotted by the makers before the gun left the factory, it would have been the easiest thing to rectify it. But it was not rectified.

This particular maladjustment can be more serious if it is associated with another of a familiar kind, that is, the self-resetting of the safety catch under the influence of recoil. In an actual case, the sportsman concerned fired his right barrel in the ordinary way, whereupon, unknown to him, his safety catch reset itself. He then attempted to fire his left, only to find, after he had given the trigger the extra hard pull that it always gets in these circumstances, that his safety catch was on. Thinking that he must have put it on inadvertently, he slipped it off, whereupon off went the gun. Nobody was hurt—but what a trap for the unwary!

I could make a considerable list of examples of inaccurate adjustment in new guns, but the moral should already be clear. No strange gun should be taken into service until all its adjustments have been checked by a competent gunsmith. No prudent buyer will grudge spending a little extra, if necessary, for the assurance this conveys.

CHAPTER TWENTY-THREE

SHOT AND SHOT SIZE

Shot for the shotgun has hitherto been made of lead or, more strictly, an alloy in which lead predominates. Lead, indeed, among the common metals, is uniquely suited to the purpose on account of its density, which gives it ranging power; its softness, which enables it to be used harmlessly in choke-bored guns; and its low melting point, which much facilitates manufacture.

Shot can be made from commercially pure lead, but modern shot is alloyed with antimony to give it additional hardness, and arsenic to increase the surface tension of the molten metal. Shot hardened with antimony is less subject to compressive damage in the gun; and since it survives its passage through the bore in better shape, it is considered to fly more truly and make better patterns than the soft variety. The proportion of antimony ranges from about 1 per cent in ordinary game shot to as much as 4 per cent in that intended for competitive trap-shooting.

The common process of making shot by dropping the molten metal from a sieve or colander at the top of a high tower is too well known to need any detailed description. It relies on the molten droplets solidifying into a truly spherical shape during their passage through the air. But good shot is also made by the short-drop process, in which the forward part of the molten droplet emerging from the sieve is cooled and solidified by immediate contact with water, whereupon the still-molten tail collapses into the solid cup thus formed and rounds itself off by surface tension to make a more or less perfect sphere.

This is the process used by amateurs for making their own shot*, some of which is of surprisingly good quality.

---

* *Gough Thomas's Gun Book*, pp. 227–30

The highest quality shot for competitive trapshooting is plated with harder metal—nickel or copper—the chief merit of which would appear to be that it inhibits the sticking together of adjacent pellets by cold welding under the intense pressure to which those at the rear of a shot charge are subjected during their initial acceleration (see fig. 94). Adherent pellets, thus produced, often separate in flight, but can be identified on the pattern plate as short strings or little clusters, which are detrimental to the evenness of the pattern.

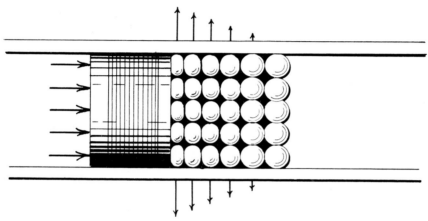

Fig. 94.   Notional view of pellets undergoing rapid acceleration in gun barrel

Iron shot.   Owing to the incidence of lead poisoning among wildfowl in America, caused by their picking up spent pellets while feeding in heavily shot-over localities, ammunition manufacturers there are under strong pressure from the conservation agencies to produce cartridges loaded with iron shot (see also Chapter 7).

Size of shot.   This is the subject of never-ending controversy, in which a main factor—confidence—is frequently overlooked.

What keeps the controversy alive is that, within considerable limits, the compensatory factors of shock and damage make the decision fairly one of personal choice and confidence.

But the limits must not be overstepped. The shot must be large enough to penetrate to a vital part, and the larger the bird the larger the shot must be to fulfil this condition. It is no use firing dust-shot at geese at normal ranges. On the other hand, the shot must be small enough to make a sufficiently close pattern, otherwise it becomes increasingly a matter of chance whether sufficient pellets will strike, however accurately the charge may have been centred on the target. Unduly large shot will certainly bring off some brilliant flukes, but, taking one shot with another, will not fill the game bag as well as will a more moderate size.

The popular sizes of shot represent the outcome of vast experience, gained over centuries. The uncommitted shooter can safely adopt them and forget the subject. They appear to be as follows:

Partridge	6 or 7	Rabbit	5 or 6	Mallard	4, 5 or 6
Grouse	6 or 7	Hare	4 or 5	Teal	6 or 7
Pheasant	5 or 6	Woodcock	7	Geese	1 or 3
Pigeon	6 or 7	Snipe	8	Squirrel	7

If, however, a man is quite confident that he does better with a different size, he would be well advised to stick to it for as long as his confidence lasts. Confidence in shooting is worth much more than marginal ballistics.

Nevertheless, shooters favouring substantially larger sizes of shot than those recommended should always bear in mind that, for the reasons set out in Chapter 4, they increase the possibility of *occasional* long-distance kills at the expense of consistency of performance, and are rightly condemned as a prime cause of wounding.

Perhaps the weightiest evidence ever assembled of the unwisdom of using unduly large shot is that contained in the report* of experiments carried out by the American Bureau of Sport Fisheries & Wildlife to determine the relative efficiencies of lead and iron shot. These remarkable experiments involved the shooting under strictly controlled conditions, of no fewer than 2,010 mallard—to the end, we may hope, that far larger numbers will in future be spared. In addition to the iron shot tested, two sizes of lead shot were used, yielding evidence that is highly relevant here.

Extraordinary steps were taken to ensure a fair comparison between the various kinds of shot used. The birds were guided, flying, along a precise course, and the gun was fired by automatic, electrical means designed to ensure that each bird was truly centred in the pattern. The great bulk of the birds were shot broadside at an elevation of about 15 degrees. Only 300 were shot head-on.

* Transactions of the 34th N. American Wildlife and Natural Resources Conference, 1969

The gun used was a fully choked 12-bore with a 30-inch barrel, and the lead-shotted cartridges were commercial loads containing $1\frac{1}{4}$ oz. of shot in each case. The two sizes tested were American Nos. 4 and 6, corresponding to our Nos. 3 and 5. The former is, of course, popular in this country for geese, but ranks as a large size for duck; whilst the latter is rather small in relation to the generally favoured No. 4.

The fate of every duck was recorded in one or other of four categories, ranging on a time scale from instant death to survival. Those alive after ten days were painlessly killed, and all the birds were examined for broken wing or leg bones, and fluoroscoped to obtain counts of imbedded shot. No less than 630 were plucked to obtain counts of entrance and exit wounds.

The results were first analysed to show the percentages of birds instantly killed at each chosen range, or which survived for certain prescribed intervals. As the record of those instantly killed will serve very well to bring out the immediate point I want to make, I give the following abstract from the report.

Killing Efficiencies against Mallard of (English) Nos. 3 and 5 Lead Shot

Range (yds.) (Broadside)	Percentages of Birds instantly killed	
	No. 3 shot	No. 5 shot
30	95	95
40	66	71
45	52	53
50	38	44
55	21	24
60	18	24
65	6	13
(Head-on)		
40	46	48
50	20	8

The striking thing about these figures is not merely the greater efficiency of the smaller shot, but the way in which its superiority was maintained right out to 65 yards. This, I admit, was more than I had expected; but it ties in with the arguments arising out of Sir Ralph Payne-Gallwey's experiments in shooting high pheasants. At 65 yards, the striking energy of a pellet of No. 5 is well below the 1·5 ft./lbs. stipulated for duck, but the smaller shot evidently made up for this— and more—by the shock-effect of its denser pattern, and the greater number of strikes that resulted.

Notwithstanding these results, the investigators realised that they did not necessarily reflect accurately the efficiencies of the different kinds

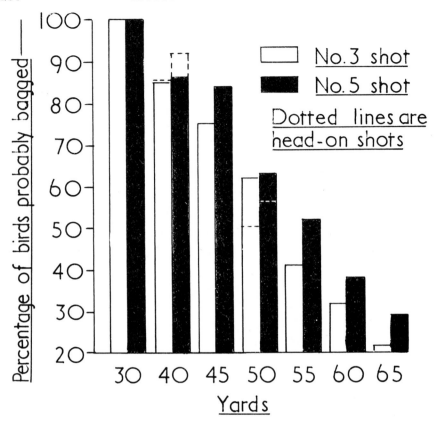

Fig. 95.   Comparative performance of No. 3 and No. 5 shot on duck

of shot in the field, in terms of birds brought to bag. They considered, and rightly, that the most important factor here is whether or not the bird had suffered a broken wing.

They accordingly re-analysed their figures so as to bring out the percentages of birds with broken wings that died within 5 minutes. I think any practical wildfowler would accept these as representing the most eminently baggable birds.

The results regarded from this angle are sufficiently significant to be worth putting in graphic form, as shown in fig. 95. It will be seen that the superiority of the smaller shot has again been maintained right over the range, including the 50-yard, head-on figure, which, in the previous analysis, favoured the larger size. This is because the denser pattern of the smaller shot was more likely to break a wing.

These experiments, in my view, are a complete answer to any argument as between No. 3 and No. 5 lead shot for duck; and they strongly suggest that No. 6 might do even better over a more restricted range, say, up to 50 yards. The No. 6-for-everything school, which includes many of the most experienced shooters, are entitled to take from them a fresh draught of confidence.

I consider that devotees of the larger sizes of shot, and more especially those who favour BB in 12-bore loads for wildfowling, should carefully ponder the significance of these results.

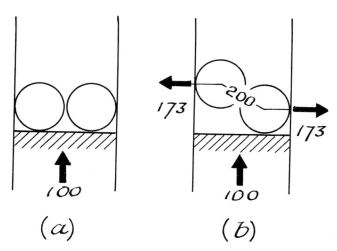

Fig. 96. Stacking of shot (theoretical)

The favoured shot

It is widely believed that certain guns tend to favour a certain size of shot, which they shoot to a better quality and more effective pattern than they do any other.

The thing that gives a gun a truly individual character in relation to shot of a certain size, is, of course, the precise conformation of the bore, from chamber to muzzle. At any point along this length, the way in which the pellets stack may be much influenced by a few thousandths of an inch more or less in the bore diameter. The forces acting on and between them, and tending to squeeze them together and against the barrel wall, will thus be considerably modified.

The principle here is well brought out by fig. 96 (a) and (b). At (a) we have two pellets sitting side by side in a bore that exactly fits them. The propulsive force of 100 is divided equally between them, and there is no component of that force tending to drive them together or against the sides of the barrel. At (b) the same pellets have been fitted into a bore slightly smaller, so that they can no longer sit side by side, but at an angle of 30 degrees, as shown. The right-hand pellet now takes the full force of 100, and squeezes its left-hand companion with a force of 200. At the same time it forces it against the barrel wall with a force of 173, and itself experiences a similar reaction. If the pellets were released from the muzzle at this stage, these side-thrusts would cause them to fly apart on divergent courses, whereas those at (a) would both fly truly forward. Such would be the remarkable effects of a minute bore reduction on two unyielding pellets in an unyielding barrel.

Fig. 97 gets nearer to actualities. It shows at (a) a portion of a correctly stacked charge under static conditions. Here I will merely say that the lines joining the centres of the pellets represent proportionately

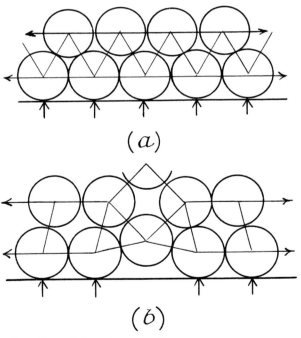

(a)

(b)

Fig. 97.   Stacking of shot (practical)

the forces acting between them, and the reactions they exert on the barrel wall.

At (b) we see a portion of a badly stacked charge, the change having been brought about by a change in the bore diameter at the point concerned. The balance of the forces acting between the pellets will in this case have been much disturbed, and some of the inter-pellet compressive forces will have been increased fully fourfold. So will the side-thrusts acting on the barrel wall. As previously, this assumes unyielding pellets.

As the bore diameter changes from one part of the barrel to another, so will the stacking situation. This will more especially apply as the charge passes through the choke; and part, at least, of the lateral dispersion undergone by the pellets as they emerge from the muzzle will no doubt depend on just how they were stacked at this critical stage. This will not be determined solely by the bore diameter at the muzzle, because the condition in which the pellets reach that point will depend partly on how they have survived abrasion and compression in their course up the barrel; and this in turn will vary according to how they stacked en route.

In practice, compressive deformation of the pellets will tend to equalise differences arising out of bore variations from one gun to another, for if only the pellets were soft enough, they would be compressed into a solid mass in any gun. But this, of course, does not happen, and the probability strongly arises that here and there a gun may be found with bore characteristics that outstandingly favour the survival, in the best possible shape, of one particular pellet size. The belief that individual guns favour shot of a particular size may thus be well-founded.

CHAPTER TWENTY-FOUR

SHOOTING AILMENTS

Shooting can afflict the shooter in several ways. It can cause bruising of the face, shoulder and fingers; it can cause headaches; and it can do permanent damage to the sense of hearing. Sometimes one or more of these troubles can prove so intractable that the victim has to give up shooting, so their causes and cures, affecting as they often do the choice of gun or ammunition, are matters worthy of careful study.

Bruising.   Even in a well fitted and correctly held gun, bruising can be caused by excessive recoil. Familiar examples are provided by those young shooters who, entertaining the characteristic delusion that success in shooting is proportional to the weight of lead discharged, fire loads out of proportion to the weight of their guns. The old rule that the weight of a fixed-breech gun should not be less than 96 times the weight of the shot charge should not be materially transgressed without good reason.

Recoil-operated repeaters constitute a special class. In the absence of effective braking of the recoiling barrel, due to excessive lubrication or incorrect adjustment of the braking ring, these guns can recoil much more severely than a fixed-breech gun of equal weight. The remedy is obvious.

Ill-fitting guns can give rise to bruising of the face or shoulder even with moderate loads. The butt must rest in the natural hollow where the upper part of the pectoral muscle affords a cushion to absorb the recoil. If the stock is too long to be thus accommodated, and if in consequence its toe rests on the scantily covered part of the upper arm where the biceps muscle ends, a most painful bruising can occur there. Stocks should preferably be as long as can be used with comfort, but no longer. Too short a stock, on the other hand, will exaggerate the effect of recoil.

204

Bruising of the face just under the cheekbone can be caused by not tucking the flank of the stock closely into the cheek when firing. It can also be caused by a stock with excessive rearward slope. This can usually be cured by adopting a level comb at the place where the cheek rests, or even one which slopes upwards to the rear. This can be done by adding to or modifying the stock without necessarily altering the drop to the comb at the effective point, or the drop to the heel (i.e. dimensions *a* and *b* respectively, fig. 85).

Bruised second finger is usually caused by an insufficiently tight, or prematurely relaxed, grip, associated, perhaps, with a stock that is too short. To help its avoidance, trigger guards should have a pronounced rearward slope. In case of persistent trouble, a small rubber cushion can be fitted over the guard at this point. These cushions are obtainable from any good gunsmith.

For other aspects of recoil, not necessarily giving rise to bruising, see Chapter 16.

Headache. Gun headaches have been widely dismissed in the past as being caused by a mild series of concussions. Churchill even went so far as to assign a single cause—failure to stiffen the neck muscles. Unfortunately, the subject cannot be dismissed so simply. Admitting the mild concussions, headaches can also be caused, wholly or partially, by noise, for the noise of a gun firing is a composite sound of great intensity. It includes the muzzle blast, chiefly noticeable with short-barrelled guns or those fitted with muzzle brakes, and what may be the significant contribution made by the note of the briefly but violently vibrating barrels, which the muzzle blast hides but does not suppress.

In the case of self-loading repeaters, there is also the noise caused by the operation of the breech mechanism. This is sometimes a metallic impact of high intensity and distressing quality; and I have known shooters to be given a headache by firing a single shot from one of these guns.

Another cause of gun headaches, hitherto almost completely unrecognised, is the fumes of nitro powder. A mere whiff of these, especially in individuals not habituated to them, can start a headache. In self-loading repeaters, the automatic opening of the breech is accompanied by a puff of these fumes, and on a still day the shooter may sniff them nearly every time he fires. I myself, in such circumstances, was at first puzzled by developing a headache, even though the recoil of the repeater was noticeably less than that to which I am accustomed. But a medical correspondent confirmed my diagnosis. 'Nitrites and nitrates', he wrote, 'are quick-acting vaso-dilators, readily absorbed from mucosal surfaces, i.e. nose and mouth. The rapid vaso-dilation produced acts on the cerebral arteries, and one gets increased cerebral blood volume and raised inter-cranial pressure.' He adds, 'I used to be RMO to a Sapper TA regiment, and I noticed that the demolition parties always complained of headaches.'

From all this, some broad suggestions emerge for curing or reducing gun headache. They are (1) the reduction of the straightforward concussion, either by a lighter load, a heavier gun or a quicker-burning powder*; (2) the reduction of noise by the avoidance of short barrels, muzzle brakes and noisy self-loaders, and the use of earplugs or muffs; and (3)—out of deference to Mr. Churchill—the stiffening of the neck muscles in the act of firing.

Damage to hearing. It is only in recent times that the damage done by shooting to upper-register hearing has been fully recognised. The matter was brought to the notice of the Service authorities by some investigations undertaken into the hearing of young marines by a Royal Naval surgeon.

It was taken up on a far wider basis in the British Army of Occupation on the Rhine, about half of whose soldiers were found to have suffered damage to their upper-register hearing by small-arms fire. The report of the BAOR investigation, published in the NRA journal, mentioned that similar damage was also caused by shotguns.

Clay pigeon shooters are nowadays fully alive to the need for ear protectors and can wear ear muffs (preferred) or one or other of the modern proprietary plugs advertised. The need is not so well recognised among game shooters; but in view of the cumulative and non-reversible nature of the damage, and its insidious approach, they should undoubtedly make more use of plugs, especially on those occasions when a considerable number of cartridges is likely to be fired.

Incidentally, ear protectors, and especially muffs, afford a striking demonstration of the contribution which noise makes to sensible recoil. When shooting very deliberately, as when testing a gun at the plate, I have found that recoil seems to be substantially diminished by using ear muffs. All the means previously recommended for the reduction of noise as a contribution to recoil should therefore be regarded as aids to the preservation of hearing.

It has been remarked as a curious fact that there is no evidence of any special incidence of deafness among the shooting giants of the late Victorian era. On 30 August 1888, for example, Lord Walsingham fired 1,550 cartridges at Blubberhouse, in Yorkshire, using $3\frac{1}{4}$ drams of black

---

* See Chapter 16, pp. 152–157

powder and 1⅛ oz. of shot in what was almost certainly a 30-inch damas-cus-barrelled gun weighing nearly 7 lb. (He objected to steel because of its 'ringing' note.) Yet he left it on record that he never had 'the semblance of a headache' afterwards or a bruise of any kind. There is no reason to think that he was unique, or that he and others like him would have remained immune to ear trouble if they had used short-barrelled guns and smokeless powder.

Aural catarrh. Occasionally a man may have to give up shooting because the report of his gun makes a really painful impact on his sense of hearing. In one such case that came to my notice, the trouble was diagnosed as aural catarrh, which, by blocking the eustachian tube, put the ear drums into a state of tension. The impact of the report on these already-tensed ear drums was understandably abnormal, but when the catarrh was cleared up by medical treatment, the patient was able to resume his shooting quite happily.

CHAPTER TWENTY-FIVE

CARE AND MAINTENANCE

The sportsman, equally with the soldier, has never lacked adjurations to look to his equipment, and in the olden days of the top-hatted shooter with his flintlock and pointers, it is open to doubt if his sport would have been possible without a degree of care devoted to his weapon that nowadays would be considered intolerably burdensome. Yet, as writers of the period testify, he often took delight in lavishing it, and now that good guns have become so valuable, it is clearly up to the present-day shooter to cultivate something of his attitude.

It can indeed be counted against the modern shotgun that it so frequently exacts no immediate penalty for neglect. But when the bill is presented—for a new pair of barrels, say, or other major repair—the owner of the gun is likely to get a shock.

Perhaps we can best consider what is needed to preserve a gun in good order and condition by thinking of the risks to which it is commonly subjected in normal usage.

On shooting days, the sportsman, more often than not, sets out in a shooting brake to join his friends. On the way, he stops for a few moments to attend to a small matter which he overlooked in the hurry of his departure, leaving his car unattended while he does so.

Having arrived at the shoot, he puts his gun together, collects his cartridges, etc., and stands chatting to his friends until the party gets its orders to move off. Meanwhile he puts his gun on the roof of his car out of harm's way. The party duly leaves for the first drive in two Land Rovers, packed pretty tightly, and disposing of their guns as best they can.

They have a very good shoot for the best part of the day, but rain sets in in the afternoon, and finally comes on so heavily that they have to pack up. Our particular man wipes his gun over with his car duster before he puts it away. and when he gets home, he cleans it to the best of his ability and gives it a really good oiling as some compensation for the wetting it has received. Moreover, he does that sort of thing with minor variations every time he goes out. He does not have his gun looked over at the end of the season, because it appears to be in perfect order, with no visible signs of rust; and anyway, he wants it by him for pigeon shooting and perhaps a round or two of informal sporting clays during the close season.

This is designedly a humdrum picture, yet it serves to pinpoint the things that need care in preserving a gun from loss, damage or the consequences of neglect.

Gun cases and covers. Our imaginary shooter travelled by brake, and if his gun was safely stowed it would perhaps have been adequately protected by a canvas cover. But not necessarily. A man I know once set out with his Henry Atkin lying cushioned in luxury on the back seat. But he had to brake suddenly, whereupon the gun shot off and fell on the floor with a force that could have broken the stock. Fortunately, the only damage suffered was a dent in the barrel where it struck the metal support of one of the front seats.

This gun was travelling uncovered, but even if it had had an ordinary canvas cover, it would not have protected it. About the only thing from which such covers do protect a gun is rubbing against something rough which might scratch the stock. A light, flat case affords infinitely better protection; and an ordinary shotgun comes apart with such remarkable ease, and can be stowed in such a case so readily, that there is little excuse for not using one every time.

A *hard-blocked* leg-o'-mutton case affords almost equally good protection, but is considerably less convenient, whilst the soft canvas leg-o'-mutton variety are little, if anything, better than full-length limp canvas covers.

There is, however, one bonus which goes with all kinds of cases that require the dismounting of the gun. It is the insurance they afford against the risk of inadvertently putting it away loaded.

The best flat cases used to be made of leather on oak. They were disgustingly heavy as well as costly. The blocked leather kind are much lighter, but even these are nowadays very expensive. I have always had a leaning towards the wooden case covered with mail canvas, which I treat with wax furniture polish until it is waterproof and scuff-proof. These cases are light, and, being rigidly compartmentalised, are strong enough to protect the contents from practically every imaginable hazard.

The more modern kind, with a plastic covering, should be even better, though many of them, with chromium plated pressed steel fittings which have gone rusty, have a cheap and nasty appearance.

Guns should on no account be left uninspected for any length of time in fabric-lined cases. If they are, they will assuredly be found to have rusted, perhaps very badly, where the fabric has been in contact with the metal.

Guns and cars. It may be remembered that our shooter left his gun on the roof of his brake, where it would be safely out of the way. So it may have been; but many a man who has done that has driven away forgetting it until the crash of its fall has jogged his memory. If a car has one of the modern flat, wide bonnets, I prefer to rest my gun on a game bag or the like just in front of the windscreen, where it cannot fail to be seen.

But our man went on in a Land Rover—a vehicle that has been described as 'the gunsmith's friend', from the amount of trade it makes in repairs. What is one to do? Here a canvas cover affords *some* protection, as well as a little moral reassurance.

Incidentally, nothing happened during the brief interval while he left his brake unattended in a hotel car park. But these vehicles are perfect display cases of their contents, and the least one can do in such circumstances besides locking the vehicle is to hide the gun case on the floor under an old mackintosh or rug.

Insufficient care. At the end of the day, the gun, as I said, was cleaned and liberally oiled; but although it had got very wet it seemed dry when it reached home, so all the care it really received, apart from the routine cleaning of the bores, was the oiling. It is practically certain that there was water left in the lockwork and elsewhere in the gun, and that in due course it would set up rusting. The extractor never having been taken out, on this occasion or any other, there would be an accumulation of powder fouling behind it, which in time could impede the closing of the gun, and even force it 'off the face'.

What this comes down to is that if the shooter is not prepared to send the gun away at the end of the season for a complete overhaul, he should at least get his local gunsmith to take the locks off and oil them, and see that all is well within; or he should fit himself out with proper turnscrews (see below) and learn how to do the job himself. Many modern imported sidelocks, especially the Spanish kind, have hand-detachable locks, which are a great help, though it is a mistake to take them off unnecessarily.

Gun cleaning. I have preserved my guns in first-class order under the worst conditions obtaining in this country, including salt water and salt mud, with the following preparations only:

(1)   Soapy water for removing salt and salt mud—hot for the metal work, and lukewarm, applied with a nail-brush, for the stock. (Never put oil on top of salt: never, that is to say, wipe a salt-contaminated gun with an oily rag until the salt has been *washed* off.)
(2)   Young's 303 for the inside of the barrels only.
(3)   Three-in-One oil for general lubrication, sparingly applied.
(4)   Vaseline mixed with medicinal paraffin and applied with a camel-hair brush for protecting non-working inner surfaces.
(5)   Boiled linseed oil plus one-third turpentine (both of 'artist's' quality) for the stock.

My normal cleaning procedure after using corrosive cartridges was as follows:

(1)   Remove visible powder residue by pushing through rolled balls of pre-cut 8-inch × 6-inch newspaper for a 12-bore.
(2)   Remove invisible residue and any leading with stiff, brass wire brush lubricated with Young's 303 and vigorously applied. (Turpentine helps if the leading is obstinate.)
(3)   Wipe out with clean flannel patch.
(4)   Apply Young's 303 with mop.

Nowadays, with non-corrosive cartridges, I merely put less effort into the second item.

I always use a piece of flannel impregnated with Three-in-One for wiping the gun over externally.

After a thoroughly wet day, I remove the extractors and locks (or the bottom plate in the case of a boxlock); shake out all possible water and mop up any that can be seen with a clean cotton rag on a little stick and with cotton pipe cleaners. The locks themselves I put somewhere where they get nicely warm but not hot. I then put the remaining components, in their disassembled and ventilated state, in a warm dry place where they can dry overnight. In the morning I examine and re-oil them. I have never had any rusting trouble.

When cleaning a gun, the barrels should always be looked over for dents. These are best detected from outside. They should be raised at the first opportunity. A badly dented barrel should not, of course, be fired.

Incidentally, it is important that the turnscrew or screwdriver used for taking out gun screws should be accurately ground to fit the fine slots in the heads. The fact that it may be a proper gun turnscrew does not necessarily mean that it will fit.

Lubrication.   Nearly every gun gets too much oil (chiefly in the wrong places) or not enough. Never use a spouted oil can on a gun—there is no part of a gun that ever needs a spurt of oil. An oil bottle with the *stem only* of a small feather in the cork or stopper is ideal.

The parts that require an occasional *drop* (repeat, drop) of oil are the under-barrel bolt; the hinge or cross-pin; the spindle of the top-lever; the space between the ejector kickers; and the legs of the extractor. Once a year, the fore-end push-rod should receive a drop—there is a hole at the top of the tube where it can go. The fore-end bolt itself should not be entirely neglected.

The parts that should never be allowed to get dry of lubricant are the parts where there is heavy frictional contact. They include (outside the gun) the exposed ends of the cocking levers; and (inside) their inner ends, where they bear on the hammers or tumblers; the sears and bents; and the mainspring and its swivel. Other moving parts should receive a mere touch of oil, as common sense dictates.

Insurance. This is the final aspect of the present subject. Your gun may be worth a lot of money: make sure that it is adequately covered in all contingencies.

CHAPTER TWENTY-SIX

MUZZLE-LOADERS

One of the saving graces of the times is our reluctance to abandon things and practices merely because they have been technically superseded. The horse, the sailing boat and archery afford conspicuous examples; so does the great and growing interest in muzzle-loading guns. Not only have we a Muzzle-Loaders' Association,* the members of which exhibit and shoot their ancient weapons at Game Fairs and the like, often in period costume, but also a considerable industry with modern factories wholly or largely devoted to the manufacture of replicas of the outstanding muzzle-loading weapons of the past, mostly intended for active shooting. The Italians appear to have taken the lead in this new industry, which evidently caters for a large demand from the United States.

Buyers of antique or replica firearms are variously inspired, but here I am addressing only those shotgunners who buy them to shoot. Their motives may go well beyond mere nostalgia. Our modern double-barrelled hammerless ejectors were evolved to meet the needs of shooting under the most sophisticated conditions prevailing around the turn of the century, and for organised shooting over preserved ground are still the most suitable weapons, and likely to remain so. There are, however, good arguments for a weapon of lower fire-power for much rough shooting. They would rest on the few shots likely to be fired in the course of a normal day, and in some cases could be urged on grounds of conservation. They would be strongly reinforced if the kind of low-fire-power gun concerned afforded a completely new interest to its owner. That is exactly what a muzzle-loader is capable of doing.

---

* The Muzzle-Loaders' Association of Great Britain (Hon Sec: De Witt Bailey II) 46 Thames Street, Sunbury-on-Thames, Middlesex

213

Since we get out of life and sport roughly what we put into them, it is not surprising to find much evidence of the enjoyment that sportsmen of the muzzle-loading days got from their more demanding, more troublesome, but in some respects more rewarding weapons. The modern hammerless ejector and the modern factory-produced cartridge have indeed largely relieved the modern shooting man of any need to care for his gun or to study the ways of getting the best out of it. They have thereby, in many cases, simply killed his interest in it.

By contrast, the old-time sportsman had to choose his fowling piece with greater discrimination and to use it with greater care. He had to study his powder, flints, caps, wadding and shot and the charges with which his gun performed best under different conditions. By way of reward for all his trouble, his successes were all the sweeter. Moreover, he commanded a more flexible weapon—one, that is to say, better adapted to a variety of purposes up to the limit imposed by recoil. These arguments, I recognise, would have little appeal to the business tycoon demanding instant week-end sport, free from all prior or incidental preoccupation, but they can be commended to many others more happily situated.

Types of muzzle-loaders

For practical purposes the only kinds of shotguns needing consideration here are single or double-barrelled guns of the flint or percussion types. Most of those in use are percussion guns, and for good reasons. They are far more readily come by; they are less demanding for reliable performance; they will shoot under weather conditions that are impossible for flintlocks; and, what is perhaps most important of all, they do not require for their successful employment the modified technique demanded by the flint. This, of course, arises from the perceptible interval that elapses between the pulling of the trigger and the discharge of the piece—evidently no fundamental bar to good shooting, as proved by the feats of the star performers of the flintlock days, but highly disconcerting nonetheless to a modern shooter brought up with modern guns.

For all that, I must confess that my own interest in muzzle-loaders is largely confined to the flint gun, which to me is a fascinating thing in its own right. In its final form, it represents the elevation of a crude and primitive principle to a well-nigh incredible pitch of efficiency, and by means that are a constant source of delight to anyone with a feeling for mechanical ingenuity and fine craftsmanship (see fig. 98).

By contrast, in the percussion gun we have a technically superior

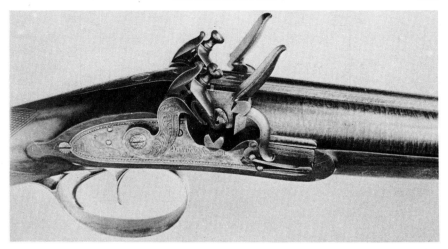

Fig. 98. The perfected form of the flintlock. This gun, by Harvey & Son of Exeter, has the Manton-type recessed chamber plugs (giving a narrower gun); vee-shaped pan; and roller on feather spring

principle requiring far less interesting means for its efficient realisation.

Whether flint or percussion, it is worth noting that single-barrelled guns have a special claim to consideration. Not only are their barrels usually much stronger, but in use they avoid certain hazards inseparable from double guns, as will appear later.

Taking into service

All muzzle-loaders coming up for use should be treated with healthy suspicion. The first question that should be asked is, 'Is it loaded?' It may well be: some long-dead owner may have finally laid it aside without drawing the charge. I once had a percussion 10-bore which I acquired in that state.

The second thing for investigation is the state of the barrels. Percussion guns are especially suspect here. The external condition may be good; so may that of the bores, as viewed from the muzzle end.

Yet they may have suffered excessive corrosion and loss of metal at the breech end, sufficient to weaken them materially. I would therefore regard it as an inviolable rule never to fire a muzzle-loader without having the breech-plugs out and inspecting the bores from end to end.

But removing the breech-plugs can be a battle, and preliminary treatment with penetrating oil, followed by a powerful wrench, heat and judicious blows with a hammer may fail to start them. For my part, not being very interested in percussion guns, I am content in such case to put the gun aside as a non-shooter, though, of course, the plug could be drilled out and replaced.

Flintlocks are another matter: their breech-plugs are usually easier to remove because they have not been subjected to the vicious corrosion of the old cap residue. For the same reason, the barrels are nearly always in better condition. If they survive critical scrutiny, inside and out, and ring clearly when suspended and struck, they are likely to be as safe as ever they were, and may be taken into service with certain precautions.

Loads

I like to test a 'new' muzzle-loader with a few light loads, working up to a heavy one, all fired at the end of a long string. For shooting from the shoulder I go back to a moderately light one, which I never afterwards exceed. I always use medium-grain powder (TS2 for 12-bore or smaller)—*never* fine-grain and *never, never* nitro.

As for what constitutes the proper load for a muzzle-loader, it must be recognised that this is primarily determined by the weight of the gun, as limiting the recoil, and not by the bore. For example, the 10-bore I mentioned, a single-barrelled gun by North of Southampton, weighed little more than 6 lb. With what we would nowadays regard as a normal 10-bore charge it would have recoiled intolerably.

I usually take as a starting point a shot charge of one-hundredth of the weight of the gun and three-sixteenths of the shot charge as the maximum powder charge. But for the best shooting with a muzzle-loader, this can often be advantageously modified out of regard for the old maxim, significantly enshrined in several other languages, 'Little powder, much lead, shoots far, kills dead.' For cylinder-bored barrels, this is the key to reduced spread and doubly increased pattern density for full-range work. So, for my 10-bore, or for a 12-bore of equal weight, I should be prepared to get the best results with, say, $1\frac{3}{16}$ oz. of shot and only $2\frac{1}{2}$ drams of powder. At the same time, and for the reasons indicated, I might be justified in using shot a size larger than originally contemplated. It is undoubtedly by such means that our forefathers, shooting with their cylinder-bored guns, seem to have shot their game as far off as we do.

Loading

The well-equipped shooter of a muzzle-loader normally loads straight from one of the powder flasks with an adjustable measuring nozzle and

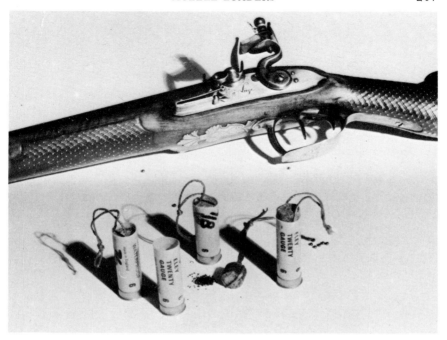

Fig. 99. 20-bore flintlock with powder and shot chargers, made from 20-gauge plastic cases, each with appropriate wad

a thumb-operated cut-off. This is a procedure which frankly gives me the shivers! It only needs a residual spark in the barrel or some scintillation among the powder residue to cause the powder to fire and the flask to blow up in the shooter's hand. All the old writers testify to the familiarity of this accident. I consider that the risk should always be avoided by detaching the charge completely from the flask before pouring it down the barrel. The best way of doing this is to put up the appropriate charges of powder and shot into small containers known as 'chargers', stoppered with the appropriate wads. The wads need to be fitted with loops of thin string, or better, perhaps, very narrow stationer's tape, to enable the wads to be withdrawn. I find that ordinary plastic cartridge cases of the same gauge as the gun make admirable chargers (see fig. 99).

Dangers
Apart from the dangers arising from bad or defective guns, or acts of folly, or causes equally operative with modern breechloaders (such as

plugs of mud or snow), the dangers to be guarded against when using muzzle-loaders are chiefly these:

(1)   In double guns, failure to re-settle the charge in the left barrel after repeatedly firing the right. If the unfired charge is thereby dislodged by recoil, so that there is a considerable gap between the powder and shot, 'it is ten to one that the barrel bursts' on being fired.*

(2)   Again in double guns, failure to put the unfired barrel to half-cock before reloading the other.

(3)   Double-charging one barrel by inadvertence. (The best precaution against this is a conspicuous band on the ramrod, which a double charge would unfailingly reveal.)

(4)   In percussion guns, inadequately cupped cocks associated with unduly light mainsprings. (With these, cap fragments can fly and endanger the eyes. Many eyes, which glasses would have saved, have been lost from this cause.)

(5)   Residual sparks or scintillation of powder residue, as previously described.

In conclusion, I strongly recommend anyone contemplating shooting muzzle-loading guns to study some of the old writers on the subject— a rewarding occupation in any case. My favourite is Blaine *(op. cit.)* who not only draws on much personal experience, but freely quotes his contemporaries, and conveys much muzzle-loading lore outside the scope of this chapter.

A last word—always wear glasses, preferably of the unshatterable kind, when firing muzzle-loaders.

* *An Encyclopaedia of Rural Sports*, D. P. Blaine, 3rd edition

CHAPTER TWENTY-SEVEN

IN THE FIELD

It is not my purpose in this chapter to attempt to instruct readers in the art of shooting. The rôle of professor in that art would, indeed, not become me. All I intend to do, therefore, is to offer some of the conclusions at which I have arrived as the result of long personal and vicarious experience.

It is well known that some of our best shots cannot give any clear or convincing account of what they do to ensure their undeniable success. They shoot superlatively well because they are liberally endowed with the necessary qualities—first-class co-ordination, a relaxed and extrovert temperament, adequate stamina, and the confidence that comes from long practice and consistent success. They do not think when they are shooting: they avoid rigid concentration, and do not let their brains breathe down the neck of their natural faculties; which, left free to express themselves in spontaneous action, assure the best degree of success of which their possessors are capable.

In saying that, I believe I have recited all the qualities necessary for successful shooting in the field. If I had to stress one particular thing, I think it would be practice.

The beginner. First, to every young beginner I would say that the making of an enviable reputation in the shooting field is something he can positively ensure. It depends on little more than the steady observance of the safety code and the sporting code.

The essentials of the safety code can be summed up in a few sentences:

(1) Remember always that a gun is a death-dealing instrument.
(2) It is always to be regarded and treated as loaded unless it is *shown* to be empty.

(3)   It must never, therefore, be pointed, even momentarily in passing, at anything you do not design to kill.

(4)   It must always be unloaded when climbing any obstacle or when your footing may be insecure, or when entering a vehicle or the curtilage of a house.

(5)   It must never be fired unless you can see where the shot will go.

The foregoing points are elaborated in various publications*, one or more of which all beginners would be well advised to study.

The sporting code may be summed up in one sentence—*Do unto others as you would be done by.* (And remember that the 'others' are not only your fellow members of a shooting party: they include all the auxiliaries—keepers, beaters, pickers-up, dogs and, rightly interpreted, the game. Have special solicitude for the dogs and the game.)

Never pursue your advantage in the field to the detriment of another's—never jockey for position, or take his bird, or press a claim to one that he thinks he has shot, or deliberately 'share' one that he is perfectly well positioned to take.

Never afflict him with explanations of your misses. He is not concerned about your performance: his own gives him quite enough to think about.

Keep quiet when there is game about. Unnecessary noise or chatter or objurgating your dog may well spoil his sport as well as your own.

Do not neglect, but rather seek out, opportunities for rendering the little courtesies appropriate from one sportsman to another, and especially to your seniors.

I take it for granted that the beginner will do all that he can to cultivate the best standard of marksmanship of which he is capable, so that he may kill his game cleanly and avoid wounding; but even if he attains only a moderate standard in this department, the enviable reputation I referred to will be his only if he attends conscientiously to the other points laid down.

The mature shooter.   To the mature shooter I can best offer some observations based on the more familiar shooting troubles encountered in my experience. These are largely matters of unsatisfactory performance in circumstances not open to immediate or easy explanation. They range from cases where there has been some external or objective change, such as a new gun, to those of a purely subjective character—

---

* 1 *The Gun Code* published by the British Field Sports Society
  2 *Gun Safety*, Major Roderick Willett (Arlington Books, London)

the 'hoodoos', for example, which can range from a few off-days to a prolonged period of paralysing inefficiency.

The two kinds of cases merge when the hoodoo attaches itself to a particular gun or cartridge without any ascertainable justification.

Cases of the first sort often arise from a change of gun in what may appear to have been auspicious circumstances. A man has shot with a particular gun for years, and with reasonable satisfaction. He then decides to treat himself to something better. He may buy a new gun 'off the shelf', with only the perfunctory sort of fitting I have described in a previous chapter, or he may have one altered or made to order, and go to a shooting school to be properly fitted. In either case, things can go wrong, and can escape immediate diagnosis by anyone who had not seen him in action with his original gun, and tested it for patterns.

The most familiar trouble is that the new gun makes tighter patterns than the old, and therefore makes greater demands than he can well meet on his standard of marksmanship.

Independently of this trouble, or, maybe associated with it, there is the possibility that the new gun may not centre its charge on the same spot in relation to his familiar line of sight.

A more tricky problem arises when the old gun was not a good natural fit, and the shooter had to adapt himself to it. At the shooting school, the coach may arrive at a good natural fitting with his try-gun, and may demonstrate its superiority by working the shooter up to a higher standard than he has previously attained. But in the interval between the fitting and the delivery of the new gun, the shooter has reverted to the old one and his old habits, so that the new gun, when it arrives, may appear to be a thoroughly bad fit. This emphasises the need for all new guns to undergo their 'acceptance trials' in the hands of the shooter concerned and in the presence of the coach who determined the fitting.

Unfamiliar guns.   Middle-aged shooters often abandon their 30 or 28-inch-barrelled guns and take to a light, short-barrelled one as a concession to their advancing years and declining stamina. More often than not the change is beneficial; but not always. The shooter may miss the forward inertia of his longer-barrelled gun and may fall into the habit of checking his swing with the other. The lesson is that major changes of this sort are risky if made without adequate preliminary trial.

The same applies to those game shooters who think they may benefit by taking to an over-and-under. I have had a succession of cases in which those who have taken to these guns are unable to shoot satisfactorily until they learn, or are advised, to shoot with the non-aiming eye dimmed or closed. The reason for the trouble is the dominant visual impression made by the side view of the stacked barrels on the non-aiming eye, which thereby tends to take charge. This trouble does not appear to arise in clay pigeon shooting, presumably because, when shooting 'gun up', the gun is put specifically under the command of the aiming eye.

Coming to the subjective cases, the most baffling thing in shooting is the hoodoo*. It is the common cold of the shooting man: few escape an occasional sniff; others suffer regular streamers, which they simply cannot shake off.

It can all start so easily. However competent a performer a man may be, the inexorable laws of chance, if nothing else, make it certain that he will occasionally have a run of misses. What happens then depends on several things. If it is at the beginning of the day—a day, it may be, on which he started out feeling fit and fine, and on top of the world— he may feel a wave of despair as the delusion takes possession of his mind that this is going to be one of his off-days. So it may be if he is not strong-minded enough to ignore the portent; yet there may be no other cause than the mental attitude induced by a few abortive shots. In all essential respects, except for this mental factor, the man may be in a condition to shoot as well as he has ever shot; but the poison has entered his system, and may take a long time to work out.

Unjustified suspicions. The blighting thing about this kind of hoodoo is that it is self-nourishing, it feeds and grows fat on its own milk. Those first few misses can spoil a day, and the recollection of it can spoil the next for fear of a repetition. And so the thing may grow like a snowball, until the wretched victim starts casting around for remedies. He may start by suspecting all sorts of things not reasonably open to suspicion— his long-familiar cartridges most probably, or his equally familiar gun, notwithstanding that both may have served him faithfully and well in the past. The suspicion that he may need a new gun is particularly insidious, for it may be strongly reinforced by a secret, acquisitive urge.

I have a steady trickle of sufferers coming to me for advice at this stage. My only qualification for offering it is that I have had a long experience of hoodoos in my own right, whereby I have become familiar with many of the symptoms and some of the remedies. Indeed, over the years I seem to have acquired a large measure of immunity to hoo-doos of the kind so far considered—those, that is to say, which have

---

* 'Hoodoo'—prob. a variant of *voodoo* (Af. *vodu* (Webster)) and used here in the sense of a malignant influence or its effect

no substantial basis, and which arise from a sheer breakdown of self-confidence.

But the hoodoo sufferer, or would-be diagnostician, needs to recognise that there are several varieties of these distressing afflictions, and that they merge into one another by insensible gradations.

First, simplest, and yet sometimes most baffling, is the kind already described, which has no enduring physical cause. It begins with something fortuitous and transient, such as a run of misses, or a temporary digestive upset. Thereafter it is a purely mental phenomenon—a loss of confidence. The victim should not delude himself with the belief that there must necessarily be some tangible reason for the breakdown in his standard of performance: loss of confidence can account for the worst shooting that ever was. The clue to this kind of trouble is its sudden onset.

Next comes the kind of case in which there *is* some enduring physical cause, the effect of which has been much magnified by a cumulative loss of confidence, as in the previous instance. This sort of hoodoo may be traceable to physical changes undergone by the shooter, or the steady onset of some maturing disability. His gun may thereby cease to fit him, or his mobility may have suffered, or his eyesight may be affected, and dominance may have switched. In cases of this sort the trouble will have arisen gradually, even though the psychological aspect may suddenly have become prominent.

Finally, there is the hoodoo with a solid material basis. The shooter is not prone to loss of self-confidence, but something has undoubtedly bewitched him, and he can do nothing right. This is a familiar case. It often arises on the acquisition of a new gun—a carefully fitted and tested gun, much better than his old one, but throwing tighter patterns, whereby performance has undergone a sharp down-turn, as I have already explained.

The first treatment I would prescribe for a hoodoo sufferer is to sit quietly and ask himself a few questions.

Have I shot well in the recent past with my present gun and cartridges? If the answer is yes, they can be given a conditional discharge straight away.

Has anything happened to me personally since I was shooting well—any noticeable loss of condition, any new complaint, *any new source of worry or distraction*? Am I undergoing any medication that could affect my reaction times?

If the answers to all these questions are negative, I would diagnose a first category hoodoo, and would endeavour to inspire the patient with new confidence on the solid basis of his past performance with his well-tried and proven equipment. With that, all he needs is to soldier on.

Sometimes a visit to a shooting school is a good idea: the instructor can often re-build confidence wonderfully by showing the shooter just how well he can shoot. But it can also be a bad idea if the instructor takes advantage of the occasion to inculcate any radically new technique in a mature shooter who has shot well in the past. If all he needs is restored confidence, better that he should not be confused by trying to change his style.

Where the shooting school can be invaluable is in the second category cases, when a skilled instructor may succeed in identifying the change or changes that have caused the loss of form, and prescribing appropriate measures to counteract them.

Two principles.   To those hoodoo victims who rely on self-treatment, I would offer two important principles. First, avoid unnecessary hypotheses: proceed so far as possible on what is assured by past experience. Secondly, if there is reasonable suspicion of some enduring physical cause, do not try to identify it by changing more than one thing at a time. A hoodoo is the worst occasion for changing a previously satisfactory gun, for changing a gun may change several things simultaneously, including fit, patterns and placement of charge. I know of no more thoroughly frazzled shooters than some who have come to me after having failed to observe this principle.

The importance of practice.   Just as there are lucky people who can eat what they like to their heart's content without ever adding an ounce to their proper weight, so, I am prepared to believe, there are shooters who can shoot to the top of their bent at any time regardless of practice.

But they are abnormal. In all physical activities requiring judgment and co-ordination, practice normally brings about striking improvements in performance, and no man need be too critical of his standard of marksmanship if circumstances have deprived him of the regular practice he needs to find and maintain his best form.

Short of serious practice, 'dry' shooting with snap-caps, and even mounting and swinging the gun at imaginary targets, or at starlings, etc., is valuable in preserving form.

What should you expect?   Within the limits of my present intent, there remains but one question against the background of which the foregoing needs to be considered. It is the question of what a man expects from his endeavours in shooting.

He may have all the physical attributes of a good shot, he may have a sound basic technique, his gun and ammunition may be above reproach; and yet, if he expects too much of himself in the way of kills to cartridges—if his expectations run too far ahead of his performance—his self-esteem will suffer and with it his confidence. In consequence he will never realise his full potential, or the pleasure he should get from his shooting, and he may even end up by becoming one of those pitiable figures, a shooting hypochondriac.

William James had something highly relevant to say in this connection. He put it in terms of a formula, thus:

$$\text{Self-esteem} = \frac{\text{Success}}{\text{Pretensions}}$$

Translated into ordinary words, this gem of truth states that self-esteem is directly proportional to success and inversely proportional to pretensions. We see examples of this all around us. If a man's pretensions are high, he needs a large measure of success to nourish his self-esteem. If his pretensions are specific—if, say, he aims to be the world champion clay pigeon shooter in a particular class—his self-esteem can survive on no lesser terms. The final competitions may show beyond a doubt that although he is not the best man in all the world, he certainly ranks as the second best—a dizzy height of attainment that would more than fulfil the hopes of any less ambitious aspirant. But not his—oh no! He is only the second-best, and the light has gone out of the day.

A game shooter, as opposed to a clay pigeon shooter, is unlikely to have any *specific* pretensions, unless he is indiscreet enough to keep a regular record of his kills-to-cartridges, and to start beating his breast if he finds his ratio running lower than he thinks it should. For all that, he may be harbouring subconscious pretensions inconsistent with the preservation of his self-esteem, and therefore of his self-confidence.

What, then, can the average shooter reasonably expect of himself? The broad answer is that he should beware of expecting too much. More specifically, he should clearly recognise that, however skilful he may be, he must be prepared to accept a considerable proportion of misses as being inevitable in game shooting over anything beyond a brief occasion or period. And by game shooting, I mean all forms of bird and ground game shooting afield.

This inevitably arises, not only from the fact that he will have a certain characteristic pattern of aiming errors, which can only be modified, but never reduced to nothing, however much he may practise; but also from the technical limitations of shotguns and cartridges.

In the course of the remarkable experiments in duck shooting described in Chapter 23 it was found that only 71 per cent of the many

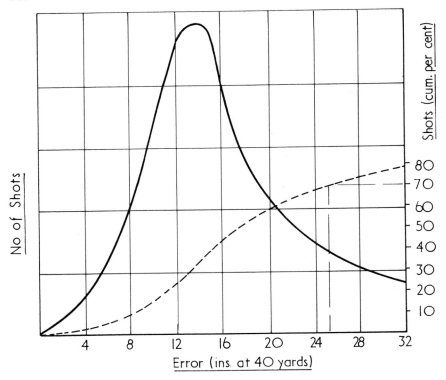

Fig. 100. Curve showing the author's characteristic aiming errors, as determined by experiment. The full line curve shows the proportionate number of shots associated with any particular error at 40 yards. The dotted curve shows the cumulative proportion covered at each stage of error

hundreds of mallard shot at 40 yards were killed instantly—and this was with 1¼ oz. of shot fired from a full choke under conditions that eliminated aiming errors.

With the smaller loads and more open-bored guns used in this country for game shooting, it is extremely unlikely that better results than those quoted would be attained against our common game birds, including pigeon.

So, the shooter who, consciously or subconsciously, harbours pretensions towards a hundred-per-cent performance, and is prone to start up a hoodoo long before approaching the 30 per cent Payne-Gallwey standard* for a whole season, had better take comfort, and pitch his expectations lower. Self-esteem, and with it confidence and perform-ance, will thereby benefit.

In conclusion, I would draw attention to fig. 100 which shows (in the form of a statistician's 'frequency curve') my personal aiming errors as experimentally determined. I believe that they may be taken as fairly representing the performance of an average shot at walked-up, going-away birds, flushed wild, and requiring quick, instinctive shooting—that is, without conscious aim.

It will be seen that I have a predominant tendency to an error corre-sponding to about 15 inches at 40 yards, and that, for a 70 per cent performance, I should require a well-filled pattern wide enough to cover an error of about 25 inches—i.e., one having a spread of 50 inches at that range. That is almost exactly the nominal spread of an improved cylinder. With any tighter patterns, the scoring would be lower.

---

* In his *Letters to Young Shooters* Sir Ralph Payne-Gallwey wrote:

'The following table is the result of several years of personal observation and careful enquiry. It gives the number of head usually killed by shooters of varied degrees of skill *under all conditions of game shooting* to every 100 shots fired:

Inferior marksman	25 per cent
Average marksman	30 per cent
Good marksman	35 per cent
Very good marksman	40 per cent
First-class marksman	45 per cent.'

These figures have been the subject of much argument, but Payne-Gallwey had what were prob-ably unequalled opportunities for forming a just opinion of the performance of the best shots in the heyday of shooting in this country. General Journée, it may be noted, gives even lower figures.

CHAPTER TWENTY-EIGHT

MISCELLANEA

There are several miscellaneous aspects of the gun which now require mention or recapitulation.

Safety catches. The limitations of these devices cannot be too widely understood. In practically all boxlock guns, they merely bolt the triggers. When applied, they do not uncock the hammers or do anything to prevent them from falling and firing the cartridge if the normal means for holding them up should fail, as fail they may, and for a variety of reasons. Faulty construction or adjustment, undue wear, the intrusion of a particle of foreign matter, the swelling of woodwork, or even a severe jolt, are all capable of causing the inadvertent discharge of a boxlock gun at 'Safe'. Sidelock guns of good quality are safer because their locks usually incorporate intercepting safety sears, which are specifically designed to catch the hammers if ever they should fall in any of the contingencies mentioned. But even intercepting sears are not infallible: the only safe gun is an unloaded gun—not merely a gun that is *believed* to be unloaded, but one that can be *seen* to be unloaded. A conventional gun with dropped barrels may be considered to comply with this condition, even if it has cartridges in the breech.

Slugs. Shotguns have, of course, been used time out of mind for firing single projectiles, ranging from solid ball (plain or patched) to the more modern Lethal, Rodda and Brenneke bullets. But none of these has enjoyed the popularity attained in recent years by the rifled slug. Indeed, in the USA, guns specially adapted for firing the slug are now available, such as the Ithaca Model 37 'Deerslayer'. This is a pump-action shotgun, bored true cylinder and fitted with rifle sights. Guns of this sort are acclaimed as the 'poor man's deer rifle' and for deer shooting in close country are highly effective weapons in the larger calibres.

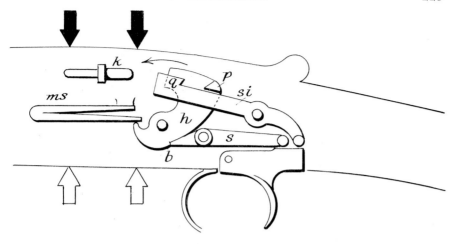

Fig. 101. Semi-diagrammatic view of a well-designed safety sear. If the hammer *h* is disengaged from the sear *s* by a jar, the projection *p* is caught in the notch *q*, thus preventing the hammer reaching the striker *k*. If, however, the sear is disengaged by the pulling of the trigger, *q* is depressed so as to clear the passage of *p*, whereby the hammer hits the striker and fires the gun. It should be noted that any jar (as in the direction of the black arrows) which tends to disengage the sear *s* tends equally to maintain the intercepting sear *si* in its correct position; and conversely with any jar coming in the opposite direction (white arrows). This feature arises from the preponderant weight of the two sears being to the right and left of their respective pivots

The appearance of the slug can be seen from fig. 102 except that it is deeply hollow, like a thimble. A 12-bore specimen when checked measured $\frac{3}{4}$ in. in length by about ·685 in. in diameter. If undeformed, it would thus pass through the constriction of a full choke, which measures, say ·689 in. When loaded in a standard game cartridge, such as a Grand Prix, this slug, which weighs 410 grains, gives the following ballistics:

	Muzzle	*25 yards*	*50 yards*
Velocity (ft./sec.)	1,450	1,305	1,175
Energy (ft./lb.)	1,910	1,550	1,255
Drop (inches)	—	0·6	2·7

The muzzle energy is thus almost exactly the same as that of the ·256 Mannlicher (1,960 ft./lb.), while the energy at 50 yards rather exceeds that of the soft-nosed Mannlicher bullet at 200 yards. The knock-down effect of one of these big slugs, travelling with such energy, is formidable. Accuracy is not good from heavily choked barrels, but from a cylinder, $3\frac{1}{2}$- or 4-inch groups at 50 yards may be expected.

Fig. 102.   12-bore rifled slug

The most likely sources of disappointment when using the slug are (1) firing at too long a range—50 yards is enough, and is a good range in wooded country—and (2) firing from a shotgun that has not been properly sighted in. This last operation is indispensable, particularly with a double gun. But the best prescription for a slug gun for woodland deer is undoubtedly a single-barrelled type, bored true cylinder, and fitted with a wide-aperture peep-sight adjusted for 50 yards.

Incidentally, a Firearm Certificate is needed to purchase slug cartridges.

Trigger pulls.   There are two bad handicaps to good shooting that are insufficiently recognised. They are soft, dragging trigger pulls; and trigger pulls which, though clean and crisp, are of unfamiliar weight. The latter are the bane of the man who uses different guns from day to day. Even if he has had all his triggers regulated to the same nominal weight, residual differences are well capable of affecting his form.

The ideal trigger pull, as has often been said, should resemble the breaking of a glass rod. For the average man, a $3\frac{1}{2}$ to 4 lb. pull for the right trigger and 4 to $4\frac{1}{2}$ lb. for the left is about correct. With cheap guns I have met some surprisingly good trigger pulls; but I have also met some very bad ones—pulls that were not only soft, but exceptionally heavy, perhaps as much as 8 lb. Such guns should not be accepted. (See also Chapter 9).

Shotgun sights.   Attempts have been made from time to time to improve the performance of the shotgun by various optical aids. The simplest are some modification of, or addition to, the familiar bead foresight. Clay pigeon shooters, for example, frequently favour an additional bead half-way down the rib. Luminous or semi-luminous foresights have also been tried, such as the 'Single point' SP280.

Ordinary low-powered telescopic sights have occasionally been used. A special application is that of a non-magnifying telescopic sight, which can be used with both eyes open, and has the effect of appearing to project a reticle or aiming mark to target distance.

The American 'Nydar' sight (no longer in production) was a variant of this idea. It, too, created an illusion of an aiming mark at target distance surrounded by a circle indicative of the extent of the spread of the shot charge. It could be used both for one-eyed and two-eyed shooting.

The 'Singlepoint' SP270 sight (fig. 103) works on a different principle. In essence, it is a source of light arranged to project an image of a small spot of light *backwards* into what is normally the shooter's aiming eye. The other eye views the target in the ordinary way.

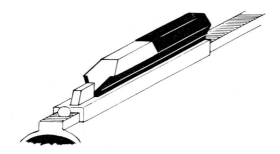

Fig. 103.   The Singlepoint SP 270 sight

The effect is that the spot appears to be superimposed on the target, thus enabling shooting to be done in near-darkness if necessary. But this requires independent illumination, as by a radio-active light source. As currently made for use with a shotgun, the Singlepoint utilises the light from fluorescent Perspex, which needs daylight for its excitation.

The Singlepoint has the disadvantage of cutting off the view of the target to the aiming eye, but at the same time appears to be immune from parallactic error due to inaccurate gun mounting, whereby the eye is not located correctly in relation to the rib.

Chromium plating of bores.   This process is much favoured by some foreign gunmakers, and is often made the subject of a sales story. But as a process capable of adding materially to the thickness of barrel walls without contributing to their strength, 'chroming' is regarded with disfavour by the British proof authorities, who have ruled 'that barrels treated in this way must be considered to have been potentially reduced in strength and be deemed to be unproved barrels under Section 110 of the Gun Barrel Proof Act'. The buyer of a second-hand gun is thus protected against the possibility of serious pitting in the barrels being filled up and concealed by deposited metal.

As applied to new guns, chroming takes the form of 'hard-chrome'— a coating of extreme hardness and microscopic thinness. It is claimed to protect the bores from corrosion, to eliminate wear, to reduce friction and thereby leading, and, by reducing the abrasion of the shot pellets, to improve patterns and to increase average pellet energy.

But, unfortunately, the kind of guns to which hard-chrome is most frequently applied are guns that have never had their shooting regulated at the time of manufacture, so that there can be no assurance that they give patterns of correct density or adequate quality. For satisfactory performance, such guns often need regulating, or at least the choke may need to be reduced. This can easily be done if the bores are left plain, but not if they are hard-chromed: the coating is so intensely hard that ordinary tools will not touch it, and some gunsmiths will not be bothered to work on barrels so treated.

For the rest, when used with modern rustless cartridges, barrels do not need the protection of plating. Nor do they need any enhanced resistance to wear: with a bare minimum of attention they often improve with age and will normally outlast the shooter. As for the reduction of friction, leading and pellet abrasion, this is dependent on the bore being adequately polished before the plating is applied. Failing that, chroming may operate seriously and most obstinately in reverse. It is never applied to best English guns except to special order, and I can only regard it as being at best unnecessary, and at worst, a nuisance and a mistake.

Bursts. It is well to bear in mind that *every* gun, irrespective of its quality and condition, has a powerful and innate tendency to burst in service; also that, although the average shooter may never come across an instance in the whole of his lifetime, *any* gun can easily be provoked into bursting by a simple act of negligence.

Bursts may occur by excessive pressure in barrels of normal strength—for example, by overloading, including the use of an unduly strong cap or primer; or by an obstruction, such as the inadvertent insertion of a 20-bore cartridge in front of a 12-bore. Even an excessively strong turnover or crimp, caused by the incautious use of glue or varnish, should be regarded as a potentially dangerous obstruction.

A special kind of excessive pressure is 'wave pressure', caused by the sudden checking of high-velocity gases in the barrel by an obstruction.

Fig. 104. Barrel burst by plug of mud or snow at muzzle. Note ring bulge which preceded burst

This causes a pile-up of the gases behind the obstruction, giving rise to a localised high pressure, which may burst the barrel, or at least cause a 'ring-bulge'. A plug of mud or snow in the muzzle of a gun is perhaps the most familiar cause of a wave-pressure bulge or burst (fig. 104). Next come cleaning implements or materials left in the bore; and after that, perhaps, some component of a faulty cartridge.

Bursts may, of course, also be caused by strictly normal pressures in barrels of inadequate strength. These include barrels never designed or proved for the pressures to which they are subjected, such as those of some of the old black powder guns when used with smokeless powder. More particularly included are these same barrels when they have been weakened by undue bore enlargement in the course of removing pitting.

Sometimes a barrel contains a flaw, such as a 'roke' formed by the inclusion and subsequent rolling out of a particle of slag in the original steel ingot. Or it may have been scored in the rib groove by a sharp tool when the barrels were struck up by the barrel maker. These flaws sometimes survive proof but subsequently cause the barrel to fail in normal service.

Protection against bursts is best afforded (1) by never using a gun which has not been nitro-proved, or one which is under suspicion of being out of proof; (2) by never using any ammunition other than that specifically stated on the carton to be suited to the gauge, chamber length and proof status of the weapon; (3) by sticking strictly to the book when home-loading; and (4) by unfailingly looking through the barrels before putting the gun together, and thereafter on every occasion when an obstruction could conceivably have been picked up, or when anything unusual is heard or felt on firing.

In the event of any untoward incident, the gun should not be cleaned until it has been inspected by a gunsmith; and the remaining cartridges from the box, and the box itself, should be carefully preserved. (For further advice on procedure in the case of a burst, see *Gough Thomas's Gun Book*, pp. 262–5.)

Misfires and hang-fires.　　Modern guns and ammunition are so reliable that it is possible for a shooter to fire many cartridges over a long period of years without experiencing a single misfire. On the other hand, I occasionally receive reports of persistent trouble from this cause.

In most cases the cartridge—and that means the cap in this context— is immediately suspected, and not unnaturally.

The normal type of shotgun cap is a simple affair. There is a little copper cup, the base of which is the part we see in the centre of the cartridge head. In the base of the cup is a shallow layer of the detonating compound, usually covered with a protective disc of thin metal foil, and then varnished. Next comes the anvil, which can be a piece of sheet brass, stamped into the form of a broad arrowhead, with its blunt point resting on the foil-covered compound. In Eley cartridges, this form of anvil has long since been superseded by an ingenious tubular anvil, roughly resembling the shape of a bishop's mitre, which appears to have cured the gas-escapes from which we used to suffer.

The cap, with its anvil, is pressed into the cap chamber, which is a slightly larger cup with a hole—the flash-hole—in its base, through which the flame of the cap emerges to ignite the powder. The caps of some Continental cartridges are of a somewhat more involved construction, intended to ensure gas-tight performance, and known as *amorçage fermée*, though the difference is not relevant in the present context.

Although the cap or primer of a cartridge is such a simple contrivance, it cannot be relied upon to detonate when it is struck unless several conditions are fulfilled. Even if it has been made and assembled faultlessly, it needs to be struck centrally, by a striker of more or less correct form, and by a blow of adequate weight. For safety's sake, caps must obviously not be made too sensitive, and to ensure that they are sensitive enough they are batch-tested in the factory by a simple falling-weight test. This alone should give pause to anyone inclined to attribute persistent misfires to the cartridges, as a matter of course.

For all that, manufacturing faults are not unknown. One hears of missing anvils, anvils assembled upside down and possibly other freaks; but although an isolated misfire may be caused in this manner, it is extremely unlikely that more than a single cartridge would be affected. When there is persistent misfiring, the gun should always be suspected first. Its potential deficiencies, already indicated, will repay closer study.

The cap does not always receive a truly central blow. For example, in old hammer guns, with relatively large, high hammers and sloping strikers, the cap receives a blow which is far from direct: it may act along a line that is 30 degrees or more away from the axis of the barrel; and unless the striker has been cleverly positioned, the indentation it makes in the cap may noticeably side-step the point of the anvil. It is for this reason that the strikers of these old guns were larger at the end than those of modern hammerless guns. Clearly, the larger the striker, the more certain it will be to hit the vital spot, though the strength of the blow will be proportionately dissipated over a larger surface.

Over-and-under guns suffer more misfires than side-by-sides—partiy because of the obliquity of their strikers and partly because the protrusion of the lower one may have to be curtailed to clear the opening arc.

But a direct and central blow is not enough: there must be an adequate punch behind it, and this may fail for several reasons. If, for example, the striker is worn, or if it was made too short in the first instance, so that there is insufficient protrusion from the breech face, the cap will not receive the full force of the blow. In an ordinary hammerless gun, there is not much latitude here for error, since the striker, even when new and unworn, does not project more than about 0·07 inch. So, if the rim recess of the barrel is of maximum depth, with worn shoulders, giving the largest possible headspace clearance, the cap will tend to ride the punch. The make of cartridge is especially relevant,

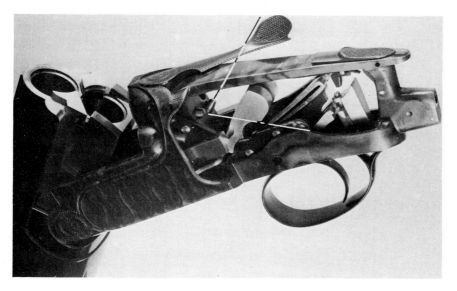

Fig. 105.   O/U action showing marked obliquity of strikers

because one kind may easily drop ·010 inch further into the chamber than another.

The cap will also ride the punch to a certain extent if, through deformation of the cap chamber or other cause, the anvil is not firmly supported, or if the cap itself is below the level of the cartridge head. This is a point for reloaders to watch.

I have left until last the most obvious cause of persistent misfires, namely, a weak mainspring, or one which is impeded in some way. In such cases, there is immediate evidence available in the shape of a weak cap-impression. Coil mainsprings are most open to suspicion of weakening, but where they are used care should be taken to avoid excessive lubrication, which, in very cold weather, can well-nigh put such springs out of action, owing to the congealing of the oil. In Arctic climates, users of bolt-action rifles and other weapons with coil mainsprings quickly learn to keep oil away from them. Even vee springs are not immune. I remember a friend's gun which misfired time and again one bitter morning. This was a best English gun with vee mainsprings; but my friend had been using Vaseline—'only a little'—to preserve the lockwork. It was enough.

To anyone who suffers a sudden spate of misfires I would say, do not do what one of my acquaintances did and throw the rest of the cartridges into a pond, with appropriate maledictions. The manufacturers would be glad to have them, complete with the carton. They are almost certain to have some interesting and enlightening comments to make, and if they have to confess that they are at fault, they will no doubt be anxious to do the right thing by the complainant.

There remains the hang-fire. Hang-fires are usually caused by the scintillation of black powder residue in the breech or flash-channel of muzzle-loading guns, and are virtually unknown with modern central-fire ammunition. I have, however, heard of very old cartridges which were prone to hang-fire, perhaps for a second or less. The conditions imaginable here were probably deteriorated caps, giving a feeble flame, and a powder also deteriorated or contaminated by grease from the wadding, in which the rate of propagation of combustion was much reduced. Intense cold would aggravate any such case.

A misfire, therefore, should always alert the shooter to the faint possibility that he has a hang-fire on his hands; and if he can remember to do so, he should keep his gun safely at his shoulder and count ten before he takes it down and opens it.

Punt guns. The professional manufacture of punt guns (fig. 106) in this country appears to have ceased. At the same time there is an undoubted revival of interest in punt gunning, and a number of amateurs

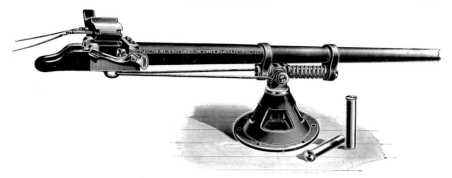

Fig. 106. A modern breech-loading punt gun by Messrs. Thomas Bland & Sons, with Snider-type breech action and spring recoil gear

with suitable resources have made their own. The more successful of these are generally constructed on the following principles.

The barrel is of seamless (solid drawn) steel tubing reinforced over the breech section by a larger solid drawn tube shrunk on. The trunnions are screwed and welded into this larger tube. The breech is a screw breech (fig. 107), and care is required to avoid unduly weakening the inner tube by the thread. The outer reinforcing tube should preferably be swaged and machined with an inwardly projecting shoulder to prevent the threaded portion of the inner tube coming back in the event of fracture. The same result can be got with a welded ring.

Cartridges are paper cartridges (fig. 108) crimped at the breech end

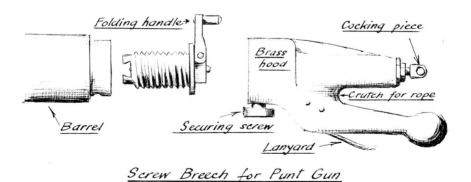

Fig. 107. Screw breech for a punt gun

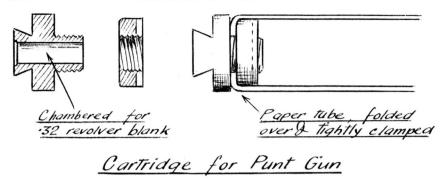

Chambered for ·32 revolver blank

Paper tube, folded over & tightly clamped

Cartridge for Punt Gun

Fig. 108.   Cartridge for a punt gun

and securely clamped between a solid brass head and a nut on a forward-projecting threaded portion. (If the breech has a right-hand thread, this thread should be left-handed.) The head of the cartridge can conveniently carry a dovetail for insertion in a corresponding recess in the breech face, whereby both are withdrawn together. The cartridge primer is a ·32 revolver blank. The only powder used should be the large-grained, black, punt gun powder. The normal load for a punt gun is a pound of shot for every 100 pounds of gun, and 3 ounces of powder for every pound of shot.

The following weights, bores and recommended charges are taken with due acknowledgment from Stanley Duncan's *The Complete Wildfowler*:

TABLE 14.   Punt Gun sizes and loads

Size of bore (inches)	Weight (pounds)	Length of barrel	Charge of shot (ounces)	Charge of powder (ounces)
$1-1\frac{1}{4}$	50–75	6′8″–7′6″	8–12	$1\frac{1}{2}-2\frac{1}{4}$
$1\frac{3}{8}-1\frac{1}{2}$	80–120	7′9″–8′0″	16–20	$3-3\frac{3}{4}$
$1\frac{5}{8}-1\frac{3}{4}$	130–150	8′0″–8′6″	22–28	$4-4\frac{3}{4}$
$1\frac{7}{8}-1\frac{15}{16}$	160–170	8′9″–9′0″	30–34	$5\frac{1}{4}-6\frac{1}{4}$
$2-2\frac{1}{8}$	180–200	9′0″–9′6″	34–40	$6\frac{1}{4}-7\frac{1}{2}$

The ideal battery.   Wherever a high degree of manual skill has to be exercised, it is recognised that, for the best results, there must be total familiarity with any implement employed. This applies outstandingly to shooting; and although some shooters, more skilful and adaptable than others, may appear to shoot well with guns that differ considerably in several respects, there is little doubt that they would do even better if they could confine themselves to a single weapon. Accurate shooting depends on precise muscular response to visual stimuli, and the shooter who uses only one gun has deep channels of habit engraved in the nervous, mental and muscular machinery involved in the process. Give him a strange gun, and somewhere along the route a departure from the habitual channel of response will need to be established before he can use it proficiently.

So, for the best results of which a given man is capable, there is no doubt that the ideal battery is *one gun*—or a matched pair, or a single gun with alternative barrels, provided that they differ only in the matter of boring.

If, in order to cope with the different kinds of sport he pursues, a man cannot avoid having several guns, it is better, from the viewpoint of performance, that the guns should be conspicuously different as to weight, balance, etc. What is most prejudicial to proficiency is to have two or more guns, similar but by no means well matched, for the same class of sport, and to use them indiscriminately.

There are some riders to the one-gun philosophy. The gun should be a good one in which the shooter has complete confidence derived from undeniable experience. It should be well balanced, and should fit him to perfection. It should throw good and consistent patterns with the potentialities and limitations of which he is thoroughly familiar. Its mechanical functioning should be smooth and easy, and free from all sources of distraction. As previously emphasised, the trigger pulls should be crisp and of suitable weight.

The ideal gun (or pair of guns) should not be too new, or rare or precious. A regular sportsman could hardly be induced to appear with some of the beautifully chiselled and gold-bedizened specimens that one sees. Their place is obviously the show cabinet, not the field. So the ideal gun, to attain that state, has had its newness worn off. By honourable service, combined with good care, it has acquired a special patina—the unmistakable mark of a seasoned campaigner.

The sportsman who owns such a gun can afford to view with detachment, not to mention complacency, the array of beautiful specimens acquired by those more interested in collecting guns than in using them.

The observation is opportune. At the end of this book, it recalls what I said at the beginning. Sporting guns, valuable as they may be, and fascinating as they undoubtedly are to use and study, are by themselves but the key to a door. Beyond it lies a whole world of associated interests, capable of enriching the leisure hours of their possessor for the best part of his lifetime. It is on that note—that consideration—that I would like to end this study of the gun.

THE PROVING OF GUNS

At the time of writing, guns proved in this country are dealt with in accordance with the Rules of Proof 1954—a system of rules, regulation and scales drawn up by the British joint proof authorities under the authority of the Gun Barrel Proof Act, 1868, and approved by the appropriate Minister.

(1) Extracts from memoranda issued jointly by the British Proof Authorities

   (a) *Information as to Barrel Enlargement—Details of Proof Sizes (Memorandum issued 3rd June, 1959)*

'Set out (below) are the nominal bore sizes under the 1954 Rules of Proof and the corresponding nominal figures under the earlier Rules of 1925:

BORE	Rules of 1925 OLD MARKING Nominal Size	Rules of 1954 PRESENT MARKING Nominal Diameter (in.)
12	12/1	0·740
	12	0·729
	13/1	0·719
	13	0·710
16	16/1	0·669
	16	0·662
	17/1	0·655
	17	0·649
	18	0·637
20	19	0·626
	20	0·615
	21	0·605
	22	0·596

'At proof if a plug gauge of ·729 in. diameter (but not one of ·740 in.) will enter the bore to a depth of 9 in., that barrel is at present marked ·729 in. and under the 1925 Rules of Proof would have been marked 12—and so on for the other bore sizes.

Rule 7 of Rules of Proof 1954 (as revised with effect from 1st September, 1966) reads as follows:

'If any Barrel of the First Class which shall be marked as proved under the Principal Act or these Rules, shall by any Process of Manufacture or by any other Means whatsoever other than the User and Wear and Tear thereof, be so enlarged in the bore that it will accept to a depth of 9 inches from its breech face, a plug gauge of the next larger diameter to that marked on the occasion of last proof or reproof, and thereby be unduly reduced in Substance or Strength, such Barrel shall be deemed unproved.'

(b) *Black Powder Guns (Memorandum revised May, 1960)*

'A gun is proved for Black Powder only (and is almost certainly over 60 years old) unless the markings on the barrel include one of the following marks and/or the words 'nitro proof':

'Shooters are therefore urged most strongly not to buy any gun not bearing the marks of nitro-proof and not to permit the continued use of any such gun in their possession until it has passed nitro-proof.'

(New Eley Magnum Cartridges. Note that normal English nitro-proof for 12-bore $2\frac{3}{4}$-inch and 3-inch chambered guns is not adequate for the corresponding new Eley Magnum cartridges, loaded with $1\frac{1}{2}$ and $1\frac{5}{8}$ oz. of shot respectively. These require guns to be submitted to a new Magnum proof; though the $2\frac{3}{4}$-inch Eley Magnum may safely be used in a 3-inch chambered gun proved to the normal nitro-proof standard.

Continental guns require to be proved to 900 kg./sq. cm. for the $2\frac{3}{4}$-inch Magnum cartridge and 1000 kg./sq. cm. for the 3-inch.)

(c) *The Repair of Gun Barrels by Welding (Memorandum issued 2nd February, 1956)*

'The Proof Authorities . . . warn members of the (gun) trade that the welding of any part of the barrel or barrels or the breech action body, breech-block or its equivalent is potentially dangerous.'

(For the full text of these and other memoranda, and much other useful information on British and foreign proof and proof marks, see *Notes on the Proof of Shot Guns and other Small Arms*, issued under the joint authority of the Worshipful Company of Gunmakers of the City of London and The Guardians of the Birmingham Proof House, and obtainable from either Proof House, at 48, Commercial Road, London, E.1, and at Banbury Street, Birmingham, 5, respectively.)

(2) Current Foreign Nitro-proof Marks

Key:

1. Austrian (Ferlach)	5. French (St. Etienne)
2. Austrian (Vienna)	6. W. German
3. Belgian	7. Italian
4. French (Paris)	8. Spanish

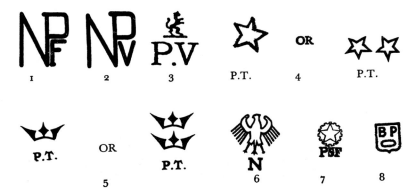

Two recently approved foreign marks are here shown to a larger scale:

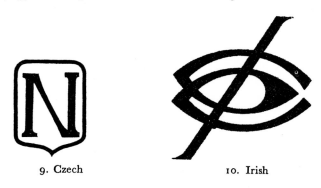

9. Czech   10. Irish

(3)   Metric Markings on Continental Guns

    (a)   *Bore and chamber length:* The nominal gauge followed by the chamber length in milli-
metres, e.g. 12/65 (12-bore, 2½ in.); 12/70 (12-bore, 2¾ in.); 12/75 (12-bore, 3 in.) Also
the bore dimensions at breech and muzzle (but breech only on Belgian guns) e.g. 18·2/
17·4 (·716 in./·685 in.).
        (To convert millimetres into inches, divide by 25·4.)

    (b)   *Barrel weight:* The finished weight in kilograms, e.g. 1·42 kg. (3·13 lb.).
        (To convert kilograms into pounds, multiply by 2·2.)

    (c)   *Proof pressure:* The nominal pressure in kilograms per square centimetre, e.g.
1,150 kg. (7·3 tons per sq. in.).
        (To convert to tons per sq. inch, divide by 157·5.)

Notes:

    (1)   Owing to differences in the methods and apparatus used for their determination, British
and Continental proof pressures cannot be directly compared.

    (2)   The proof pressures stamped on Continental guns or quoted in their test certificates
must not be confused with the service pressures stamped on those made and/or proved
in Britain. The former are test pressures: the latter are working pressures.)

METRIC EQUIVALENTS

The following table gives the approximate metric equivalents of the more common quantities associated with shotguns and their ammunition and their appropriate conversion factors. (See also Appendix One (3)).

WEIGHTS

Guns

(To convert pounds to kilograms multiply by ·45)

$$5\tfrac{1}{2}\text{ lb.} = 2\cdot5 \text{ kilograms}$$
$$6 \quad = 2\cdot73$$
$$6\tfrac{1}{2} \quad = 2\cdot95$$
$$7 \quad = 3\cdot18$$

(To convert kilograms to pounds multiply by 2·2)

Shot

(To convert ounces to grams multiply by 28·35)

$$\tfrac{7}{8}\text{ ounces} = 23\cdot4 \text{ grams}$$
$$1 \quad = 28\cdot35$$
$$1\tfrac{1}{8} \quad = 31\cdot9$$
$$1\tfrac{1}{4} \quad = 35\cdot4$$
$$1\tfrac{1}{2} \quad = 42\cdot5$$
$$1\tfrac{3}{4} \quad = 49\cdot5$$

(To convert grams to ounces multiply by ·0352)

Powder

(To convert grains to grams multiply by ·065)

$$20\text{ grains} = 1\cdot3 \text{ grams}$$
$$22 \quad = 1\cdot43$$
$$24 \quad = 1\cdot56$$
$$26 \quad = 1\cdot69$$
$$28 \quad = 1\cdot82$$
$$30 \quad = 1\cdot95$$

(To convert grams to grains multiply by 15·38)

LENGTHS

Barrels

(To convert inches to centimetres multiply by 2·54)

$$
\begin{array}{rl}
25\ \text{inches} &= 63\cdot5\ \text{cm.} \\
26 &= 66\cdot0 \\
27 &= 68\cdot5 \\
28 &= 71\cdot0 \\
29 &= 74\cdot0 \\
30 &= 76\cdot2
\end{array}
$$

(To convert centimetres to inches multiply by ·394)

Chambers

(To convert inches to millimetres multiply by 25·4)

$$
\begin{array}{rl}
2\ \text{inches} &= 51 \\
2\tfrac{1}{2} &= 63 \\
2\tfrac{3}{4} &= 70 \\
3 &= 76
\end{array}
$$
(To nearest mm.)

(To convert millimetres to inches multiply by ·0394)

FIREARMS AND THE LAW

The following is an abstract of the Home Office and Central Office of Information pamphlet, *Firearms—what you need to know about the law* (1969 HMSO Dd 571811), based on the Firearms Act 1968 and here duly amended to cover changes resulting from the Courts Act 1971 and the Criminal Justice Act 1972. It is reproduced by permission; and although it is believed to provide authentic guidance at the date of publication of this book, it is not to be regarded as a substitute for the relevant statutes.

FIREARMS—WHAT YOU NEED TO KNOW
ABOUT THE LAW

In general, if you wish to acquire, possess or use any firearm you must obtain a certificate from the local chief officer of police. There are certain exceptions set out below.

(1) AIR WEAPONS

If you are 17 years of age or over you may buy or hire most types of air gun, air pistol, etc., and the ammunition for them, without restriction. It is an offence liable to 6 months' imprisonment or a fine of £400 or both to sell an air weapon to a person under 17. You may give or lend it to anyone over 14; but to make a gift of an air weapon to anyone under 14 is an offence liable to a £100 fine. (See section 5 below: 'The Law and Young People'.)

Certain types of air weapon are declared specially dangerous by the Secretary of State; these may not be obtained unless you have a firearm certificate (see section 3 below).

(2) SHOT GUNS

You may not possess, purchase or acquire a shot gun unless you have already obtained a shot gun certificate from your local police. They may refuse one if they consider that your possession of a shot gun would endanger public safety or if such possession is forbidden by the Firearms Act. If you obtain a shot gun without holding a valid certificate you are liable on conviction to a maximum of 6 months' imprisonment or a £400 fine or both.

You may not sell, lend or give a shot gun to anyone who has not got a shot gun certificate. The maximum penalty for doing so is 3 years' imprisonment or a fine or both.

You may not make a gift of a shot gun to anybody under 15 years of age. The maximum penalty for doing so is a fine of £100.

There is no restriction on the possession, purchase, or acquisition of shot gun ammunition by persons over 17.

These prohibitions are subject to the following exemptions. You do not need a shot gun certificate if:

  (i) you borrow a shot gun from the occupier of private premises (including land) and use it thereon in his presence

  (ii) you use someone else's shot gun on artificial targets at a place and time approved by the local chief officer of police

  (iii) you are visiting Great Britain from abroad for a total of not more than 30 days in any 12 months

  (iv) you possess a Northern Ireland firearm certificate for a shot gun

  (v) you are in possession of a weapon (for which someone else holds a certificate) in a theatrical or film production

  (vi) your weapon is 'an antique firearm' which has been sold, transferred, purchased, acquired or is possessed as a curiosity or ornament

  (vii) you are under instructions from another person who holds a certificate and you are carrying a weapon for his/her use for sporting purposes only

  (viii) you use a weapon for drill or target practice as a member of a rifle club or cadet corps approved by a Secretary of State

  (ix) you are engaged in the business of a registered firearms dealer

  (x) you are in possession of a weapon in the course of the business of an auctioneer, carrier, warehouseman or slaughterer of animals

  (xi) you are in possession of a weapon *on board* a ship, or as a signalling apparatus *on board* an aircraft or at an aerodrome

  (xii) you are in possession of a weapon (for which someone else holds a certificate) for starting races at an athletics meeting

NOTE: For the purposes of this section a shot gun is 'a smooth bore gun having a barrel not less than 24 inches in length not being an air gun.' The restrictions on shorter shot guns are set out in Section 3 below.

(3) RIFLES, PISTOLS AND REVOLVERS, SPECIALLY DANGEROUS AIR WEAPONS AND SHOT GUNS WITH BARRELS LESS THAN 24 INCHES LONG

You may not possess, purchase or acquire any of these weapons (nor any other firearm not mentioned in Sections 1 and 2 above) unless you have already obtained a firearm certificate from your local police. They will not issue a certificate unless they are satisfied that you have good reason for having it, that public safety is not endangered, and that you are fit to be entrusted with a firearm. The chief officer of police may impose conditions, and may revoke a certificate.

If you gain possession of any of these weapons without a certificate, you are liable on conviction to a maximum of 3 years' imprisonment or a fine or both.

You are not allowed to possess, purchase or acquire most types of ammunition for these weapons unless you have a firearm certificate.

You may not sell, lend or give any of these weapons (or most types of ammunition for them) to anyone who has not got a firearm certificate. The maximum penalty for doing so is 3 years' imprisonment or a fine or both.

You may not lend, or make a gift of, any of these weapons or any ammunition for them to a child under 14 years old; and you may not sell them to anyone under 17. If you do, you are liable on conviction to a maximum of 6 months' imprisonment or a maximum fine of £400 or both.

Exemptions. You do not need a firearm certificate if you are in any of the exempted categories (v) to (xii) mentioned in section 2 or if you are in charge of a miniature rifle range or shooting gallery where the weapons used are air weapons not classified as 'specially dangerous' or rifles not exceeding ·23 inch calibre.

(4) PROHIBITED WEAPONS

Continuous-fire weapons (for example machine guns) are generally prohibited, as are weapons which discharge gas or any harmful substance and similar weapons and ammunition. You may not possess, purchase or acquire them without a written authority from the Home Office or the Scottish Home and Health Department, in addition to a firearm certificate.

(5) THE LAW AND YOUNG PEOPLE

If you are under 14 years of age you may not possess, purchase or acquire any firearm or ammunition, nor may anyone give or lend you any. But there are the following exceptions to this general rule.
  (i) You may possess and use firearms and ammunition
       a. as a member of an approved club; or
       b. when you are shooting in a shooting gallery where only air weapons or miniature rifles are available.
 (ii) You may possess and use any air weapon if you are not in a public place and are using it under the supervision of somebody over 21; but you may not use it for firing a missile beyond the premises or land where you are being supervised.
(iii) You may carry a firearm or ammunition under the instruction of another person who holds a certificate and for his or her use for sporting purposes only.

If you are 14 or over, you may be given or lent an air weapon or its ammunition and, if you have a firearm certificate, you may be given or lent any firearm or ammunition covered by section 3 above.
If you are under 15 and have a shot gun certificate (see section 2 above), you may have with you an assembled shot gun provided you are supervised by a person over 21 or the shot gun is in a gun cover securely fastened.
If you are 15 or over and have a shot gun certificate (see section 2 above), you may be given a shot gun as a gift.
If you are under 17 you may not purchase or hire any firearm or its ammunition.
If you are under 17 you may carry an air gun or air rifle in a public place, but only if it is in a gun cover securely fastened.

(6) APPEALS

If the police refuse to grant, vary or renew a firearm or shot gun certificate, in England and Wales you may appeal to the Crown Court on giving notice within 21 days to the Chief Clerk and the chief officer of police; in Scotland you may appeal to the sheriff.

(7) OFFENCES

It is an offence to infringe any of the above requirements. There are also the following specific offences created by the Firearms Act:

Offence	*Maximum Penalties*
(i) To trade in any way in firearms and shot guns without being registered with the police as a firearms dealer	3 years or a fine or both
(ii) To shorten the barrel of a shot gun to less than 24 inches in length	5 years or a fine or both

(iii) To convert in any way an imitation firearm into a lethal weapon	5 years or a fine or both
(iv) To possess a firearm or ammunition with intent to injure a person	life or a fine or both
(v) To use real or imitation firearm to resist arrest	life or a fine or both
(vi) To carry a real or imitation firearm with intent to commit a crime	14 years or a fine or both
(vii) To supply a firearm to anyone who is prohibited from having one	3 years or a fine or both
(viii) To carry without lawful authority or reasonable excuse a loaded shot gun or air weapon or any other firearm (whether loaded or not) together with ammunition suitable for use in that firearm	5 years or a fine or both
(ix) To trespass without reasonable excuse with a firearm:	
(a) in a building	5 years or a fine or both
(b) on land	3 months or a £200 fine or both
(x) To acquire, possess or use any firearm or ammunition for 5 years after release from any detention or imprisonment of 3 months or more	3 years or a fine or both

(8) THE PROOF OF FIREARMS

Proof is the compulsory testing of every firearm (except air weapons) to ensure its safety before it is first offered for sale. Reproof is the similar testing of a firearm which has gone out of proof by reason of alteration or wear.

The Gun Barrel Proof Acts 1868 and 1950 lay down that no small arm may be sold, exchanged or exported, exposed or kept for sale or exchange or pawned unless and until it has been fully proved and duly marked with a recognised proof mark. The maximum penalty for such offences is a fine of £20 for each unproved barrel.

The offence of dealing in unproved arms is committed by the seller, not by an unwitting purchaser.

If you are doubtful about the proof of your firearm, you should take it to a gunmaker or to the Proof House, 48 Commercial Road, London E1, or to the Birmingham Gun Barrel Proof House, Banbury Street, Birmingham 5.

If you are in any doubt about firearms seek advice from the police.

Never take risks with firearms! Take out an insurance policy against accidents.

Visitors from abroad
If you are visiting Great Britain from abroad and stay for a total of *not more than 30 days in any 12 months*, you do not need a shot gun certificate. *Otherwise all the restrictions in this leaflet apply to you.*

Import and export of firearms
Both imports and exports of firearms are controlled in Great Britain. Details may be obtained from the Department of Trade: Import Licensing Branch, 1 Victoria Street, London SW1; Export Licensing Branch, Sanctuary Buildings, 20 Great Smith Street, London SW1.

BIBLIOGRAPHY

Principal works consulted:

The Modern Shotgun by Major Sir Gerald Burrard–(1931)

Tir des Fusils de Chasse by General Journée–2nd edition (1902) and 3rd edition (1949)

Sporting Guns and Gunpowders Parts I and II–(1897–1900)

The Mysteries of Shotgun Patterns by G. G. Oberfell and C. E. Thompson–(1960)

The Gun and its Development by W. W. Greener–9th edition (1910)

High Pheasants in Theory and Practice by Sir Ralph Payne-Gallwey–(1914)

The Lyman Shotshell Handbook–1st edition (1969)

The Shotgun Stock by Dr. Robert Arthur–(1971)

INDEX

Accuracy, problems of, 187
Actions, 141
  bar, flexure of, 142, 144
  boxlock, 26, 27
  sidelock, 27, 28
  sliding breech (Darne), 28
  trigger-plate, 29
Adjustomatic, 81
American cartridge components, 105
Armalite, 39
Armi Famars, 27
Automatics (self-loaders):
  gas-operated, 39
  long-recoil, 39
  manually-operated, 37
  recoil-operated, 39
  short-recoil, 39
  weight of, 39
AYA, 33, 41

Balance, 45, 158
  a dynamic quality, 158
  data, 163
  definition of, 160
  measuring, 161
  optimum, 164
Balling, 87, 88, 89
  crypto-, 87, 88, 92
Barrels, 131
  aluminium alloy, 131

chamberless, 137
chambers, 134
chopper lumped, 132
chromed, 131
cones, 135
fibre-glass, 131
length, 137
material, 131
monobloc, 132
parts and assembly, 131, 133
rifled for shot, 65, 134
sleeving, 138
top extensions, 144, 145
Battery, the ideal, 238
Beauty, 48
Benelli, 39
Blaine, D. P., 218
Bolt-action, 46
Bolt, under-barrel, 145
Bores, 24
chromium plating of, 231
Boss, 47
Boxlock, 27, 148
  safety of, 149
  strength of, 149
  variant forms, 151
Browning, F. N., 39
BSA, 116
Burrard, Sir Gerald, 52, 55, 126, 152, 153
Bursts, 232

Caps, 87
Care and Maintenance, 208
  cases and covers, 209
  cleaning, 46
  guns and cars, 210
  insurance, 212
  lubrication, 211
Cartridges, 83
  bad, effect of, 60
  case:
    functions of, 84
    length of, 85
    paper, 83, 84
    plastic, 83, 97
    plastic (bio-degradable), 85
  crimp closure, 63
  Dispersante, 65
  Eley, 83, 86
  imported, 99
  manufacture of, 92
  Maximum, 95, 96
  new developments, 97
  spreader, 65
  two-inch 12-bore, 85
  Wanda, 98
  Winchester, compression-formed, 98
Chamberless gun, 99
Chambers, 83
  cone, 99
  contamination of, 84
Choice of gun (performance), 51
Choice of gun (type), 43
Choke, 71
  anomalies, 72
  automatic, 79
  best degree of, 77
  definitions of, 72
  for trapshooting, 78
  invention of, 75
  recess, 71
  trumpet, 71
  types of, 74
  variable, 79, 81, 82
  Winchoke, 82
Chromium-plated bores, 231

Churchill, 126
Clay pigeon guns, 113
  borings, 114
  effect of expansion on, 115
  MPI of, 115
  release triggers, 117
  testing of, 117
  triggers and trigger pulls, 117
Cleaning, 210
Coloroll Company, 85
Cutts Compensator, 81

Darne gun, 26, 45, 46
Drilling, 26
Duncan, Stanley, 238
Durability, 47

Ejectors, 31
  Baker, 31, 32
  Deeley, 31, 32
  Holland & Holland, 31
  optional, 33
  Southgate, 31
Eley reloading notes, 106
Energy:
  minimum striking, 53
  striking, 54
Eugeny Petrov, 72

Field, in the, 219
  aiming errors, 227
  practice, importance of, 224
  success v. pretensions, 225
  the beginner, 219
  the mature shooter, 220
Field, The, 75
Fitting, 171
Flintlock, 19
French Ammunition Society (SFM), 101

Game charges, pellets in, 58
Gape, 45
Garwood action, 126
Greener G.P. gun, 30
Greener, W. W., 75
Gun cleaning, 211

Gun fitting, 171
Gun-rifle, 26
Guns:
    choice of (performance), 51
    choice of (type), 43
    clay pigeon, 113–17
    conventional, 26, 41
        boxlock, 27
        hammer, 26
        over-and-under, 30
        self-opening, 122
        side-by-side, 26
        sidelock, 27
        single-barrelled, 30
        sliding breech (Darne), 28
        trigger-plate action, 29
    magnum, 118–22
    Paradox, ball and shot, 31
    punt, 236
    repeaters:
        bolt-action, 39, 46
        gas-operated, 39
        manually-operated, 37
        pump, 37, 39, 114
        recoil-operated, 39
        weight of, 39
    second-hand, 49
    special (for boys, women, elderly
        and disabled shooters), 127
Gun Trade Association, 49

Hammer gun, 26
Hang-fires, 234
Hartman, Barney, 185
Heat-haze, 189
Historical background, 17
Holland & Holland, 126
Home-loading and reloading, 100
    black powder loads, 104
    equipment, 101
    IMI, Notes on, 106–12
    precautions, 101
    procedure, 103
Houiller, 84

IMI, 53, 154

International Proof Commission
    (CIP), 134

Jointing, 143
Journée, General, 90, 136, 157

Kerné, 119

Lancaster, 126
Law, firearms and the, 245
Lead poisoning, 99
Lefaucheux, 21, 84
Litter problem, 85
Loads, 93
    black powder, 104
    high velocity, 97

Magnum guns, 118
    small bore, 119
Maintenance, ease of, 46
Manipulation, ease of, 45
Manton, 162, 163
Martini action, 30
Matchlock, 17
Metric equivalents, 243
Mirage, 189
Miscellanea, 228
Misfires, 234
Muzzle-brake, 79, 153
    principle of, 156
Muzzle-loaders, 213
    Blaine, W. D., 218
    commissioning, 215
    dangers, 217
    loading procedure, 216
    loads, 216
    Muzzle-Loaders' Association, 213
    replicas, 213
    types of, 17–20, 214

Newton, Isaac, 152
Nitro proof, 50, 241, 242
Nydar sight, 231

Oberfell & Thompson, 69
One-gun philosophy, 239

Operation, quietness of, 46
Over-and-under, 30, 113

Pape, W. R., 75
Paradox ball and shot gun, 31
Patterns, 60
    close range, 65
    factors affecting, 62
    minimum, 53
    percentage for all borings, 54
    spread, 74
    testing for, 64, 117
    voids, 68, 69
Payne-Gallwey, Sir Ralph, 199, 227
Pellets in game charges, 58
Perazzi, 29, 46
Percussion muzzle-loaders, 21
Performance:
    comprehensive diagram, 55
Pinfire, 21
Poly-choke, 81
Pointability, 180
Portability, 46
Powders, 85
    Amberite, 154
    deteriorated, 101
    Nobel-Glasgow, 85
    progressive, 87, 94
    storage of, 101
Proof and proof marks, 50, 240
Pulls, trigger, 117
Pump guns, 37, 39, 114
Punt guns, 236
    sizes and loads, 238
Purdey, 35, 126

Range:
    extreme, 59
    maximum effective, 52
    maximum killing, 51
Recoil, 152
    brake, 153, 156
    dynamic, 152–4
    fallacy, 154
    pathological cases, 156
    reducers, 155

sensible, 152–4
    velocity of, 152, 153
Reliability, 47
Reloading, 100–12
Repairability, 47
Repeaters, 22, 37, 38, 42
    bolt-action, 39, 46
    gas-operated, 39
    manually-operated, 37
    recoil-operated, 39
    weight of, 39
Ribs, 182, 185, 186, 192, 193

Safety, 45, 219, 220
Safety catches, 228, 229
Second-hand guns, 49
Self-loaders (see Automatics)
Self-opening actions, 35, 126
Shooter's Year Book, 53
Shooting ailments, 204
    aural catarrh, 207
    bruising, 204
    damage to hearing, 206
    headache, 205
Shot, 54, 88, 196
    cold-welding of, 89, 197
    cubic, 65
    favoured size of, 201
    iron, 197
    killing efficiencies of, 199
    manufacture of, 196
    plated, 88, 197
    plomb-disco, 65
    sizes of, 196, 197
    stacking of, 202
Sidelock, 27, 148
Sighting the shotgun, 184
    gun fitting, 184
    line of sight, 185
    superelevation, 185
    tension, effect of, 185
Sights, 230
    bead, 230
    luminous, 230
    Nydar, 231
    Singlepoint, 230, 231

sights—*continued*
  telescopic, 231
Single barrel, 30
Singlepoint sight, 230, 231
Single triggers, 33, 34
Skeet, 76
Sliding breech (Darne), 28
Slugs, rifled, 228
Smith action, 126
Stanbury, Percy, 185
Stocks and fitting, 171
  American, 175
  chequering, 177
  grip, 175
  gun measurements, 172
  minimum adaptation, principle of,
    173
  stock bolts, 178
  terminology, 172
  the natural stock, 173
  vital measurements, 174
  wood, 177
Striking energy, 53, 54, 57
Stringing, 53

Take-down and reassembly, 46
Target, aiming, 78
Transportability, 46
Trigger-plate action, 29, 46

Triggers:
  double selective, 35
  pulls of, 230
  release, 35
  single, 33, 34

Variable choke, 79
Vision, problems of, 165
  contact lenses, 170
  idiosyncracies of, 167
  master eye, 165, 168
  shooting glasses, 169
  theory of master eye, 168
  training for mastery, 168

Wadding, 62, 87
  cork, 87
  felt, 87
  Kleena, 88
  obturating power, 87
  plastic, 63, 88, 112
Wanda cartridges, 98
Warping of double guns, 189
Weight and recoil, 44, 152
Westley Richards, 126
Wheel-lock, 19
Wildfowlers, 44, 49, 58
Winchester, 34, 39, 98, 131
Winchester cartridge, 98
Winchoke, 82